Living the Gospel of Jesus Christ

Series Preface

Regnum Studies in Mission are born from the lived experience of Christians and Christian communities in mission, especially but not solely in the fast growing churches among the poor of the world. These churches have more to tell than stories of growth. They are making significant impacts on their cultures in the cause of Christ. They are producing 'cultural products' which express the reality of Christian faith, hope and love in their societies.

Regnum Studies in Mission are the fruit often of rigorous research to the highest international standards and always of authentic Christian engagement in the transformation of people and societies. And these are for the world. The formation of Christian theology, missiology and practice in the twenty-first century will depend to a great extent on the active participation of growing churches contributing biblical and culturally appropriate expressions of Christian practice to inform World Christianity.

REGNUM STUDIES IN MISSION

Living the Gospel of Jesus Christ

Orthodox and Evangelical Approaches to Discipleship and Christian Formation

Edited by Mark Oxbrow and Tim Grass

First published 2021 by Regnum Books International

Regnum is an imprint of the Oxford Centre for Mission Studies
St. Philip and St. James Church
Woodstock Road
Oxford OX2 6HR, UK
www.ocms.ac.uk/regnum

09 08 07 06 05 04 03 7 6 5 4 3 2 1

British Library Cataloguing in Publication Data
A catalogue record for this book is available from the British Library

ISBN: 978-1-5064-8371-9
eBook ISBN: 978-1-5064-8393-1

Typeset by Words by Design

Cover photo: Beit Saleem Community Based Rehabilitation Centre, Jofeh, Balqa, Jordan. Picture © Mark Oxbrow

The editors wish to acknowledge the generous financial support of the Lausanne-Orthodox Initiative and its supporters towards the publication of this volume.

Distributed by 1517 Media in the US, Canada, India, and Brazil

CONTENTS

FOREWORD

In a broken and divided world, one which is building walls, and in which we avoid and evade anyone and everyone with whom we might differ, we as co-chairs of the Lausanne-Orthodox Initiative (LOI) are so happy to offer a book encouraging the body of Christ to defy the world's norms, and to run *towards* one another, faithfully 'living the gospel of Christ'.

Orthodox and Evangelicals each bring a variety of strengths, approaches and rich contributions in their understanding and experience of worshipping and knowing Christ; together, these can impact our world powerfully for the Kingdom. We can take every opportunity to preach about the love, forgiveness, and new life found in Jesus Christ to unbelievers, but it is *'living the gospel of Christ'* that truly demonstrates who Jesus is: the One who raises the dead to life. We need to be living this *gospel* of Christ in the *body* of Christ.

This is an incredibly important issue, because it highlights and demonstrates that as we extend grace and love within the family of God, we are more equipped to extend this same grace and love to those outside. This book offers an important perspective, showing what this looks like between Evangelicals and Orthodox and how, as a result, we all become stronger as one, with a deeper faith in the Lord. The essays included motivate every Orthodox and Evangelical to be a 'humble learner' (disciple) of the other, in order to live as a community of disciples serving our Lord and the world. This is what LOI is all about: building one another up in the mission of God, with the Spirit of God at the centre.

We have much to learn as disciples of Christ, and this book will surely inspire us towards achieving what Jesus desired for his people: 'That they may be one even as we are one, I in them and you in me, that they may become perfectly one, so that the world may know you sent me and loved them even as you loved me' (Jn 17.21-23). What beautiful, deep, and practical insights it gives into our wonderful gospel!

Leslie Doll / +Angaelos

1. Introduction

Revd Canon Mark Oxbrow and Dr Tim Grass

Some years ago, I (Mark) visited the Orthodox Theological Academy in St. Petersburg and the Biblical Leadership Training Centre in Krasnodar, southern Russia, in quick succession, and in both places, I listened to almost identical stories. In each institution, one Orthodox and the other Evangelical, faculty members told me that their greatest challenge was not the academic standard of their students, nor training them in liturgical practice or pastoral ministry, but rather the moulding the Christian character of their students. At that time, it was in the first decade after the fall of communism in Russia, both traditions were experiencing a growth in their ecclesial community which brought with it a great need for new leaders. With many of the theological schools having been closed for many decades under the former regime, it was difficult enough to find teachers of theology, philosophy, philology, patristics and pastoral studies, but the challenge I was hearing about ran much deeper. The Orthodox academy and the Evangelical training centre each had very able students, academically high fliers, who were failing morally, failing to be shaped in the image of Christ, even failing to see any need to change the character in the way they dealt with their families, finances and work ethics. I do not recall using the word 'discipleship' once during those conversations but that was what we were discussing. More than first-rate theologians or even pastors, these churches needed top-rank disciples of Jesus Christ.[1]

The sub-title of this book, *Orthodox and Evangelical Approaches to Discipleship and Christian Formation*, reminds us that if the gospel is to make sense in our contemporary world, it will need to be lived visibly by disciples who bear, in humility and sometimes to martyrdom, the image of God in Christ Jesus. In a recent publication, Alan Kreider[2] has claimed that during the first three centuries of the undivided Church, the Christian faith spread faster and further than in the following centuries of Constantinian Christendom, not as a result of preaching or effective evangelical campaigns but as a response to the integrity of the lives of Christian people, often living

---

[1] In later years, both these institutions developed more effective ways of shaping the character of their students as well as their minds. The Biblical Leadership Training Centre (BLTC) in particular moved to an interesting discipleship model of training, in which students spent half the week in the classroom and half in local church ministry, while at the same time living in a community setting with one of the faculty staff so that they were mentored over their years in college in a small group by an experienced Christian leader.

[2] Alan Kreider, *The Patient Ferment of the Early Church* (Grand Rapids, MI: Baker, 2016).

under pressure and sometimes persecution. Kreider reminds us[3] that when Cyprian is asked to provide Quirinus with a 'list of precepts' of the Christian faith,[4] Cyprian does not list doctrinal statements but rather 120 principles of Christian living, including economic sharing, visiting the sick and non-violence. It was the act of living the gospel of Jesus Christ which helped the undivided Church grow in the first three centuries, and it is this same commitment to an honest living out of the gospel which will carry the Church forward into the hostile contexts of our contemporary world as salt and light for people who hunger for hope.

As Orthodox and Evangelical partners in the Lausanne-Orthodox Initiative address this topic of discipleship in this current volume, we do not do so alone. It seems that in recent decades the Spirit of God has been drawing Christians of every tradition into a deeper reflection on, and commitment to, discipleship. In November 2013, very early in his pontificate, it was Pope Francis who, in his encyclical *Evangelii Gaudium*, called the Church to live as a 'community of missionary disciples'[5] who walk closely with Jesus whilst serving the world; a call he has kept up ever since, as he himself attempts to live out the gospel in radical ways. Just over two years later, at their 2016 meeting in Lusaka, Zambia, the Anglican Consultative Council called all Anglicans globally to a 'Season of Intentional Discipleship and Disciple-Making'.[6] At Pentecost that year, the Great Council of the Orthodox Churches in Crete, in its statement on mission, reminded all Orthodox believers that '[t]he conveyance of the Gospel's message according to the last commandment of Christ, *Go therefore and make disciples of all nations, baptising them in the name of the Father and*

---

[3] Kreider, *Patient Ferment*, 161-63.

[4] See *Ad Quirinum 3* in the English translation by Ernest Wallis, in A. Roberts and J. Donaldson, eds, *Ante-Nicene Fathers*, vol. 5, online at: https://en.wikisource.org/wiki/Ante-Nicene_Fathers/Volume_V/Cyprian/The Treatises_of_Cyprian/Three_Books_of_Testimonies_Against_the_Jews/Book_III/H eads, accessed 14 April 2020.

[5] *Evangelii Gaudium*, 120. For a fuller exposition of Pope Francis's teaching on missionary discipleship, see Pope Francis with William P. Gregory, *Go Forth: Toward a Community of Missionary Disciples* (Maryknoll, NY: Orbis, 2019).

[6] In introducing this call, the Anglican Archbishop of South-East Asia, Moon Hing Ng, wrote: 'Our lives reflecting the image of God, will attract and change others. To hold the good news of the Gospel of Jesus Christ to ourselves is a supreme act of selfishness. As we follow and are shaped by the life of Jesus, that selfish possessiveness of our relationship with him will be dissipated and we will naturally begin to include others in that love-relationship. Exclusivity has no place in the family of God; all God-centred relationships are inclusive, and our evangelism has nothing to do with numbers and power but everything to do with love, generosity, inclusion, and the all-encompassing life and love of God': John Kafwanka and Mark Oxbrow (eds), *Intentional Discipleship and Disciple-making: An Anglican Guide for Christian Life and Formation* (London: Anglican Consultative Council, 2016), viii.

of the Son and of the Holy Spirit, teaching them to observe all that I have commanded you (Mt. 28.19) is the diachronic mission of the Church.'[7] The World Council of Churches was next to follow, with the 2018 Conference on World Mission and Evangelism in Arusha, Tanzania, meeting under the banner 'Moving in the Spirit: Called to Transforming Discipleship'. This deliberately ambiguous title invited the assembled church and mission leaders both to transform the way we live as disciples of Jesus Christ and by so doing to then allow that discipleship to transform the communities and the world in which we live – all as a response to the living Spirit of God in our midst. In his welcome, the WCC General Secretary, Rev Dr Olav Fykse Tveit, said: 'The terminology of discipleship brings a fresh and challenging dimension to our reflection and practice of being "pilgrims". We are not moving as pilgrims just to move. We are moving to make a difference, to bring transformation.'[8] A year later, in November 2019, the World Evangelical Alliance held its first General Assembly for eleven years to 'launch a new era (decade) of disciple-making and inter-generational leadership across nations and regions'.[9] The Orthodox and Evangelical contributors to this volume seek to encourage and deepen this commitment of our diverse Christian communities to discipleship, to living the Gospel of Jesus Christ.

Drawing on papers originally delivered at a number of Lausanne-Orthodox Initiative (LOI) conferences (see further details below), this volume, in LOI's tenth anniversary year, builds on the initiative's core commitment to partnership in mission. Over the past decade, participants in the LOI 'pray for each other and study Scripture together; encourage mutual understanding, respect and appreciation of one another's tradition and practice; promote collaboration in mission wherever this is possible; build short-term and long-term mission partnerships; and facilitate the exchange and sharing of resources for mission'.

In a divided world, the LOI has a strong commitment to discovering a 'unity in diversity' which will enhance the participation of each of us in the mission of God. Our desire to be together is not driven by a desire for some sort of tidy uniformity or simple coherence in the Church, but by a deep theological conviction that, as beings made in the image of God, we can never be complete without 'the Other'. On the opening page of his *Communion and Otherness: Further Studies in Personhood and the Church,*

---

[7] The statement goes on to remind believers that '[t]his mission must be carried out not aggressively or by different forms of proselytism, but in love, humility and respect towards the identity of each person and the cultural particularity of each people': https://www.holycouncil.org/-/mission-orthodox-church-todays-world, accessed 23 May 2020 [italics original].

[8] *Handbook for CWME, Arusha, Tanzania 2018* (Geneva: WCC Publications, 2018), vi.

[9] https://jakarta2019.org/en/about/, accessed 11 June 2020.

John Zizioulas draws a vivid picture of what many of us have experienced as different Christian traditions relate to each other:

> In our culture, protection from the other is a fundamental necessity. We feel more and more threatened by the presence of the other. We are forced and even encouraged to consider the other as our enemy before we can treat him or her as our friend. Communion with the other is not spontaneous; it is built upon fences that protect us from the dangers implicit in the other's presence. We accept the other only in so far as he or she does not threaten our privacy or in so far as he or she is useful for our individual happiness.[10]

As Orthodox and Evangelical Christians, many of us have lived with that fear of the dangerous Other: we have built our fences, preserved our separate identities, and written excluding boundaries into our statements of faith. From a firm foundation in Trinitarian theology, Zizioulas breaks down the dividing walls and opens up for us the life-enhancing possibility of a mutual indwelling (*perichoresis*) without any loss of distinctive identity. For those of us on this 'LOI journey', this is the experience to which we bear witness, that when we lower the fences, begin to appreciate the Other for who they are, we do not need to become like them but their otherness begins to enrich our 'being myself'; we find our true self in the interaction with, the valuing of, the vulnerability to, the Other.

An Evangelical scholar who also encourages us down this road is Miroslav Volf, who takes up a very similar theme: a passion for the otherness of the Other born of his own bitter experience of being caught up in the prejudices, fear and violence of the Yugoslav civil war. In *Exclusion and Embrace*, Volf draws for us the powerful image of the costly divine embrace of the Other which is set as a pattern for all who live the Gospel of Jesus Christ.

> When God sets out to embrace the enemy, the result is the cross. On the cross the dancing circle of self-giving and mutually indwelling persons opens up to the enemy; in the agony of the passion the movement stops for a brief moment and a fissure appears so that sinful humanity can join in (see John 17:21). We, the others – we, the enemies – are embraced by the divine persons who love us with the same love with which they love each other and therefore make space for us within their own eternal embrace.[11]

Living the Gospel of Jesus Christ is about being embraced by the divine Other, embracing the others in the Church whose difference will enrich our own being ourselves, and then together bearing a living witness to the others who have yet to allow themselves to be embraced by the divine Other. As Mikhail Bakhtin has written, 'My communion with the other opens up "the possibility of creation" and the recognition of my call to assist the other to fill in the apophatic gap of non-self-sufficiency that every self faces. For

---

[10] John Zizioulas, *Communion and Otherness: Further Studies in Personhood and the Church* (London: T. & T. Clark, 2007), 1.

[11] Miroslav Volf, *Exclusion and Embrace: A Theological Exploration of Identity, Otherness and Reconciliation* (Nashville, TN: Abingdon, 1996), 129.

what God is for me, I must be for the other.'[12] For Orthodox and Evangelical disciples learning to embrace each other, this is why mission becomes so central to our being.

Many picking up this book may be unfamiliar with the story and calling of LOI. So, in best narrative theology fashion, here is the story. In 2010, the Lausanne Movement convened a global congress of four thousand Evangelicals in Cape Town. Four Orthodox were invited as part of a small team of observers. Sessions explored the greatness of the love of God for the world, and the urgent challenges facing Christians who seek to go into all the world to live and proclaim the good news. Some speakers were burdened by the spiritual needs of traditionally Orthodox countries such as those in Eastern Europe, but in describing such nations as 'unevangelised' they overlooked the historic presence of Orthodox Christians (and of Evangelicals who had often suffered for Christ alongside Orthodox under Communist rule). One Orthodox observer (now a co-chair of LOI) raised this with some Evangelicals who had invited him to lunch (amongst whom was the other current co-chair of LOI), and, to cut a long story short, LOI was born.

Our calling is expressed in the LOI Commitment:

> The goal of the Lausanne-Orthodox Initiative is to reflect constructively on the history of relationships between Orthodox and Evangelicals in order to work towards better understanding, and encourage reconciliation and healing where wounds exist. Through this process, Evangelicals and Orthodox are mutually enriched and strengthened in the work of mission, working towards mutual respect, support and co-operation in the spirit of our Lord's prayer for His Church in John 17.

> To achieve this goal the Lausanne-Orthodox Initiative is committed to encouraging members of its two traditions to: pray for each other and study Scripture together; encourage mutual understanding, respect and appreciation of one another's tradition and practice; promote collaboration in mission wherever this is possible; build short-term and long-term mission partnerships; and facilitate the exchange and sharing of resources for mission.

Two aspects of this commitment call for comment: firstly, it is relational, and secondly, it is missional. Relationships have been a major part of the problems which have bedevilled contact between Orthodox and Evangelical traditions over the last three centuries. There is no need to repeat the saga of those problems here. But we believe that with God change is possible. Evangelical board members of LOI have found that it is possible to enjoy deep and honest relationships of Christian fellowship with Orthodox believers, and vice versa. Such relationships have drawn us closer to Christ, and we seek to create space in our consultations for others to experience the same blessing, and to learn from them as they share their own experiences of

---

[12] M. M. Bakhtin, 'Author and Hero in Aesthetic Activity', in M. Holquist and V. Liapunov (eds), *Art and Answerability: Early Philosophical Essays* (Austin, TX: University of Texas Press, 1990), p. 56.

relationship-building. As a small example of this, we rejoiced recently to hear of the first inter-tradition marriage to result from one of our gatherings.

LOI is also missional in its ethos. Other Orthodox-Evangelical dialogues have explored theological issues, but, as might be expected from an initiative with roots in the Lausanne Movement, we focus on how we can work together in the mission of God. This, we believe, is what marks out LOI, what represents its distinctive calling from God for the benefit of the Church and the world which God loves. Mission has often been the contested ground on which conflict between our two traditions has broken out: what one person calls 'sharing the good news', another calls 'proselytism'. To overcome this, we need to understand one another, and to respect one another but, in doing so, we may also find that we can learn from one another, and as we build relationships, we may come to love one another. All this can become a reality without compromising our convictions or our desire to remain faithful to Christ. St Paul's picture of the Church as the body of Christ (1 Cor. 12) illustrated to the self-sufficient Corinthians that they needed one another, and that even those who thought themselves highly gifted needed the less respectable members of the body in order to function effectively. We may be familiar with that in the life of local congregations; but it applies too between Christian traditions.

So what does LOI actually do? Is it just a talking shop, or a space for formal contact? We hope not, and we seek to go beyond merely holding a consultation every year. That said, those gatherings are at the heart of our work. Invited participants – mission workers, hierarchs and church leaders, academics, and others – come together for a residential gathering to explore how we can learn from one another and equip ourselves more adequately for our part in God's mission. These gatherings are deliberately structured to allow plenty of time for joint prayer and study of the Scriptures, but also for informal conversation. I (Tim) have long wanted to write a book about the history of food in Christianity, which I plan to entitle *From Agape to Alpha* – but what began partly in jest is rooted in the conviction that when we eat and drink together, relationships are often formed and deepened.

The COVID-19 pandemic has affected our plans, but LOI is committed to facilitating 'listening visits' to areas where relationships are challenging, to learn about those situations and to reflect on how the initiative might be able to encourage those who minister there. We also continue to develop other aspects of the work, and to keep in online contact with those who share a vision for Orthodox-Evangelical collaboration in God's mission for our fractured and fearful world. That involves communicating with a wider audience: sharing resources of interest to those engaged in Orthodox-Evangelical encounters, at all levels, passing on stories of such engagement and its practical outworking, and promoting improved mutual understanding. This book is part of that aspect of our work.

Our first volume, *The Mission of God: Studies in Orthodox and Evangelical Mission* (Regnum, 2015), comprised papers from the first two

LOI consultations, both held at the Monastery of St Vlash in Albania, at the invitation of His Eminence Archbishop Anastasios. We have been greatly encouraged by its reception around the world.

The articles in this book were taken from subsequent LOI gatherings. A global consultation in Finland during 2015 considered 'The Gospel as Good News'. The following year, we met in Ethiopia for a regional gathering under the title 'Witness, Peace and Unity'; even though we met during a state of emergency, there was joy at being able to encounter Christians from the other tradition in a way some never thought possible. Arising from interest expressed at our meeting in Finland, a consultation on 'Theological Formation for Mission' brought together theological educators from around the world at Cambridge, England, in 2017. Our first gathering in North America took place at Holy Cross Orthodox Seminary near Boston in 2018, when we looked at 'Discipleship and Christian Formation'. Most recently, we met in Egypt in 2019, at the Monastery of St Bishoy, to explore the topic 'Christian Witness: "A life worthy of the gospel of Christ" (Philippians 1.27)'. This was a regional consultation for the Middle East and North Africa.

This volume focuses on three distinct but interlocked aspects of *Living the Gospel*. Firstly, four Orthodox and three Evangelical authors explore the meaning of the gospel in their own tradition, with a particular focus on the contribution of St Paul to defining why the Incarnation, life, death and resurrection of Jesus is good news, as well as how we can learn from each other's traditions and experience the richness of exploring together the depth of what it means to live the gospel.

In part two, the focus turns to the formation of disciples. St Augustine of Hippo (354-430) famously wrote on the catechesis of new believers. It is interesting to note, as we reflect on living the gospel, that Augustine was just as concerned about the character of the teacher and how he was to form Christian character and lifestyle in his disciples as he was about the content of the teaching. He concludes his Prologue to *On Catechizing Beginners* with the wonderful reflection, 'our greatest concern is much more about how to make it possible for those who offer instruction in faith to do so with joy. For the more they succeed in this, the more appealing will they be'.[13] In this section, Evangelical and Orthodox authors first reflect on their respective understanding of the discipleship process and then on how the Bible is taught in each tradition – also a central concern of Augustine.[14] This section ends with two case studies, the first by two authors who have taught together from their different traditions, in Russia, and the second a study of Orthodox-Evangelical encounter in the Middle East.

---

[13] Augustine of Hippo, *Instructing Beginners in Faith*, trans. R. Canning (New York: New City, 2006), p. 59.

[14] See, for example, Augustine of Hippo, *On Christian Doctrine*, Book 2, 'What is Required for a Faithful Study of Scripture', trans. E. Hill as *Teaching Christianity* (New York, New City, 1996), p. 135.

The third and final part of the volume takes us into the more practical and demanding arena of living the gospel, living as disciples, in contemporary society. The concept of liminality, formulated by Arnold van Gennep in 1909, has more recently been adopted by a number of theologians to speak about the context in which disciples of Jesus Christ find themselves: the 'betwixt and between', being of this world and yet not of this world. Turner speaks of the liminal state positively as allowing spontaneity, freedom and a release from externally imposed societal norms,[15] but Lee reminds us that modern liminal states may be 'open-ended, ill-defined, and quite often imposed on those undergoing them'.[16] Our first two contributors to this section address the challenges of discipleship in this enforced liminal space, on the margins of society. Our attention is then drawn to the continent with the fastest growing number of disciples of Jesus Christ, as we consider the future of African discipleship. The last three chapters remind us that from the very earliest days of the Church, living the gospel has been closely associated with martyrdom. Staying in Africa, two authors, one Evangelical and the other Orthodox, reassess the life and martyrdom of St Mark and his contribution to living the gospel. The volume closes with a sensitive reflection on the blessings of persecution which comes out of Egypt, a land where for centuries discipleship, witness, persecution and martyrdom have gone hand in hand.

We would like to thank the authors for their co-operation in this project. Their excitement about it has fuelled our own. We also thank the co-chairs of LOI, His Eminence Archbishop Angaelos and Mrs Leslie Doll, for their foreword. Finally, it is a pleasure to work with our publisher, Regnum Books, who have not only handled this project professionally but encouraged us by their interest.

What struck us when we first drafted a list of contents was how well everything fitted together. Volumes of essays can sometimes be a very mixed bag, in which any overall theme is difficult to trace. But we are excited as editors about this book's potential as a resource to enrich our thinking about Christian discipleship, whether we are Orthodox or Evangelicals, whether as church leaders or in our personal discipleship. It is rather like looking at a precious stone from different sides. The gem's different facets are part of the one stone, and the authors share that one goal, of becoming more like Christ as we walk with him in discipleship of heart, soul, mind, and strength. Read on; and we hope that you will be blessed (and hopefully challenged) as you do so.

---

[15] Victor Turner, 'Frame, Flow and Reflection: Ritual and Drama as Public Liminality', *Japanese Journal of Religious Studies* 6 (1979), 465-99.
[16] Sang Hyun Lee, *From a Liminal Place: An Asian American Theology* (Minneapolis, MN: Fortress, 2010), 33.

2. What is the Gospel in Eastern Orthodoxy?[*]

Dr Bradley Nassif

'In the beginning was the Word. And the Word was with God, and the Word was God ... And the Word became flesh and dwelt among us' (Jn 1.1, 14). In these few lines, the apostle John summarizes the central theme that permeates the whole of Eastern Orthodox life and thought: *In the incarnate Person of Jesus Christ, and his Trinitarian relations, is found the mystery of salvation.* Every other Christian doctrine either prepares for, reveals or grows out of this reality. Hence all Christian conversation about the meaning of the gospel must begin with a shared understanding of the Incarnation of Jesus Christ in his trinitarian relations and what that means for the message that Christians preach and the life that we live within the various cultures of the world.

In accordance with the trinitarian and christological dogmas of Nicaea and Chalcedon, I will attempt to clarify in this essay the Orthodox Church's understanding of the gospel as it relates to the Incarnation as the supreme mystery that lies at the centre of the Christian faith. Because the saving gospel is embodied in the very person of Jesus Christ, the Incarnation explains why humans, as well as the whole of creation, need salvation and why salvation can only be appropriated through union with the risen Lord. As we will see, the gospel is discerned by discovering its content, gifts and demands. I will focus in this article mainly on the content of the gospel and secondarily on its gifts. Regrettably, there is not space to explore the demands of the gospel for discipleship or its social relevance. Other Orthodox colleagues will develop those subjects in subsequent chapters.

The Gospel in Salvation History

Before articulating the content of the gospel, a few words are in order to place the gospel in its biblical, historical and liturgical context. The term most often employed by the Church Fathers to describe the history of salvation is the Greek word *oikonomia*. In its classical context, the term refers to the management of a household. According to Fr John Meyendorff, '[a]mong the Greek Fathers *oikonomia* has the standard meaning of "incarnation history"'.[1] So in patristic usage, *oikonomia* describes the providence of God which governs the course of

---

[*] Scripture quotations in this chapter are from the Holy Bible, New International Version®, NIV® Copyright ©1973, 1978, 1984, 2011 by Biblica, Inc.® Used by permission. All rights reserved worldwide.

[1] John Meyendorff, *Byzantine Theology*, 2nd ed. (New York: Fordham University Press, 1979), 88.

human history towards the Incarnation of the Word who will save fallen humanity and renew the entire physical cosmos.

Incarnation history is grounded in the relationship between the old and new covenants. The old covenant is the one God made with Israel. But in Old Testament history, that covenant was not meant for Israel alone. Rather, the covenant was meant to be a bridge to the rest of the world. Israel was chosen to be the channel of revelation through which YHWH would reach all the other nations of the world (Gen. 12.3; Gal. 3.28). The creation of the heavens and the earth in Genesis 1–2 eventually reached an eschatological climax in a divine promise of renewal when God said: 'I am about to create new heavens and a new earth' (Isa. 65.17; 66.2). The New Testament reaffirms the continuing validity of the Old Testament's hope of a renewed creation (2 Pet. 3.13; Rev. 21.1; Rom. 8.19-22). That new creation belongs to the eschatological Kingdom of God which was fulfilled in the earthly ministry of Jesus, and will one day be consummated in the age to come. Jesus is the one through whom God has formed a new covenant people through his life, death, resurrection, ascension and sending of the Spirit at Pentecost.

In the present age, that new covenant is established in the Eucharist, in which Jesus took bread and wine and declared them to be 'the new covenant' in his blood (Mt. 26.26 and parallels). The eucharistic meal is celebrated every Sunday in the Divine Liturgy of the Orthodox Church. It is there that the Kingdom of God becomes the North Star that guides the eschatological proclamation of the Scriptures and the partaking of communion. The first words of the opening petition of the liturgy are: 'Blessed is the kingdom of the Father, and of the Son and of the Holy Spirit.' Here the Church's liturgical theology is revealed as kingdom theology; and kingdom theology is gospel theology. The gospel lies at the very centre of the Orthodox liturgy and permeates its entire structure and content.[2]

The four Gospels unanimously bear witness to the coming of the Kingdom of God and the new creation through the person of Jesus of Nazareth. In and through Jesus, the living God has opened the door of this new creation he has been preparing, and has invited all to enter. In the Synoptic Gospels, the name given to life in this new creation is the 'Kingdom of God', while the Gospel of John describes it as 'eternal life'. Yet all four Gospels bear a collective witness to the reality that God is rescuing the whole creation, and individuals within it, through the eschatological coming of the King of the kingdom. Through his birth and life and, climactically, through the cross, Jesus brings the kingdom by defeating sin, death and the devil. Through his

---

[2] For the centrality of the gospel in the Church's liturgy, see my essays 'Orthodox Spirituality: A Quest for Transfigured Humanity', in Bruce Demarest (ed), *Christian Spirituality: Four Views* (Grand Rapids, MI: Zondervan, 2012), 27-55; and 'The Beauty of Holiness: Deification of the Passions in the Divine Liturgy of St. John Chrysostom', in Dale Coulter and Amos Yong (eds), *The Spirit, the Affections and the Christian Tradition* (South Bend, IN: University of Notre Dame Press, 2016), 65-86.

resurrection, his death has saving meaning. Through his ascension into heaven, Jesus completes the process and now sits in glory interceding with the Father on our behalf in anticipation of the Second Coming. Thus the story of salvation history is what constitutes the gospel for St Paul as well as the rest of the New Testament writers: 'But when the set time had fully come, God sent his Son, born of a woman, born under the law' (Gal. 4.4; cf. 1 Cor. 15.1-8).

Why Does Anyone Need the Gospel?

At the centre of creation is a trinitarian God. It is out of God's trinitarian relationships, and for communion with those trinitarian relationships, that we humans were created and redeemed. God exists in an eternal communion of trinitarian love between Father, Son and Holy Spirit. Our original vocation in creation was to become like God: 'Then God said, "Let us make human beings in our image, to be like us"' (Gen. 1.26). Adam and Eve were called to grow eternally in the 'likeness of God. In Orthodox vocabulary, this is known as 'glorification', 'deification' or *theosis.*

Adam and Eve were also tasked with overseeing the earth and the created order as the realm of the Kingdom of God. This is the 'royal priesthood' of our divine calling as children of God. Sin, however, brought both physical and spiritual death to the human race (Gen. 3; Rom. 5.12), as well as dominion by the flesh and the demonic powers of darkness. The union which God created between himself and Adam and Eve (and between them) was broken through sin. Humanity and creation stood in need of healing and renewal.

The Mystery of the Gospel

In Orthodoxy, as in the New Testament, the gospel is a many-sided mystery. Its description' – impossible to define narrowly – is simultaneously simple, comprehensive and complex. The gospel constitutes the very essence of the Christian message. It is a vast canopy that embraces the following acts in God's relationship to humankind: the story of creation, humanity made in the 'image of God', the fall into sin, Israel as the nation through whom God's Messiah would come, the climax of the Incarnation, the eschatological Kingdom of God, the cross, the resurrection, the ascension, Pentecost, the Church as the new messianic community, the sacraments, spiritual life, social engagement and missions. These are some of the essential elements of the gospel that relate to a believer's saving union with Christ. To be united to Christ means that we are joined to the incarnate Person of Christ himself, and by this union we participate in the very life and love of the Trinity. Paul identifies this mystery as 'Christ in you, the hope of glory' (Col. 1.27). The mystery of Christ's union with his Church lies at the core of the good news that Paul preached and was willing to suffer and die for: 'And pray for us, too, that God may open a door for our message, so that we may proclaim *the mystery of Christ,* for which I am in chains' (Col. 4.3). 'Pray also for me, that whenever I open my mouth, words may be given me so that I will fearlessly make known *the mystery of the gospel,* for which I am an ambassador in chains' (Eph. 6.19-20).

The supreme mystery of the gospel is the Incarnation of the Word (Jn 1.14). God, in the person of Jesus Christ, takes upon himself our humanity in order to save us in the humanity he assumed. C. S. Lewis repeats the central conviction of patristic Orthodoxy when he observes that the Incarnation lies at the centre of the Christian gospel: 'The Central Miracle asserted by Christians is the Incarnation ... Every other miracle prepares for this, or exhibits this, or results from this.'[3] Important as the death and resurrection of Christ are, without the supreme mystery of the Incarnation, the crucifixion and resurrection would not have their saving power. The Incarnation is much more than simply a necessary pre-requisite to the work of Christ. The very *person* of Christ *embodies* the gospel!

'Who do people say that I am?' (Matthew 16.15)

'In the mind of Eastern Christians,' said Fr John Meyendorff, 'the entire context of the Christian faith depends upon the way in which the question "Who is Jesus Christ?" is answered.'[4] That answer is given in Scripture and the saving dogmas of the Ecumenical Councils (325-787 AD). Those dogmas bear witness to the meaning of the gospel. The identity of Jesus Christ, and his trinitarian relations, constitute the heart of the Church's christological, trinitarian and iconoclastic controversies in the age of the Ecumenical Councils. It is important to note that the councils were not producing abstract philosophical speculations about correct formulas of christological chemistry. On the contrary, the Ecumenical Councils were the by-product of the practical concerns of church life and worship. The councils produced dogmas that originated from the pastoral concern of church leaders regarding the meaning of the gospel. The dogmatic decrees and ecclesiastical canons which resulted from several centuries of protracted theological debates centred on the salvation that was achieved through the person of the incarnate Lord in his trinitarian relations. In other words, the dogmatic conclusions of the Ecumenical Councils were all about the saving truths of the gospel.

The Gospel and the Ecclesiology of the Ecumenical Councils

Without going into great detail on this subject, there are at least two points to be made concerning the ecclesiology of the Ecumenical Council which most Evangelicals seem to overlook when claiming allegiance to the Councils of Nicaea and Chalcedon. The first is that the churches which gathered at the

---

[3] C. S. Lewis, *Miracles* (New York: Touchstone, 1996 reprint of 1947 edn), 143.
[4] Meyendorff, *Byzantine Theology,* 151.

Ecumenical Councils were in eucharistic communion with each other. The earlier teachings of Ignatius of Antioch, concerning local bishops as touchstones of unity, continued to shape the ecclesiological principles that governed the Ecumenical Councils. The local churches that were present at the councils were represented by bishops who shared the same faith and were in eucharistic communion with one another. This 'eucharistic ecclesiology', as it has been called, existed before, during and after the actual gathering of the councils, except, of course, in cases where a bishop was recognized as being heretical.

The second ecclesiological principle that was in play during the Ecumenical Councils was Irenaeus's doctrine of apostolic succession. The Church's true bishops were (and are) those whose ordination stood in historical succession with the apostles whose authority originated with Jesus. Historic succession, however, is no guarantee of truth. So there existed in the councils not only a historical succession of episcopal ordinations, but also, and even more importantly, the succession of apostolic truth that lived in each local community headed by its own local bishop. Both successions (historical and theological) were necessary *pre-conditions* for each bishop's participation in the Ecumenical Councils, even if the truth question was still to be discussed during the proceedings.

These basic ecclesiological realities remain central to an Orthodox understanding of the gospel today. Christian truth is ultimately recognized as a communal witness, not an individual one. Even in cases where individuals, such as Athanasius who almost single-handedly bore witness to the consubstantiality of the Father and Son, or Maximus the Confessor who defended the two wills of Christ, the wider Church eventually affirmed the truth these individuals were upholding. As I have shown elsewhere, the mind of the Church is formed, and informed, communally.[5]

The Saving Ontologies of the *Homoousion* and the Hypostatic Union

The Nicene Creed (325/381) and the Chalcedonian Definition (451) are foundational to Orthodox soteriology and thus to the very content of the gospel. The incarnate Son of the Father, in his trinitarian relations, lies at the heart of these two conciliar statements (in tandem, of course, with the other Ecumenical Councils which surrounded them). For example, the Nicene Creed declares the saving significance of the Incarnation: 'Jesus Christ … of one essence (*homoousion*) with the Father … Who for us humans and for our salvation, came down from heaven and was incarnate of the Holy Spirit and the Virgin Mary, and became human'. In the fifth century, the four negative adverbs of the famous Chalcedonian Definition laid boundaries around the mystery of the union of the

---

[5] Bradley Nassif, 'Tradition, Catholicity and the Mind of the Church', in Mark Oxbrow and Tim Grass (eds), *The Mission of God* (Oxford: Regnum, 2015), 215-23.

two natures of Christ with the aid of apophatic language.[6] Here we have the Church's *de facto* recognition of its inability to exhaust the mystery of the Incarnation:

> … one and the same Christ, Son, Lord, Only-begotten,
> to be acknowledged in two natures,
> without confusion, without change,
> without division, without separation.

Chalcedon, however, was not the final word on the christological debates in the Christian East. Against the heresy of monothelitism (the belief that Christ had only one divine-human will), the Sixth Ecumenical Council (680-81) formally attested to the complete integrity of, and cooperation between, the human and divine wills of Christ:

> We also proclaim two natural willings or wills in him and two natural operations [modes of action], without separation, without change, without partition, without confusion, according to the teaching of the holy Fathers – and two natural wills not contrary [to each other], God forbid, as the impious heretics have said [they would be], but his human will follows, and does not resist or opposes, but rather is subject to his divine and all-powerful will.[7]

The Christology of St Maximos the Confessor lies behind this conciliar statement. Maximos advanced the work of Chalcedon by distinguishing between the 'natural' and 'gnomic' (deliberative) wills. He maintained that Christ has a natural will that followed its created instincts towards union with God, but he did not have a gnomic will which is characterized by hesitation and deliberation between two or more options. Christ never deliberated whether to do the will of the Father or not. He sinlessly followed the natural will of his fallen, but healed, humanity. In his incarnate life, Christ did for us what we could never do for ourselves. His obedience to the Father through the natural operations of his human will, in synergy with the divine will,

---

[6] The Church's use of apophatic (negation) and cataphatic (affirmation) language as paths to the knowledge of God is explained by Andrew Louth, 'Apophatic and Cataphatic Theology', in Amy Hollywood and Patricia Z. Beckman (eds), *The Cambridge Companion to Christian Mysticism* (Cambridge: Cambridge University Press, 2012), 137-46. The Chalcedonian Definition condemned Apollinarianism, Nestorianism and Eutychianism, which in various ways undermined either the full humanity of Christ or the unity of humanity with divinity.

[7] Deno John Genakoplos, *Byzantium: Church, Society, and Civilization seen through Contemporary Eyes* (Chicago, IL: University of Chicago Press, 1984), 152. The heresy of 'aphthartodocetism' (the belief that Christ's body was incapable of death and corruption) explained such passages as Lk. 2.52 (Jesus grew in wisdom and stature') as divine pedagogy and not real growth from ignorance to knowledge. The Church's opposition to aphthartodocetism indicates a biblical and Chalcedonian perception ('the preservation of the properties of each nature') that Christ's humanity was identical to ours in every way except sin: John Meyendorff, *Christ in Eastern Christian Thought* (Crestwood, NY: St Vladimir's Seminary Press, 1975), 86-89.

makes it possible for us to obey God when we become united to his redeemed humanity.

These Christological realities carry soteriological implications. In becoming human, the Son of God assumed a human body, a human soul, a human mind, and a human will. In taking up our full humanity, the hypostatic (personal) union of the divine and human natures in Christ brought about a reconciling, atoning union within the being (ontology) of the Saviour. As 'the only mediator between God and humans' (1 Tim. 2.5), the Son of the Father took our full humanity into the very life of God, destroying the separation between God and humanity within his very being. The Incarnation recreated and reoriented our fallen humanity back to a proper relationship with God which Adam and Eve had lost in the Garden of Eden.

The last of the Ecumenical Councils (787) visualized the gospel through iconographic depictions of Christ made possible because the Word was made flesh. Icons, in other words, are the Church's 'visual gospel'. The ultimate theological justification for the use of images in liturgy and devotion is the Incarnation. Icons bear witness to the saving reality of the God who became human. To reject the icons is to implicitly deny salvation itself. St John of Damascus sums up the Orthodox position with brilliant Christological insight:

> In former times God, who is without form or body, could never be depicted. But now when God is seen in the flesh conversing with men, I make an image of the God whom I see. I do not worship matter; I worship the Creator of matter who became matter for my sake, who willed to take His abode in matter; who worked out my salvation through matter. Never will I cease honoring the matter which wrought my salvation! I honor it, but not as God.[8]

Jesus Christ: The Centre of the Gospel

What the Orthodox want to say through the Ecumenical Councils is that Christ, in his trinitarian relations, is the defining centre of the gospel, and of all Christian belief. Everything in the Christian faith depends on knowing who Christ is and becoming united with him. Jesus reveals the nature of sin, salvation, the Church, reconciliation of the cosmos, missions, and every other dimension of reality. Fr John McGuckin elaborates on the expansive embrace of the Incarnation in Orthodox soteriology:

> In Orthodox understanding, incarnation does not simply refer to the act itself … it stands more generically for the whole nexus of events of the life, teachings, sufferings, and glorification of the Lord … As such, the theological concept of incarnation is a profoundly soteriological term: it always has reference to the dynamic effects of God's involvement in the cosmos. It is also an obviously Christocentric way of approaching the concept of salvation … [W]hen one approaches a theology of salvation through the medium of the

---

[8] *Saint John of Damascus, Three Treatises on the Divine Images* (trans. Andrew Louth; Crestwood, NY: St Vladimir's Seminary Press, 2003), §16.

incarnation of the Logos, one soon finds the argument turns into the profoundly related areas of Trinitarian doctrine of God and transfigured anthropology.[9]

Two fourth-century Church Fathers sum up all we have said thus far. St Gregory Nazianzius succinctly states the saving work of the full humanity the Son of God assumed: 'Whatsoever has not been assumed has not been healed.'[10] St Athanasius expresses the wondrous soteriological exchange between God and humans as a consequence of the mediatorial work of the God-man: 'God became human so that humans might become God.' Or, more literally, 'God became humanized so that humans might become divinized.'[11]

Through the Ecumenical Councils, the Church Fathers proclaimed and protected the Church's understanding of the Person of Christ. The Incarnation shows us in the clearest way possible that God, the holy Trinity, wants to join humanity to himself by uniting us with Jesus Christ. That is the 'good news' of the gospel, to which I now turn.

The Gospel's Call: Union with the Incarnate Son

The content of the good news of the gospel cannot be limited to a single soteriological doctrine, whether it be the Protestant emphasis on justification by grace through faith or the Orthodox emphasis on deification (*theosis, divinization*). The work of Christ is more comprehensive than either of these. Fr Theodore Stylianopoulos underscores how holistic the doctrine of salvation is in the New Testament:

> The New Testament features an array of participatory, forensic, expiatory, ethical, sanctifying, and transformational concepts pertaining to the understanding of salvation. The richness of salvific language contravenes exclusive concentration on any single concept or principle. For example, Paul's teaching of justification (*dikaiosis*) cannot be isolated from other concepts such as redemption (*apolytrosis*), reconciliation (*katallage*), sanctification (*hagiasmos*), transformation (*metamorphousthai and kaine ktisis*), glorification, and union with Christ (*en Christo*).[12]

What, then, is the connection between deification[13] and the Incarnation? By uniting our humanity with the God-who-became-human, there is a

---

[9] John McGuckin, 'Incarnation', in John McGuckin (ed), *The Encyclopedia of Eastern Orthodox Christianity* (2 vols; Malden, MA: Wiley-Blackwell, 2011), 1.338.

[10] Gregory Nazianzius, *Letter 101 to Cledonius*.

[11] Athanasius, *On the Incarnation of the Word*, §54.

[12] Theodore G. Stylianopoulos, *The Making of the New Testament: Church, Gospel, Canon* (Brookline, MA: Holy Cross Orthodox Press, 2014), 54.

[13] Misconceptions about the Orthodox doctrine of deification need to be dispelled to avoid misunderstanding. Unlike Neoplatonism, Mormonism or Hinduism, deification does not involve the loss of our individual identity by reabsorption into a divine Being. On the contrary, those who are divinized remain in an 'I-You'

transformative healing of our fallen humanity (1 Pet. 2.24) that makes it possible for us to regain what was lost in the Fall, and to begin living here and now in the eschatological blessings of the age to come (Rev. 21.1-4; 22.1-5). St Paul teaches that all the saving benefits of the gospel have taken place 'in Christ'. Redemption and forgiveness are in him' (Eph. 1.7); believers are made alive 'in Christ' (1 Cor. 15.22); they are justified in Christ' (Gal. 2.17); they are relieved from condemnation because they are 'in Christ Jesus' (Rom. 8.1); they are sanctified 'in Christ Jesus' (1 Cor. 1.2); and 'in Christ Jesus' humans become the adopted children of God through faith (Gal. 3.26). In other words, salvation is accomplished not only *by* Jesus Christ, it is also accomplished *in* Jesus Christ. Salvation is found in our union with the divinized, new humanity that Christ has assumed and restored to communion with the Father.

The Cross and Resurrection

> For the message of the cross is foolishness to those who are perishing, but to us who are being saved it is the power of God. (1 Cor. 1.18)

James Payton Jr provides an elegant and masterful synthesis of the Orthodox vision of salvation.[14] Based on the ontology of the Incarnation, the death and resurrection of Christ constitute the climactic work of salvation through which physical death and the cosmic defeat of evil are accomplished (Rom. 1.1-4; 8.31-34; 1 Cor. 15.1-4; Jn 12.31). Christ's death on the cross on our behalf was an atoning sacrifice for the sins of the world.[15] Christ did for us what we could never do for ourselves. The gifts or benefits of his cross and resurrection are rich and varied: union with God, justification, redemption, reconciliation, adoption, sanctification, a new humanity, the fruit of the Spirit, a new creation and more. The cross also demands radical discipleship, most notably recorded in the Sermon on the Mount (Mt. 5–7). The Christian life is a life of daily dying to sin and increasing in newness of life (Rom. 6.1-11; 12.12). The resurrection of Christ is the ultimate 'good news' of the gospel. 'Christ is Risen!' is the victorious

---

relationship with God. We do not lose our creaturely status. The distinction between the Creator and the creature remains eternally. In addition, the doctrine is not merely a patristic teaching; it is a scriptural one: Jn 10.34-36; 1 Jn 3.2-3; 2 Pet. 1.3-4; 2 Cor. 3.18; Rom. 8.29; Mt. 17.1-8 and parallels. For an exegesis of these texts, see James R. Payton Jr, *Light from the Christian East* (Downers Grove, IL: IVP, 2007), 137-42.

[14] James Payton Jr, *The Victory of the Cross: Salvation in Eastern Orthodoxy* (Downers Grove, IL: IVP, 2019). Payton elaborates on themes I am unable to develop here due to limitations of space, including the work of the Spirit.

[15] For a fuller account of the work of Christ on the cross in Orthodoxy and its relation to Evangelical theology, see Bradley Nassif, 'The Evangelical Theology of the Eastern Orthodox Church', in James Stamoolis (ed), *Three Views on Eastern Orthodoxy and Evangelicalism* (Grand Rapids, MI: Zondervan, 2004), 27-87, especially 37-41.

source and goal of all the Church's liturgies and spiritual life. It is the basis of the believer's ever-growing deification into the image of Christ (Rom. 8.29; 2 Cor. 3.18).

Notice also in Paul's writings how the death and resurrection of Christ belong together: 'He was handed over to die because of our sins, and he was raised from the dead to make us right with God' (Rom. 4.25 NLT). The gospel requires both. At the cross, Jesus won the victory over the powers of darkness, and granted forgiveness of sins (Col. 2.11-15). But without the resurrection, the cross remained powerless for the forgiveness of sins (1 Cor. 15.17), and in fact there would be no gospel (1 Cor. 15.1-3).

The Gospel as the Church's Story

In the Church Fathers' exposition of the gospel, the Incarnation takes place within a biblical story that has many parts.[16] If any are left out, or if one part is given undue emphasis, the story will not come out as its author intended. How the story is told makes all the difference to how the gospel is known. The story of the gospel cannot be reduced to emphasizing a few propositions about the substitutionary work of Christ on the cross, justification by faith and the need to repent and believe, crucial as those things are. Rather, the gospel involves the whole plan of salvation history (*oikonomia*). It starts with God himself and then moves on through creation, the fall of the human race, the establishment of the covenant with the nation of Israel through whom the Messiah would come, the climactic fulfilment of salvation in the Incarnation of the Son through whom God's Kingdom is given and the Church of God is formed, followed by the proclamation of the gospel through the Church and ending with the eschatological consummation of the entire cosmos. Once again, the gospel is the work of the triune, intrapersonal God to restore us to union with himself and to communion with others, for the good of the world. This God does by forming a community through which the image of God is restored, through the cross, resurrection, ascension and Pentecost.

Finally, we return to the reality that the gospel is appropriated through the Church. The gospel is not a disembodied voice that has power to change people's lives all by itself, as if it were a text message sent from heaven. Instead, the people of God proclaim the gospel of the Kingdom of God by calling all to know Christ through repentance, faith and baptism into the body of Christ (Acts 2.38; 22.16; Rom. 6.1-12). Baptism is the occasion on which

---

[16] Biblical scholars today have used the story model to explain the overarching narrative of Scripture. This seems to be a helpful model to use because it comports well with the way the Church Fathers did their theology. Even though the Fathers did not have all the storylines organized in the neat and orderly way often found today, their reading of the biblical text was coherent as they sought the overall soteriological purpose (*skopos*) of the scriptural narrative. Examples include the exegetical commentaries of St John Chrysostom and St Athanasius's treatise *On the Incarnation of the Word*.

Christ, the Living Gospel, is appropriated by faith through the work of the Spirit. Discipleship follows baptism and becomes a daily 'death and resurrection' with Christ. At the centre of this worshipping community lies the bread and wine of the new covenant (Mt. 26.26; 1 Cor. 11.24). The Eucharist is central to the ongoing appropriation and proclamation of the gospel. Just as the Exodus and the Passover meal became the central communal act of commemorating the deliverance of the children of Israel from bondage, so also in a much greater way does the celebration of the Eucharist proclaim the salvation wrought by the death, resurrection and Second Coming of Christ: 'For whenever you eat this bread and drink this cup, you proclaim the Lord's death until he comes' (1 Cor. 11.26; 10.16). The Christian Church, therefore, is the locus of God's work in the world today. It is a eucharistic community that becomes most fully itself when it is gathered around the Lord's Table, presided over by a bishop in apostolic succession (or one of his appointed representatives) who calls on the Holy Spirit to bring to reality what it celebrates in word and sign. The primary language of the gospel is the language of Scripture expressed in the Church's preaching and eucharistic meal.

The Gospel in Orthodox Parishes Today

Finally, no presentation of the gospel in Orthodox perspective is complete without addressing the gospel to the internal life of the Church. The Church itself tells us that no formal membership in the community can ever guarantee salvation. Saints Symeon the New Theologian, Makarios of Egypt and other spiritual writers remind us that it is possible to be religious, but lost. Whether through lifelong commitment or through an instantaneous experience, an authentic form of Christian existence is one which appropriates the gospel by experiencing a personal Pentecost that is rooted in the sacramental life of the Church.[17] It is not only that the gospel, therefore, leads to the Church; the Church leads us to the demands of the gospel: 'For whoever wants to save their life will lose it, but whoever loses their life for me and for the gospel will save it' (Mk 9.23-24). This means that every pastor, parish council member, church school teacher and parishioner must come to terms with their own personal relationship with Jesus Christ before attempting to lead others to the knowledge of God.

An internal mission of spiritual renewal must be given top priority in the local Church. It is not enough for priests and bishops to offer parishioners more liturgies or 'try harder' sermons. The challenges facing the Church today can only be encountered by a robust biblical vision of the gospel. One of the most urgent needs in world Orthodoxy today is the need to

---

[17] Kallistos Ware, 'Personal Experience of the Holy Spirit According to the Greek Fathers', paper presented at the European Pentecostal/Charismatic Research Conference held in Prague, 10-14 September 1997, online at: https://silouanthompson.net/2008/08/experience-of-holy-spirit/.

(re-)evangelize our own people. This can be done in a variety of contexts, such as the confessional, personal counselling, hospital visitation and similar occasions for pastoral care. All of us – lay and clergy alike – must make the gospel as clear and central as it was to Jesus. It must be articulated in such a way that people inside and outside the Church can easily understand it. Authentic Christian experience flourishes in the Church whenever the gospel is consciously elevated in each of its life-giving liturgies and sacramental acts. 'At the core of the Orthodox tradition', writes Fr Theodore Stylianopoulos, 'whether we turn to the Eucharist or the lives of the great saints, the same truth has primacy, namely, Christ and the Gospel ... The challenge of rediscovering the centrality of the Gospel, as well as of energizing the evangelical ethos deeply enshrined in the Orthodox tradition, is our highest task.'[18]

---

[18] Theodore G. Stylianopoulos. *The Way of Christ: Gospel, Spiritual Life and Renewal in Orthodoxy* (Brookline, MA: Holy Cross Orthodox Press, 2002), 49. Stylianopoulos is Professor Emeritus of New Testament at Holy Cross Greek Orthodox Seminary in Brookline, MA, and this is an excellent resource for reclaiming the centrality of the gospel in Orthodox parishes. Aside from his debatable eschatological views, see practical suggestions for Church renewal in two works by Fr Eusebius Stephanou, *Pathway to Orthodox Renewal* (Fort Wayne, IN: Logos Ministry for Orthodox Renewal, 1978); and *Sacramentalized but not Evangelized* (Destin, FL: Orthodox Brotherhood of St Symeon the New Theologian, 2005).

3. Gospel as Foundation for Mission:
The Theological Basis

Dr C. Rosalee Velloso Ewell

Introduction

It is never very interesting to start with a caveat, yet it seems the title of this article warrants one rather desperately. Gospel. Foundation. Mission. Theological basis. One could spend a lifetime reflecting and writing on just one of those terms, let alone on all four put together. To add to our challenge, the request for the original presentation was for *the* theological basis, as if there were just one, if one at all.

Shaped in the post-modern, anti-foundationalist tradition, in which fundamentalism and relativism are basically understood as two sides of the same coin,[1] I prefer to shy away from an idea of a (or 'the') basis, and to focus on the terms 'Gospel' and 'Mission' as we think together about how these relate and how they shape our theologies and practices in our ever-changing world.

An implied notion of story or narrative in words such as 'Gospel' and 'Mission' will help to illustrate the ways in which we learn to hear God's call and to participate in mission together. The context for this presentation was a gathering of the Lausanne-Orthodox Initiative, in which the practices of listening and learning to one another's stories and building friendships with people of different traditions help to reinforce and strengthen the possibilities for greater co-operation and service to God in the future. I am very grateful that such an initiative exists!

As Baptist pastor and scholar H. Stephen Shoemaker has argued, humans are *homo narratus*.[2] We are story-formed creatures; whenever we neglect or make less of our own or of someone else's story, we are being less than human. God works through narratives, through transforming the scripts of our worlds, our contexts, and our lives. The Gospel and Mission are intimately related to such transformational narratives. Indeed, together, they are the 'master' narrative of transformation.

In order to think theologically and biblically about the relationship between Gospel and Mission in the context of these dialogues and this initiative, I will briefly examine some characteristics of what we are calling 'The Gospel of Jesus Christ'. Following this, we will consider some of the

---

[1] James Wm McClendon Jr and Nancey Murphy, 'Distinguishing Modern and Postmodern Theologies', *Modern Theology* 5.3 (1989), 191-214.
[2] H. Stephen Shoemaker, *Godstories: New Narratives from Sacred Texts* (Valley Forge, PA: Judson Press, 1998), xiii-xvi.

implications of such characteristics for how we understand mission. The conclusion will offer some pointers or suggestions for how reframing some aspects of our theology of mission might help us better understand and learn from one another. Furthermore, I would argue that a very serious implication, which follows from understanding the fullness of the gospel, is that our understanding of mission is shaped not by our agendas, but by coming alongside one another and listening to what God has to say to us as we serve God's world for the sake of God's Kingdom.

Gospel Traits

The Particularity of the Gospel

It is not any good news we have received or any good news we proclaim. It is the particular news, the particular story of God the creator, the God of Abraham, Isaac and Jacob, the God who raised Jesus from the dead. It is the story of the formation of a particular people at a particular point in time and with a particular mission; we will get to the mission later.

History matters in all our considerations of the gospel. Essential to the gospel is the narrative of the shaping of this particular people in history, the people through whom all the nations will be blessed. It is a history and a story that culminates in a very particular person.

The angel Gabriel visited one town, one virgin. It is a story that reaches its climax in the person of Jesus of Nazareth. We do not proclaim any messiah, but Christ crucified and risen.

Too often in the history of the world, and certainly in the history of Christian mission, the particularity of the gospel story has been lost or neglected, sometimes with dire consequences. Paying attention to such particularities is not a denial of the many contexts in which the gospel takes root, nor is it necessarily an imposition of one cultural context upon another. Rather, as was mentioned earlier, it is paying attention to the story-formed character of the good news of Christ. All stories have contexts and histories within which God works. Taking such contexts seriously makes us even more able, more open to the ways in which the good news shapes, and is shaped by, other contexts.

As Latin American theologian René Padilla wrote, in Jesus of Nazareth God contextualized himself. 'God does not shout his message from the heavens; God becomes present as a human being among human beings.'[3] As we consider the many characteristics of the gospel and their implication for mission, it is necessary always to keep such contextualization in mind.

---

[3] C. René Padilla, *Mission between the Times: Essays on the Kingdom* (Carlisle: Langham Monographs, 2010), 103.

The Universality of the Gospel as a Challenge to our Identities

Yes, the gospel is very particular, but it is also global, universal. What comes to mind when you think global? Perhaps our tendency is to think big:

> Big as in large-scale – mega-cities, mega-churches, massive numbers of people and crowds, the Olympics or the World Cup.

> Big as in diversity – people from all over, different people, different languages and cultures.

> Big as in big problems – global warming, global hunger, global war.

> But global gospel or global mission?

Generally, such terms might be deemed colonial or seen as an imposition. And yet ... the gospel is indeed global, universal, and about the transformation of all of the cosmos. Consider the global scope of God's promise to Abraham: 'Go from your country and your kindred ... and I will bless you ... so that you will be a blessing ... and in you all the families of the earth shall be blessed' (Gen. 12.1-3). In the Gospel of St John, 'For God so loved the world ...' is about as global as one can get.

The scope of the gospel challenges the ways that shape the church's identity (and our own identities). The particularity of our histories, of wars both theological and missiological, of divisions within peoples and denominations has the tendency to push us towards protecting what we see to be 'our way of life'. This was the challenge at the tower of Babel.

The people at Babel had two main concerns that are very similar to concerns we see today and in every age across the globe. These were:

- The concern over identity – Who are we? Will people remember our name? What if we are not valued?
- The concern over security – the concern of fear and vulnerability – What if we are scattered and dispersed? What if we become exiles or homeless?

These are very real fears and concerns in the world today, both in terms of people's physical well-being and the challenges faced by churches in war-torn areas or places of persecution. These are also spiritual and psychological fears of many people and many churches in the West. Too often we want the power and the fame and we fear being scattered and unknown. The good news of Jesus challenges these fears and pushes us towards a different understanding of mission.

The solution to their fears in Babel was all about themselves; it was this sense of 'we can take care of this on our own'. They had no concern for God or for seeking God's wisdom and saving help. They had technology (bricks and mortar: Gen. 11.3) and they used it without any concern for the earth or for the consequences of their use of these resources to secure their identity and safety.

In contemporary terms, the sin of the people at Babel was the sin of empire: it is the grasping for power and control, making others look up to oneself or one's church, and trusting in one's own strengths rather than pointing to Jesus and being dependent on God. Historically, in the context of

Christian mission, this type of sin has played itself out in various ways. It can be seen in coercive attempts to 'convert' others to the gospel; in the self-centred focus that the church often has on itself and on securing its own goals rather than God's; and even in the church's fear of 'mixing' with others who might make it different or who could upset the status quo. Unity that is based on uniformity, fear and a sense of determining one's own identity is not the unity of the good news of Jesus.

The sin of Babel also shows itself in more subtle ways, such as the presupposition that Western forms of Christianity are the standards by which other cultures' adherence to the gospel should be judged. In general terms, the missionary movements that grew rapidly in the nineteenth and twentieth centuries took the good news of the gospel around the world, but with them they carried their own cultural trappings and presumptions that 'church' must look the same whether it is located in cold northern Europe or tropical Latin America. The problem is not that the missionaries and evangelists were culturally bound; being of a particular culture is part of what it means to be human. Rather, the danger was twofold: first, there was the failure to recognize one's own cultural 'boundedness' – Western Christianity is just as 'native', 'cultural' and 'ethnic' as African or Asian Christianity. Second, and related to this first point, they sometimes failed to see the need to retell the gospel story within the particularities of the cultures to which the good news was taken, or they denied and trampled upon other cultures thinking that such was the way to preach Jesus. I believe these are still dangers that any church faces today, but especially those who have power or wealth; Christian witness is about Jesus, not about making everyone look the same or look like us. We need one another to be able to see our own blind spots and we need to pray often for discernment and care as we seek to be faithful to Christ in ever-changing landscapes.

Wherever the gospel is taken – east, west, north or south – it is culturally bound *and* it challenges cultures. It is the story of God's dealings with a particular people and coming to us in a Jewish man of the first century, but it also challenges and changes the landscape of the culture to which it is introduced. Jesus challenged the religious landscape of his day and challenges ours today. If the gospel does not challenge and transform all our fallen cultures, it has not truly taken root in such cultures.

The desire for power and fame were some of the sins of Babel. These remain challenges to genuine Christian unity today. Whenever the church points first to itself rather than to its Lord, it is behaving like Babel, making a name for itself, rather than trusting the gospel. According to the biblical text, it is specifically for this reason that the people decide to build the tower (Gen. 11.4), and it is also because of this that God decides to confuse their language and scatter them all over the earth. The text does not contain one verb of judgement or condemnation. Rather, there is the suggestion that the type of oneness for which humanity strives is that type which leads to total independence from God. At Babel the people took no notice of God, but God took notice of them. If the church is pointing to itself or to its ministries rather than looking to God or pointing others to Jesus, then it is failing in its obedience to the gospel, it is failing in its missionary task. If it is failing in its work of evangelism, it is failing in unity as well, for unity and evangelism must be bound together.

In John 17, Jesus prays that the disciples be one for sake of their witness, so that the world can come to know Jesus and, through Jesus, know the Father. At Babel the people failed to see that God is the only one through whom true unity is possible.

The universality of the gospel transforms who we are because we are invited into a bigger story, a story not of our own choosing, a story we were not even a part of. The gospel destabilizes our identities. Who are we? We are strangers, foreigners listening in to God's conversation with a particular people and then hearing God say, 'Boo! I have news for you. It's not all about you or your church or your plans, but about how I'm going to make all things new through Jewish flesh.' It is so new, so universal that even God's people have to reorient themselves according to this good news. The gospel de-centres us in order to re-centre us. It is universal in that it reaches its climax in God coming in the form of human flesh to include us into that global story.

'Remember that at one time you were without Christ' (Eph. 2.12). This reorientation, this re-centring around Christ is for all. Both Jew and Gentile have to be reconfigured in the person of Jesus Christ.

The Surprising Gospel

We are called to plant seeds, to witness to God's amazing love and the sacrifice of Jesus, but 'how the Spirit will grow the plant from that seed is not for us to determine'.[4] That plant might look really different from what we have known or even what we like. The gospel calls into question all our attempts to control, to lead as we see fit, to determine outcomes according to our desires or according to our understanding of how things should be. The gospel, by definition, resists any attempt to be colonized or to become empire. It is good news because it is the Spirit of God that is given as gift to the whole world and it is through this Spirit that we are sent out.

In the book of Jeremiah, we read the prophet's famous letter to the exiles: plant gardens, build houses, marry, have a family. And then the surprising promise: in these things you will find the peace, the *shalom* of the city in which God has placed you; in doing these things you will find your own salvation (Jer. 29.7). This is the kind of surprise that the people do not like. As we know from Jeremiah's story, there is resistance and refusal to follow God's call to mission to the city, and they return to Egypt, their place of slavery. The gospel of surprise might also be a gospel that asks the church

---

[4] Rose Dowsett, lecture to the Lausanne Theology Working Group, Arab Baptist Theological Seminary, Beirut, Lebanon, 17 February 2010.

today to be faithful, to practise mission in ways that are difficult and that demand greater humility. Yet it is in such faithfulness that God also surprises us.

We should expect to be surprised. It is in our story. God has promised to surprise and has done so again and again. Just as the disciples huddled in fear behind locked doors after the crucifixion and were surprised at the appearance of Jesus, so are we guided today by that same Spirit with which Jesus empowered them. It is the Spirit that led them to the wonder that was Pentecost and guides us still today. Just as at Pentecost or on the road to Emmaus, the gospel will surprise us. Expect the unexpected.

The Missionary Gospel or the Gospel Mission

From that first calling of Abraham to the laws of Moses to Jeremiah's instructions to plant gardens and build houses, this gospel was always about showing in word, deed and character that there is only one true God. The particularity of the laws had a purpose, a global purpose, that Israel should show to the nations through its own living what it means to welcome the stranger, to care for the widow and the orphan, to care for the land and let it rest. If we lose this evangelistic nature, we've lost the gospel. It is evangelistic, inviting the whole world to join their many stories with the story of Jesus, each part being joined to the whole, but each part maintaining its distinctiveness. To understand evangelism within the framework of the global gospel is like looking at the parallel yet contrasting images of Pentecost and Babel. At Babel we see languages that divided, that confused, that tore apart. At Pentecost we see a picture of fire and languages, still as diverse and multi-faceted as Babel, but languages that reconcile, that worship and that serve. So in the book of Revelation there are peoples gathered as different as we are today, all sitting at that table to feast. These are snapshots of the missionary character of the gospel.

Jesus asks us to obey, to be faithful to God's calling. Such obedience, while not always easy, is based on love. The gospel's missionary impetus is joyful. Think of a child who does something for a parent simply to honour the parent, unconcerned about the results or the effectiveness of her actions. She does it out of love. So we too are called to live this gospel and to tell others about it simply because we love God, because God first loved us.

The missionary gospel recalls the early narratives of God's shaping of a new people, the narratives of the early church and the lives of the saints. We are called to be holy, set apart, as St Peter writes. Yet being set apart in mission is not about retreat or being exclusive. Rather, God's Spirit is setting us apart for God's purposes in this world, with our many differences, with our many roles. Some of us are set aside with priestly functions, some with hosting, others with feeding, with healing, with praying.

If our starting point is the good news of Jesus and our obedience to that we see both gospel and mission from another perspective. If we start with the fact that mission belongs to God, then we are free not only to learn and to be with one another, but we are also free to allow others, and especially to allow God's Spirit, to guide and to shape our mission, rather than controlling the outcomes ourselves.

Perhaps one of the gifts that these conversations can give us and can give our different contexts is the gift of a renewed hope in the work of the Spirit in mission. A secondary gift might be a renewed commitment to mission, to sharing the story of Jesus and to inviting others to join their lives to that grand story.

The missionary character of the gospel requires that our faithfulness to God is carried out with others. Just as Peter needed Paul to help him see where he was making a mistake regarding the laws for the Gentiles, so we need one another. As we are drawn by the Spirit into closer communion with Christ, we are also drawn closer to one another. Within the context of mission praxis, sometimes being close to one another is difficult or uncomfortable. But drawing away from such difference also means pulling away from Christ who is at the centre.

Matthew the tax collector and Peter the fisherman were not natural friends. There was nothing in their world, in the politics or economics of their society, which would make them friends, let alone partners in mission. Yet this is precisely the power of the gospel in mission: bringing people together and joining their stories to the grand story of God's mission to redeem the world is only possible because of the gospel. It is the good news that compels us towards mission and it is the gospel that enables such mission.

Early in this chapter, I mentioned narrative and story. We have looked at a few snapshots, a few brief stories from our Holy Scriptures that shed light on the gospel and our participation in God's mission. My prayer is that we keep some of these images always in our minds. The calling of Abraham, confusion at the tower, gardens planted and houses built in Jeremiah, an angel, a virgin, the death of the Messiah, fire at Pentecost, the scandal of Gentile inclusion into the promises of another people, a banquet table. In the richness, the diversity and the particularity of these scenes, we can begin to glimpse the kingdom of the global gospel.

4. The Good News of the Gospel

Archpriest Michael J. Oleksa

Christ is Risen!
Xpucmoc Bockpec!
Kristuussaaq Unguirutuq!
Kristos nuosi kuolesta!

The paschal greeting and its response is the essence of the gospel, the good news and the inspiration, impetus, beginning and end of Orthodox mission. As Fr Alexander Schmemann noted many years ago, 'Without exaggeration, the celebration of the Resurrection lies at the heart of Orthodox worship. The Church dedicates a hundred days of the calendar year to preparing for and celebrating the Christ's victory over sin, darkness and Death itself and another fifty to keeping the memory of that triumph "alive" throughout the year.'[1] As the Apostle Paul noted, 'If Christ is not risen, we are fools and ought to be pitied' (1 Cor. 15.12-19). Without the resurrection, there is no Christian faith. The disciples would have remained a frightened group of disillusioned followers, hiding behind locked doors. Their encounter with the risen Lord transformed them into courageous evangelists and eventually martyrs. Their certainty in the 'fact' of the resurrection propelled them to the far corners of the earth, proclaiming the 'good news': 'Death is overthrown! Christ our God is Risen!'

Nothing in Christendom compares to the Orthodox observance of Holy Week and Pascha, the Passover from 'death to life and from earth to heaven', as the paschal hymn affirms. For the forty days following, the Paschal Troparion is sung literally thousands of times: 'Christ is Risen from the Dead, trampling down Death by death, and upon those in the tombs, bestowing Life.' And here is the good news for all people everywhere: Jesus, by his death on the cross, has destroyed death itself forever and for everyone. The Church declares that his victory includes all, 'Christ is Risen and not one

---

[1] I have been unable to trace the source of this quotation, but for similar points, see Alexander Schmemann, 'The Sanctification of Life', in *The Liturgical Life of the Church: The Third Annual Teacher's Religious Conference of the Metropolitan Council Religious Education Committees*, St Vladimir's Theological Seminary, 25-27 July 1963, 4-5, online at:
https://signorthodoxchurch.ca/publications/schmemann-liturgical-life-church/.
Shortly after his death in 1983, CBS broadcast an Easter programme from St Vladimir's Seminary, 'The Spirit of St Vladimir's', which begins with Fr Alexander making the same comment: https://www.youtube.com/watch?v=qycRfRzTo9Q.

dead remains in the tombs, for Christ being risen from the Dead has become the First Fruits of those who were asleep.'[2]

Death has been abolished for all people everywhere. We are all given eternal life. We are all destined to live in eternity with God, with Christ in his everlasting kingdom. If the mission begins by announcing this gospel, there is no need to convince those who hear this 'good news' of their sins, faults and transgressions first. We start at the end and move backwards from there.

How did God destroy death? By entering it himself. How did he do that? By dying as a criminal, executed by crucifixion. Why did he submit to such a humiliating death? Because he himself is humble and because he loves all people, sinners though we are, including those who have died in past generations. He came to earth seeking Adam whom he loved and, not finding him, descended into Hades to find and rescue him. God became man to enter death and destroy it 'from within'.

God is life and the source of all life. He is light and in him there is no darkness or shadow. When light enters darkness, the darkness is destroyed. When life enters death, death itself is abolished. The cross is the means by which 'Joy has come into all the world.'

The Anselmian model begins with very different premises: We humans are sinful because we have violated God's law and, as criminals, deserve to be punished. We have no excuse for our misdeeds and God is angry with us and will punish us. But he sent his Son into the world to take upon himself all the punishment we ourselves deserve. Following this paradigm, mission must start by convincing those to be converted that they are condemned, but there is a way out, an escape, which God has provided.

Ancient Church Fathers had some problems with this approach, first complaining that this requires belief in an angry Father who is ready to punish rather than forgive us. His demand for justice overrides is mercy, kindness and love. And mission must begin by presenting the 'bad news' first: you are all guilty and deserve punishment! The Fathers also ask what kind of father sends his son to be horribly tortured and murdered? What kind of God is this?

If we focus instead on the victory over sin, darkness and death as the essence of the gospel, there is no need to insist on universal guilt and damnation at the start of the mission. But if we are all granted eternal life, how then should we prepare for it and live now? What changes need to be made? How will the direction of our lives be influenced by this 'good news'? For the repentance (*metanoia*) the gospel demands is not a feeling of guilt or sadness, but a change of direction, an adjustment of our purpose, aim and goals.

If we are all destined to spend eternity with God, with Christ, with the angels and saints of all ages, and with each other, how does that change the

---

[2] St John Chrysostom, *Catechetical Sermon.*

way we live here, now, on earth? How do we relate to God, and to each other, once we accept that Christ is risen and we will all, in the end, be taken into his eternally and infinitely loving embrace, for 'our God is a consuming fire' (Heb. 12.29)?

From this perspective, salvation is about relationships. If we are in a loving, personal relationship with God, with Christ and with our neighbour – the least of these – then being forever with them will be joy, delight, happiness, bliss, ecstasy. But if we have rejected God, abused, exploited and violated our neighbour, we will nevertheless spend all eternity with him and with them. Hell is not so much a place to which we are condemned. It is a spiritual condition in which we have decided to remain. 'The Kingdom of God is within you!' (Lk. 17.21).[3] Yes, and also the potential for the reality of hell.

'Damnation' is not so much a juridical prison term to which we are sentenced by the righteous judge as a spiritual condition into which humans have already placed themselves. It is awkward, even painful, to be in the presence of some we dislike or have offended, or who has insulted, offended or harmed us or someone we know or love. At the extreme, imagine Hitler or Stalin forever in the presence of all their victims! Faced with Infinite Love, how will they endure that fire? But it is the fire of love that radiates and warms, enlightens and glows in the hearts of those who love, but the same fire becomes painful, burning those who continue to hate, who justify their sins against love and retreat into their separate, self-righteous and deluded individuality.

In the beginning, the Genesis account reminds us, God created and blessed everything, calling it 'very good'. All was holy, blessed and consecrated except that one infamous tree, unblessed and without any connection or reference to God, to life. It is the image of living without him. But life without Life is death and this is what Adam and all humans choose. We are born into a reality that is alienated from God, separate from him and in which, therefore, everyone and everything dies. Salvation requires the restoration of that broken relationship, a resumption of unity and of communion with God.

This derives from another biblical truth, that humans were originally created in the image and likeness of God. The Orthodox Church affirms that people have retained the image of God in their freedom and creativity. They are not compelled by instinct or driven to make exclusively 'fight or flight' decisions, as the animals are. We can freely decide our actions and therefore are responsible for the consequences of those actions. The image of God as freedom has been retained and this is liturgically celebrated when the celebrant offers incense to the icons made of colour and wood and then turns to the people and censes them, the living images of God, as well.

---

[3] Some English translations have 'among you', but both renderings put the focus on the 'presence' of the Kingdom here and now, not only in the future.

But the likeness has been lost. We have lost our similarity to God who is love, who is holy, who is all-merciful, patient, humble, kind and forgiving. And we see most clearly what God is in the person of the only-begotten Son, Jesus Christ. He is the pattern, the paradigm, the ultimate revelation of what God *is*, and therefore of what we are supposed to be or become. And when we compare ourselves to him, we recognize how far we have missed the mark, the target, the goal. Repentance comes when we see the need for readjustment of our attitudes, beliefs, behaviours and priorities.

What is God 'like'? He is Father, Son and Holy Spirit, a unity of three divine persons. Why is this important for all Christians? Because if God is a unity of persons, we, as billions of human persons, were created to embody that kind of unity among ourselves. The three divine persons are 'one in essence and undivided'. They are all three God, yet we insist that God is one God. How can three be one? This is a mathematical impossibility! But the Son and Holy Spirit so love the Father, that without any reduction in their divinity, they freely fulfil the will of the Father. Love makes God *one*.

It is in this likeness that humans were created. But sin is the disruption of that sort of unity. When asked why he ate the fruit, Adam virtually blames God – 'The woman you gave me' (Gen. 3.12) – and she blames the serpent: 'I was tempted' (Gen. 3.13). Sin is division, conflict, violence, egotism, self-affirmation and self-aggrandizement, the distortion of 'personality' (in communion and unity with others) and its devolution into 'individuality' (autonomous and separate beings). A classic Orthodox analysis recently published, succinctly presents the Orthodox perspective on this in a treatise: 'I love, therefore I am.'[4] Persons are saved as they enter into increasingly sincere and caring relationships with each other. But there is no such thing as *individual* salvation.

This unity in faith and love towards which we strive, with all people everywhere, our contemporaries and our ancestors, as well as all future generations yet unborn, will not be empirically achieved in this world, but it is already manifest, iconically, in the Divine Liturgy. Here, the believers gather at the Lord's Table in his future kingdom to eat and drink there together, to become partakers of the one bread and the one cup. On earth we 'represent' (that is, 'make present again') the cherubim who surround the heavenly throne and we sing their hymn, join their worship. In worship we unite with the saints and angels and with God himself. Food and drink are restored to their original function, as means of contact and communion with him.

---

[4] This phrase comes from the teachings of Archimandrite Sophrony who emphasized the need for a personal relationship with God, with God initiating the relationship. For the story of his life and an analysis of his ministry as a *starets* or spiritual advisor, see Nicholas V. Sakharov, *I Love, therefore I Am: The Theological Legacy of Archimandrite Sophrony* (Crestwood, NY: St Vladimir's Seminary Press, 2002).

In Alaska Native cultures, Aleut, Eskimo and Indian, the universal belief is that humans are poorly equipped to live in this Arctic environment. When they first arrived, the animals advised them to return to wherever they came from, noting that they could not run as fast as most of the animals, could not catch anything with their stubby fingers, could not fly without wings or feathers and were going to die of hypothermia since they had no fur. But when the humans refused to leave, the animals had to devise some way of helping them to survive. They offered to give the humans their fur and feathers for cover, for clothing and their bodies as meat to sustain them in exchange for gratitude and respect. This is a sort of 'natural covenant' which hunter-gathering tribes have made with the fish and wildlife whose self-sacrifice sustains them.

The gospel made perfect sense to these people. But now the pattern is revealed as divine. God becomes flesh to offer himself as a sacrifice to nourish us with the bread of eternal life. On the eve of Pascha, the Orthodox Liturgy includes the entrance hymn: 'Let all mortal flesh keep silent and with fear and trembling stand, pondering nothing earthly minded. For the King of Kings and Lord of Lords comes to be slain, to give Himself as Food to the Faithful'.

Wherever the gospel has taken root, has been accepted sincerely, the Orthodox mission has presented the good news primarily as the fulfilment of what that society already believed, rather than as the overthrow of their traditional beliefs. Missionaries, such as those who arrived from Valaam, Finland, on Kodiak in 1794, spent their first months among the Alutiiq people, seeking to discern what they already believed about God, about the world and the human condition. They discovered that the 'Americans', as they called them, already believed in one supreme heavenly God, and believed further that all people were descended from the same original parents, had a story of a world-wide flood, and knew most of the Ten Commandments. The missionaries decided they could build on this foundation.[5]

Perhaps even more remarkably, Fr Ioan Veniaminov, when encountering the undeniable spiritual powers of a local Ungangan Aleut shaman, interviewed him and concluded that this man was in communication with angels. Christian missions bring a part of God's revelation that no one could have surmised – that God became man and lived on earth and was crucified,

---

[5] Cf. Paul D. Garrett, *St. Innocent: Apostle to America* (Crestwood, NY: St Vladimir's Seminary Press, 1979); James J. Stamoolis, *Eastern Orthodox Mission Theology Today* (Maryknoll, NY: Orbis, 1986), 33-4; James J. Stamoolis, 'Innokentii Veniaminov', in Mircea Eliade and Lindsay Jones, eds, *Encyclopedia of Religion*, revised ed., vol. 7 (Detroit, MI: Macmillan, 2004); James J. Stamoolis, 'Missions, Orthodox', in *The New Catholic Encyclopedia*, revised ed. (Detroit, MI: Thomson / Gale. 2003); Michael Oleksa (ed), *Alaskan Missionary Spirituality* (Mahwah, NJ: Paulist Press, 1987); Michael Oleksa, *Orthodox Alaska: A Theology of Mission* (Crestwood, NY: St Vladimir's Seminary Press, 1992).

buried and risen. Not to steal, kill or lie seem to be universal commandments, easily discerned when people, any people, try to live harmoniously together. But to love your enemies is a uniquely Christian doctrine, illogical though it may be. No tribe ever arrived at this conclusion analytically. It makes no sense! But when the missionaries brought this commandment to them, they accepted it with joy. Inter-tribal fighting and wars ceased. The good news brought peace where there had been war, and forgiveness where there had been hatred.

Why must we forgive and be reconciled? Why must we treat each other with kindness and respect? Because we are going to spend eternity together!

There is, therefore, in Orthodox piety and theology, very little emphasis on Christ's suffering. On icons of the crucifixion, he is universally depicted as asleep, dead, not in agony, not suffering. There are no services during the time on Holy Friday he is hanging on the Cross. The Church maintains total silence before this mystery. But at the time of his life-creating death, he is buried, the shroud carried to the tomb where he rests for three days. And gradually, this death will be revealed, in the rites and hymns of the Church, as not the ultimate defeat that it seemed at first to be – the murder of God and Satan's greatest possible triumph – but the ultimate victory of love, light and life over hatred, darkness and death.

The goal of mission is, therefore, a call to unity. Competing 'missions' are therefore a contradiction. Christ's final prayer was for his disciples to be one as he is one with the Father, 'I in them and Thou in me' (Jn 17.23). A 'mission' that divides Christian from Christian cannot succeed. One might say that it cannot truly be Christian, for its activities preclude fulfilling the Lord's will as expressed in his prayer.

Orthodox receive the Eucharist using a formula 'for the remission of sins and unto life everlasting'. Sins are forgiven to the extent that we repent of them, turning from those temptations and habits to become increasingly more like God, like Christ. This is a lifelong struggle in this world, which is why we must 'deny ourselves, take up our cross and follow' (Mk 8.34). There is an inescapable ascetic dimension to Christian life, the struggle to turn our innate self-love outwards, away from our own desires, wishes, programmes, ideologies and projects, and towards others, towards God and our neighbour.

The Church reserves 100 days to remember and celebrate the resurrection each year. She also has over 170 days of fasting. But this fasting should not be understood in exclusively dietary terms. The true fast is fasting from sin, from evil, from pride, from impatience, from indifference. Let us abstain from passion as we abstain from food, as the Lenten hymn advises. The world, the cosmos which God so loves, is being ravaged by uncontrolled, unbridled human greed, consuming the earth and its resources at an alarming rate. If we truly love God and love our neighbour, we cannot sit silently by and allow this devastation to continue. The gospel must necessarily include a call to self-control, to the voluntary limiting of our self-centred impulses to own, control and dominate.

It is true that God gave humanity the right and even the command to 'fill the earth and subdue it' (Gen. 1.28), but this was when we were still obedient to his will and in loving communion with Him. The 'fall' of man, the severing of his ties to God, was a disaster of a cosmic order. Not only did human beings become mortal beings, and therefore in unavoidable dog-eat-dog competition with all other humans, but mortality became the law of nature, all creatures devouring each other in order to survive. This cycle has been broken by the resurrection. Pascha is good news to the whole creation.

And the mission of the Church extends to all of nature. The Orthodox bless nearly every created thing: plants, animals, food, land, water, rivers and oceans. The mission of the Church extends beyond a concern for humans to the whole of nature, for God blessed it in the beginning and our sin blinds us to its inherent sanctity. Environmental pollution is more than a social or economic tragedy. It is a sacrilege, poisoning the world God called 'very good' and blessed, and which Christ renews. The Spirit hovered over the waters in the beginning and he descends on the waters at the baptism of Jesus in the Jordan, revealing Father, Son and Holy Spirit at the riverside.

The most recent state-wide debate in Alaska arose around the controversial 'Pebble Project', a copper and gold mine at the headwaters of the world's largest wild salmon fishery. Only the Orthodox spoke out against this potential degradation of a huge region in South-West Alaska in theological and religious terms. The unanimous resolution of the Diocesan Assembly declared that the Church would invoke God's blessing on any development that would enhance the lives of our people, but could not invoke such a blessing on any 'development' that threatened to pollute and poison the lakes and rivers upon which we had performed the Rite of the Great Blessing of Water every year for two centuries. Such environmental damage was termed a 'sacrilege' – a term the Pebble Project's leaders adamantly rejected. They even called the headquarters of the Orthodox Church in America, complaining that this was not an appropriate characterization of their mine. 'Is this really the doctrinal position of the Orthodox Church?', they demanded rhetorically. The response was, 'Well, yes, it is!' But no other church or denomination supported us.

This world is being transformed into God's Kingdom, like a caterpillar in a cocoon. Heaven is not some spiritual, distant place somewhere in the clouds. It is this world 'made new'. This process is already under way. At every Liturgy, God uses bread and wine, food, to connect himself to us. The bread is more than flour, water and yeast. The flour comes from wheat, the wheat from a field somewhere on earth, where the soil had to be fertile, the sun had to shine, the rain had to fall, the wind had to blow, the farmer had to sow and the harvest had to be gathered. Then the wheat had to be ground, packaged and shipped. All that cosmic as well as human energy is being offered to God on the altar. The wine comes from grapes whose cosmic biography is parallel, the sun shining, the rain falling, the wind blowing, the fertility of the soil given by God. It takes the whole creation to celebrate the

Eucharist. Our communion with God is dependent on the viability and sustainability of the earth.

There are sins against the creation, just as there are sins against other people. We can violate God's will and plan by allowing the world, the cosmos, which he so loved and came to reclaim, to sanctify and to transfigure, to be poisoned and polluted while the Christians remain silent. Our 'green' Patriarch and now Pope Francis have joined to call upon all believers of all faiths to unite in maintaining the inherent sanctity of the whole creation. This too is our mission.

If there has been conflict, even hostility between missions anywhere, this situation undermines the success of any of them. Sin is division, a rupture of communion, a break in loving relationships. Salvation, then, is unity, a restoration of communion, a return to loving relationships. Only to the extent that we can accomplish this can we be truly 'missionaries' and bring the essence of the gospel to others. Our divisions undermine our proclamation. Our ignorance of, and indifference to, each other render our 'gospel' hypocritical at best, unbelievable at worst.

At least let us be united in paschal joy! No matter what doctrinal differences may continue to plague our situation, let us not allow these to disrupt the common work in which we must all be engaged: the mission to the world and to all creation, to proclaim the triumph of God and his victory over sin and death itself, the good news of the resurrection and eternal life for all.

5. Learning from Paul Together: How New Insights into Paul's Teaching Can Help Move Us Forward in Mission[*]

Rt Revd Prof. N. T. Wright

Introduction

I have spent a good deal of time over the years trying to help build bridges between different Christian groups and churches and I remain convinced that one of the best ways forward is to read the Bible together and – perhaps paradoxically! – not least the letters of St Paul. I say 'paradoxically' because Paul has often been a figure of controversy, both in his own day of course and ever since the sixteenth-century Reformation, when he was more or less claimed as a patron saint by the Protestant Reformers even though they often disagreed amongst themselves as to how exactly he should be interpreted.

Before we get properly into Paul himself, however, let me say a word or two about the theme which I have been asked to address; about three words in particular, 'Mission', 'Teaching' and 'Together'. These are all important for Paul himself and for us today, but they all need sharpening up. (I should say at the outset that I am taking for granted throughout this chapter a good deal that I have argued at more length in various published works.)

First, 'Mission'. The mission of the Church – or, more properly, the mission of God through the Church, the ongoing tasks for which the living God 'sends' and equips the Church – can only be properly understood in the light of a fully biblical eschatology. This means firmly embracing the biblical vision of new creation, of new heavens and new earth, inaugurated when Jesus announced God's Kingdom and rose from the dead after defeating the powers of darkness, and to be consummated when he returns in glory to make all things new. The mission of the Church *derives from* that inauguration, energized by the same Spirit by whose power Jesus was raised, and *points forward to* that consummation, anticipating it, demonstrating its life-transforming reality even in the present time, calling men, women and children to share in the new life, communal and personal, which is already a reality and which will be fully revealed at the last.

I anticipate that this holistic new-creation vision and all that follows from it may be startling to many Western Protestants, for whom 'eschatology'

---

[*] This article was originally published as N. T. Wright, 'Learning from Paul Together: How New Insights into Paul's Teaching can help Move us Forward in Mission', *St Vladimir's Theological Quarterly* 62.4 (2018), 317-32. We are grateful to the editor for permission to republish it here.

often focuses on 'going to heaven when you die' on the one hand and a 'second coming' on the other hand in which Jesus will snatch his people away from the wreck of the present world and take them to 'heaven' at last. This Western vision, deeply rooted (albeit with variations) in the Middle Ages, gives rise to a sense of 'mission' simply in terms of 'saving souls for heaven', despite the fact that the Bible nowhere speaks of the future in those terms. I suspect in fact that a certain amount of resistance to what I and others have done that goes under the loose title of 'new perspectives' on Paul – there is no single 'new perspective', but a variety – has come not so much from problems connected with the traditional doctrine of justification, though that of course matters as well, as from what to many appears as a radical redrawing of the ultimate future. And I suspect that many Orthodox theologians will recognize the biblical picture I am sketching as far more consonant with their own traditional emphases than with those of Western theology. As in some other matters, I am perhaps standing like a typical Anglican halfway between different groups.

This already highlights the need for the second word: 'Teaching'. We are a group of theological educators,[1] and as such our vocation is to continue a noble tradition unbroken since the days of the apostles. When Paul and others speak of 'teachers' in the Church, what were they teaching? One obvious answer is that they were teaching people to read; many non-Jews of Paul's day would be functionally illiterate, and the Church was eager from the beginning to get Christians to read the Scriptures and to understand the great story into which they had, to their own surprise, been adopted. Few would disagree with this, but the new insights which I and others have been exploring in Paul have often come as we have tried to tune in to the way he and other second-temple Jews were reading their scriptures, and in particular to the great scriptural story in which they believed that they were now caught up. A great many of the traditional puzzles and problems which people have encountered in reading Paul have arisen because it has been assumed that he was addressing the questions which much later generations wanted to address – particularly, in modern Western thought, those I mentioned above, of 'how can my soul get to heaven?', or, in Luther's question, 'how can I find a gracious God?' But the trouble is that Paul and his contemporaries were not asking exactly those questions. Ultimate salvation on the one hand, and assurance of divine grace and mercy on the other, are and were of course vital. But the way these questions have normally been asked ignores the central element of teaching which we see in, for instance, some of the great speeches in Acts, and also by strong implication in Paul's letters themselves: that what had happened in Jesus of Nazareth meant what it meant within the context of the long story of Israel, the single narrative stretching from Abraham to the Messiah and now, through the Spirit, out into the wider

---

[1] The paper on which this article is based was delivered at a LOI consultation for theological educators in Cambridge during September 2017.

world. For Paul, it is this narrative that makes sense of and undergirds the Church's mission: one of his favourite texts was Isaiah 49, where the 'servant' is commissioned to bring God's light to the nations. Saul the Pharisee thought in terms of the 'present age' and the 'age to come'; for Paul the Apostle, the 'age to come' had broken in to the present age in Jesus, so that now the powers of the age to come had been released upon the world, commissioning and equipping the apostolic mission. As far as I am concerned, the most important new insight into Paul's teaching to arise in recent generations has been the discovery of the way in which Paul's apocalyptic eschatology makes sense as the sudden and shocking fulfilment of the age-old scriptural promises, generating a new moment, a new time, in which new things would happen, chief among them (as far as Paul was concerned) being the creation of a new covenant family, the Jew-plus-Gentile single community which, indwelt by the Spirit, was to be the model, the advance sign, and in part the means, of God's eschatological purposes for all creation. Perhaps I should just say that this vision emerges most clearly in the letter to the Ephesians, and that I regard the Western scholarly prejudice against Ephesians as arising exactly from the long-running and deep-seated Western distortions of biblical theology of which I have already spoken. The Mission and the Teaching thus go together.

'Together', indeed, is my third key category. One would not know, from many Pauline interpreters, that the unity of the Church was one of Paul's overriding passions. The famous doctrine of justification, used in the sixteenth century and later as a means of dividing the Church, was itself actually designed to affirm the unity of all believers across lines of ethnic and other divisions. That is clear particularly from its first exposition in Galatians 2, where Paul confronts Peter because Peter has given in to pressure from hard-line Jewish Christians and has separated himself from table-fellowship with Gentile Christians. Paul's response, in a brief articulation of justification, is that *all who share Messiah-faith belong at the same table.* All alike have died with the Messiah and have come through to new life in him, and that new shared life is the one and only source and marker of their identity: 'I through the Law died to the Law that I might live to God; I am crucified with the Messiah, nevertheless I live, yet not I but the Messiah lives in me'. Plenty of detailed questions remain, of course, but the thrust of the passage is clear: what matters is that we belong *together*, we eat together, we pray together, we believe together. Again, it often goes unnoticed that whereas even the vital doctrine of justification is stated only in three of the letters, and there quite briefly, every letter, including Philemon, insists on the unity of the Church and is working hard to achieve it through what Paul names 'the ministry of reconciliation'. Whether it is Jewish and Gentile in Galatians and Romans, rich and poor in Corinthians, competing factions in Philippians, different ethnic groups in Colossians, a master and a slave in Philemon – at every point we find Paul standing in the middle and saying 'But we must do this *together.*' So here we are: mission, teaching and togetherness.

There is of course one other major concern for Paul, and that is holiness. The community that has come through the death and resurrection of the Messiah, that is indwelt by the Spirit, that is in its very existence a sign and foretaste of the coming time when the creator will flood the whole creation with his glory – this community has the responsibility to model the life of new creation, of creation restored. The eschatology I spoke of above funds this vision of holiness, which cannot be reduced – as it has so often been reduced in Western thought – to detached ethical principles or rules on the one hand or to the mere cult of 'authenticity' or 'spontaneity' on the other hand. Right from the start Paul's communities were challenged to live differently from the world around them. This meant in one sense living Jewishly – particularly in their rejection of idolatry and sexual immorality – though granted the crucified and risen Messiah the Jewishness had been radically redrawn so that ethnic-specific customs had become irrelevant. (This is a particularly important point today when sexual morality, upon which Paul insisted, is often put in the same level as food-laws and circumcision, which Paul declared to be 'matters indifferent'.) Of course, holiness is fairly easy if you do not care about unity; you just split over every disagreement. Similarly, unity is fairly easy if you do not care about holiness; anything goes and we shrug our shoulders and ignore it. One of the biggest challenges for me about the new insights into Paul's teaching, and one of the most vital to grasp if we are to move forward together in mission, is that combination of unity and holiness. The world will take no notice of a divided church. The world will take no notice of an unholy church. Paul's theology is directed again and again at equipping and exhorting the Church to be united and holy so that the world may see that Jesus is Lord, that in raising him from the dead God has launched his new creation, and that there is in consequence a different way to be human. All mission flows from that, as the Church announces Jesus as Lord and explains what that means not least by reference to the new way of life which has been unveiled and which the Church itself is supposed to be modelling.

So much by way of a long introduction. I now want to move into my two main sections, expanding what I have said into the areas of eschatology and mission on the one hand and justification and mission on the other. In both, I am again drawing on the Pauline insights which I and others have developed in recent years.

Eschatology and Mission

When you buy a new commentary on a favourite book of the Bible, if you are anything like me you turn at once to certain particular passages to see what the writers will do with them. With commentaries on Paul's letter to the Romans, one obvious point is 10.4: what does Paul mean in saying that the Messiah is the end of the law … or is it the goal of the law? Does the Messiah abolish the law or fulfil it, or what; and how does Paul's subsequent use of Deuteronomy explain what he means? For me, an equally important point is the place of Abraham in the argument of Romans 4 and Galatians 3. Many exegetes assume that Abraham is simply an 'example', or a 'proof from Scripture', an ancient instance of someone who was 'justified by faith', offered without any sense of a larger narrative which has Abraham as its starting-point and the Messiah, and the believing community, as the newest elements. Some have tried to resist the idea of a grand biblical narrative, supposing that it reduces grace to the mere outworking of historical progress; but this is a pernicious distortion, combining elements of Reformational protests against 'works' (and hence against 'history' – that strange connection would take too long to unpack just now) with elements of early twentieth-century protests against immanent Hegelian progress-schemes. When we grasp the thought-world and particularly the narrative world of second-temple Jews such as Paul, and then see how, for him, the good news of Jesus the Messiah, crucified and risen, made the sense it did within that world, Abraham cannot simply be a random example. The two key points are that for second-temple readers of Genesis Abraham was the divine answer to Adam, or rather the start of the divine answer to Adam, requiring the full answer in the later achievement of the Messiah. The nexus between Abraham and the house of David is clear in many texts; I think of Psalm 2, so vital for Paul and other early Christians, in which the Abrahamic promises of inheritance are globalized so that David will now inherit the whole world. This fits exactly with Paul's sense that Isaiah 40-55 has now come true and is coming true: the work of the Servant has accomplished the divine purpose to end Israel's long exile and restore creation itself. That is why mission is now the name of the game.

The trouble for us here is that most Western exegetes until recently have ignored the four themes which were so obvious in the first century but so opaque to later ones. I start with three interlocking ones and then return to the fourth.

First, the principle I just mentioned: God's purpose through Abraham was to rescue the human race. Second, the point of rescuing the human race was that God always purposed to work within creation *through his image-bearers*, so that saving people from sin and death was not simply for their own benefit but so that through renewed humans God would rescue creation itself. That is the underlying logic of Romans 8, which by anyone's account must be seen as central to Paul. Third, Paul invokes again and again the biblical prophecies which speak of God's frustrated judgment on the people of Israel, resulting in exile – not just the exile in Babylon itself but the much longer exile, spoken of in Daniel 9, in which most Jews of Paul's day believed they were still living. The exiles, still enslaved under foreign overlords, longed for the much-promised New Exodus, and not only Paul but most of the New Testament writers insist that this is what has happened in the events concerning Jesus. (The reason they can all be so sure of this is of course because Jesus himself chose Passover as the moment to do what had to be done.) The different stories all fit together: the exile of Israel is the long outworking of the exile of Adam and Eve from the Garden, and the New Exodus is therefore the rescue of Israel – in the person of the Messiah as he defeats the powers of darkness and is raised from the dead – and with that the rescue of the human race as a whole.

Here is a point of paramount importance in many current debates, not least as they affect the mission of the Church. People have often supposed that Paul had discovered what he took to be a new or superior form of religion, that he rejected something we call 'Judaism' because it now seemed to him an inferior form of 'religion', and that Christian 'mission' would then consist in propagating this new kind of 'religion'. That perception carries all the marks of nineteenth-century philosophy and none of first-century history (a mistake which is reinforced when educational institutions, and indeed broadcasting institutions, treat anything to do with 'Christianity' as a branch of 'religion', with 'religion' defined in an eighteenth-century way rather than a first-century way). What mattered for Paul was not *comparative religion* but what we may call *messianic eschatology*. Any Jew of the period, faced with the claim that this or that person was Israel's Messiah (there were many such claims, culminating with the Bar-Kochba rebellion of AD 132-135), would know at once that it constituted an eschatological and theological claim – and indeed a global claim, because Israel's Messiah was to be the Lord of the whole world. One could not say 'This man is Messiah; so follow him if you feel like it'. To say 'this man is Messiah' necessarily means 'This is where the One God is acting for the salvation of Israel and thereby of the world, and this constitutes a worldwide summons to faithful allegiance'.

This does not, then, mean that something called 'Judaism' (again, beware of nineteenth-century constructs!) is deemed to be somehow 'inferior' as a system or pattern of religion; on the contrary, the claim only makes sense as the *validation* of everything that first-century Jews like Paul had held dear (the ancient purposes and promises, the long covenantal narrative). The symbols of Jewish identity themselves – circumcision, Sabbath, food laws – were set aside, not because they were irrelevant or 'legalistic' but because they were forward-looking signposts to the reality which had now been unveiled. To cling to the signposts is to imply that you have not yet arrived at the reality; but the point of Paul's gospel was that the reality had dawned in the events concerning Jesus. In him, the promises to Abraham had been fulfilled; Adam and Eve had been rescued, and with that new creation had been launched; Israel's exile was over and 'Israel' itself had been transformed, as so many scriptures had promised, into a new worldwide family. This story, with this fulfilment, is the necessary substructure for Paul's mission; and, I would submit, for ours as well. Fresh teaching in all these areas is urgently needed if we are to understand our shared mission as *both* the announcement of Jesus as the crucified and risen Lord, demanding the personal response of obedient faith, *and* the inauguration of new creation, with signs of healing and hope pointing forward to the eventual renewal of the whole cosmos.

I mentioned a fourth element, which could be a course of lectures in itself but which I will state very briefly. For Jews of Paul's day, the Temple was the central symbol of history, covenant, hope and above all divine presence. Recent research has shown again and again how from Genesis and Exodus onwards the Tabernacle and the Temple were seen in terms of *new creation*: the wilderness Tent, and then Solomon's Temple, were understood as the *microcosmos*, the 'little world', not an escape from creation into a separate 'religious' space but the place where heaven and earth came dangerously together, thereby functioning as the sign and foretaste of the promised new creation. (Within a larger biblical theology, this is of course why there is no temple in the new creation in Revelation 21 and 22: the new creation *is* the new temple, with the New Jerusalem as the Holy of Holies within it.) All this (and much more detail), as many scholars have now argued, was easily present to many Jewish minds in the first century, and makes a great deal of sense both of Jesus' focus on the Temple and of Paul's fresh use of Temple-imagery. This theme joins up with the narrative I sketched a moment ago, because part of the point of the long-awaited 'return from exile' was that Israel's God himself had promised to return to his people in power and glory (notably in Isaiah 40-55 but in many other books as well, including so-called 'post-exilic' writings like Zechariah and Malachi) but had not done so yet. I have argued at length in *Paul and the Faithfulness of God* (chapter 9) that this theme of the return of YHWH to Zion is central to Paul's Christology and pneumatology, offering a window on early trinitarian theology which I would hope might prove exciting for Orthodox and Evangelical alike. But my point here is that this also provides the eschatological context for understanding Paul's fresh use of Temple-imagery (e.g. in 1 Corinthians 3 and 6) in relation to the Church and the individual Christian, with unity the theme of chapter 3 and holiness the theme of chapter 6. Once again, what we are looking at is not simply a miscellaneous metaphor, a mere verbal allusion, but a deep-rooted theological theme: that the living God has come to dwell in our midst in and as Jesus, Israel's Messiah, and now comes again to dwell in the hearts and lives of his faithful community. *The very existence of this community therefore constitutes the mission of God in the world*, though of course we must quickly add that since the Spirit is the same Spirit that blows through all creation we must not and cannot limit the Spirit's work simply to 'what is going on in the church'. There is also the danger that some might suppose this would limit 'mission' to 'ecclesiology', but this would simply be to miss the point: ecclesiology – the biblical understanding of the Church – simply is the *outreach* of new creation in the midst of the old. (That is why suffering is also, for Paul, a constant feature of apostolic life, as the old world, called to account by the new, strikes back in unpleasant ways.) The Church, seen as the Temple where the Spirit dwells (as in Ephesians 2 and elsewhere – and actually this theme is present in much of Romans as well, though normally unnoticed), is the sign and means of new creation, and if for a moment the Church forgets this vocation, it is turning itself into something else (a 'religion', perhaps?).

Paul often simply takes this missionary focus of the Church's life for granted. He himself is involved in the apostolic task, but (perhaps surprisingly to us) he seldom speaks of others sharing in this work. Philippians is the obvious exception, where he envisages Christians 'speaking the word with boldness', and 'holding forth the word of life' (both passages have difficulties but the overall thrust is, I think, clear). But part of the missionary point is that the Church is to 'do good to all', to be generous, to rejoice with those who rejoice and weep with those who weep, to 'remember the poor', to show the example of a public life worthy of the gospel, in other words, to live as a sign of contradiction to the ways of the old world and a sign of hope that there is a new way to be human, a way of outgoing love and refreshing holiness. The history of the second and third centuries – when the Romans were doing their best to stamp out this new and subversive movement – indicates that the project succeeded beyond, perhaps, the wildest dreams of Paul and his colleagues. The Church really was the missionary body of the Messiah.

Justice and Justification

I turn now to my second main topic, which dovetails at many points with what I have already said. Once we understand the second-temple world of Bible reading, with its great sprawling narrative from Abraham to the Messiah, with exile and return as a major feature and the Temple, and the return of God to the Temple, as providing the theological depth, we can focus on the question of justification in a new way. Justification has been, of course, at the heart of some of the puzzles about the so-called 'new perspective' on Paul, and though this is not the time or place to expound that whole theme in any detail I hope I can not only shed some light on the controversy but also show how such reflection might help focus and fuel our shared missionary calling.

The word 'justification' has suffered from becoming first a technical term and then a contested technical term in ways that have not allowed its original range of meaning to shine through. (Like everything else in this article, this is of course a long and complex story which I here drastically abbreviate.) Once again my sense is that the Western tradition has done us no favours here – ironically, since the doctrine of justification was one of the key focal points of the Reformation. As Karl Barth himself observed in the *Church Dogmatics* (long before anyone was talking about 'new perspectives' and all that!), Luther allowed his view of what was wrong with Rome to skew his exegesis of Galatians by reading it as though Paul's Jewish opponents were more or less like late medieval Roman Catholics; and many of Luther's successors to this day have continued with various forms of the same mistake. The problem can be focused by suggesting that for Luther and the other reformers what mattered above all was the *forensic* sense of 'justification': as in Romans 3, all humans are in the dock, God is the judge, all are found guilty – but then, astonishingly, the verdict is reversed on the basis of the death of Jesus on the one hand and 'faith' on the other. There are several exegetical problems with this account of Romans; and it is noticeable in particular that it is *only* in Romans where the 'forensic' meaning stands out (and only in Romans 1-3, not in Romans 4 or the 'justification' passage in 9-10). We cannot transport the 'lawcourt' meaning into Galatians 2 and 3, or into Philippians 3, both of which are about 'justification' but without hinting at a lawcourt setting. In addition, in each of the key passages, Paul combines talk of 'justification' with talk of 'being in the Messiah': Romans 3 speaks of being justified 'through the redemption which is in Messiah Jesus', Galatians 2 speaks of being 'justified in the Messiah', and Philippians 3 aspires to be 'found in him' (that is, in the Messiah), 'not having my own righteousness but that which is through Messiah-faith'. Many Reformational accounts of 'justification' (with Calvin a notable exception) have managed to split off 'justification by faith' from 'being in the Messiah'. For Paul, they belong together.

The problem here is deep-rooted. As I have argued in *The Day the Revolution Began*, the essentially Platonic eschatology of 'going to heaven' has been coupled with an essentially moralizing anthropology in which keeping (or not keeping) the moral law is the clue to 'going to heaven' – so that those who do not keep it need some other way, namely to be 'justified in the Messiah' and/or 'by faith'. But this does no justice to Paul's arguments. For Paul, as for all serious Jews of the period, the primary human failure was not 'sin' but idolatry, and the primary result was not simply not 'going to heaven' but the failure of the whole human project, including the divine mandate to look after creation. 'Sin' still matters, of course; it is what happens when humans worship idols, thence distorting their own humanity and that of others with them. Ultimate 'eternal life' still matters, of course; only it will be resurrection life in God's new creation, with responsibilities ('the royal priesthood'), not simply disembodied bliss. This double distortion has then produced distorted views of what the cross achieved, a problem I have addressed in the book just mentioned. But my point for our present purposes is that by focusing on the moralistic problem, and then shrinking 'justification' to the lawcourt in which that problem is addressed, the tradition has failed to notice the two other focal points of Paul's 'justification' language.

First, this language is (in general terms) 'relational', which (in specific terms) takes us into the sphere of covenantal theology: the question is, who is really a member of the family of Abraham, the family promised in the foundation covenant of Genesis 15 which Paul expounds in Romans 4 and Galatians 3? (We remind ourselves that the point of the covenant was that Abraham's family was God's answer to the problem of Adam – in other words, that to be within the covenant family was to be declared to be 'in the right', with sins forgiven; this is not, in other words, something to be played off against 'sin and forgiveness'.) The main thrust of Paul's 'justification' argument in Romans 3-4 and 9-10, and also in Galatians 2 and 3, was not 'this is how you get to heaven' but that *believing Gentiles are every bit as much members of the Abrahamic covenant family as believing Jews.* The unity of the covenant family was threatened in Galatia (and was anticipated in the warnings of Philippians 3). That unity needed to be nailed down firmly in Romans if the later exhortations in the letter were to have full value.

But if 'justification' language is not only forensic but also covenantal (indeed, forensic *because* it is covenantal), it is also *cosmic*. In the largest sense, the creator God intends to put all things right in the end: this is the promise of the Psalms (e.g. 96, 98), a promise built in to creation itself and never rescinded in favour of any cosmic dualism such as that embraced by Gnosticism. To understand how this works we need once again to invoke eschatology: God *will* put all things right at the last; God *has*, as a past event, launched this project in raising Jesus from the dead; and, in the present, *God puts humans right so that they can then be part of his putting-right project for the world.* This is what is missed in many traditional doctrines, but is a point central to Paul, not least to Romans (this is what is happening in Romans 8, as redeemed humans share Jesus' sonship and the 'glory' spoken of in Psalm 8, namely, the glorious rule of the 'son of man' over the creation). The larger point of a Hebraic vision of 'justice' – not so much a punitive 'judgment', though that is implied for the recalcitrant, as the 'judgment' for which creation longs, as in the Psalms – is the long outreach of what Paul means by the *dikaiosyne theou*, the 'righteousness of God': God's covenant faithfulness *through which creation is to be restored by means of the restoration of the human race.*

It ought to be clear from this that a 'mission' which is simply aimed at bringing people to faith in Jesus and so assuring them of eternal salvation has only done half the job. Yes, coming to explicit faith matters. Yes, this faith functions as the badge which assures the believer, and his or her fellow believers, that this person is a true member of Abraham's covenant family, and 'those he justified, them he also glorified'. But justification is a middle term in a much larger story than normally envisaged. And that larger story is, once again, the story of creator and cosmos, of God and the world. 'Justification' forms part of the missiological mandate of the Church, not because that mandate is simply to get more people into 'heaven' but because the mandate is to bring signs of new creation to birth even in the present age, signs that point forward towards, and indeed truly partake in, the reality of the new creation which will be complete upon Jesus' return to put all things right and to transform his people so that their bodies are 'like his glorious body' (Phil. 3.20-21, again echoing Ps. 8). Those who themselves have been 'put right', as the Spirit works through the gospel to bring them to faith and to the transformation of identity signalled in baptism, are called by that very same event to be part of the mission of God to and for the world.

Conclusion

It is time to sum up after this very brief account of some ways in which recent insights into Paul and his teaching can help move us forward together in mission. My argument, obviously, has been that as we learn more about the actual historical context of Paul's work, and particularly about the Jewish narratival world which makes sense of so much of his writing, we can see in these two ways (and no doubt several others) that the mission of the Church is given fresh grounding and shaping. And I hope we can see that, contextualized as all this is within Paul's concern for the unity of the Church, this ought to be almost by definition something which the different parts of today's Church can and must agree on and work on together. There has not been time to provide all the nuancing and shading required by recent scholarly debates; for that I must refer to other work.

I hope I have said enough to start some fresh trains of thought and particularly, granted our overall theme, to suggest some ways in which that word 'together' might become more of a reality. One of the joys of my episcopate in Durham was to see how shared Bible study could be one of the great ecumenical instruments: we still have difficulties about meeting at the one table (and Paul would be as horrified by that as he was with Peter in Antioch), but there should be no theological difficulties about shared reading of Scripture. It can be done very simply; the thing is to start, at the local level, not just with church leaders. And, as we read together, there is again no reason why we should not do mission together: why we should not, together, engage in projects of generous and healing love and hope in the wider communities where we find ourselves? No church restrictions prevent us getting together to do prison visiting, hospice care, work among migrants of whatever sort, running youth employment schemes, campaigning for local or global justice, providing safe spaces for women and children at risk … and so on, and so on. Once we grasp the great story which, by its climax in Jesus and in the energy of the Spirit, is now the story not of Israel only but of a worldwide family; once we grasp the truth that our own justification by faith is part of God's larger project to put the whole world right – then there should be nothing to stop us. As together we learn from Paul, we ought to find that his teaching should both encourage and inspire us to move forward, again together, in our mission in the world.

Of course, all this assumes that we will be worshipping and praying Christians. For Paul, the constant invoking of the One God as Father and Son in the power of the Spirit was basic and essential. That was not my assigned topic, but I am anxious that because I had not mentioned it you might imagine that I considered it unimportant. Clearly Paul was keen that all Christians from whatever backgrounds would be able to worship together, with one heart and voice; that, after all, is the final rhetorical climax of Romans (15.7-13). All that we do in our teaching and our mission ought to have that as the ultimate aim, though it may take some further sudden moves on the part of the Spirit before we can see our way to such unity on the ground. But let us at least do together all that we can. Let us constantly thank God for the unsearchable riches of the Messiah, for the good news that the power of evil has been radically defeated and the new creation decisively launched. These are the great truths of the faith. Our different traditions have sometimes expressed them differently, but the more we learn of Paul and the other early Christians the more I believe and hope that we can come together, work together, pray together, and thereby demonstrate in mission to the world that Jesus is Lord.

6. Learning from Paul Together:
An Orthodox Response[*]

Very Revd Dr John A. Jillions

In approaching this topic, I would like to thank Bishop Tom for his rich, inspiring, thought-provoking and hopeful presentation. It is an honour to bring a response from an Orthodox perspective to an exposition by such a widely respected biblical scholar. Wright begins by saying that bridge-building between different Christian groups and churches has been one of his aims over the years. In his article, now with the Orthodox Churches, he is building a bridge with Paul. As he notes at several points, for some Evangelical Christians what he and other Pauline scholars have uncovered is new and controversial. But for the Orthodox there is a familiar ring in much of what he says. So my first response is that he is opening up an *old* bridge that has not been used for some time and needs maintenance.

In Wright's chapter there is much with which I wholeheartedly agree and which requires little comment but this brief response will look at some of the issues that most struck me and where Orthodox experience might shed further light or provide a slightly different view on Paul, mission and bridge-building.

Before getting into the response, I also want to acknowledge how grateful I was to be back in Cambridge for the consultation at which this material was first presented. I owe a deep debt of gratitude to Tyndale House, and its then Warden, Dr Bruce Winter, who welcomed me in the mid-1990s when I was doing my PhD on St Paul while attached to the University of Thessaloniki and travelling periodically to Greece to work with my supervisor, Professor Petros Vassiliadis. Dr Winter became a second mentor to me, and Tyndale House became a friendly and uplifting scholarly home for three years.

Let me now respond to Bishop Tom's paper in detail.

1. We begin the bridge-building with a shared love of Paul, and a desire to see him read and studied much more closely at the level of our congregations. St John Chrysostom expressed this well in fourth-century Constantinople, at the start of his lengthy series of sermons on Romans.

---

[*] Originally published as John A. Jillions, 'An Orthodox Response to N. T. Wright's "Learning from Paul Together"', *St Vladimir's Theological Quarterly* 62.4 (2018), 333-47.

Scripture quotations in this chapter are from the Revised Standard Version of the Bible, copyright © 1946, 1952, and 1971 the Division of Christian Education of the National Council of the Churches of Christ in the United States of America. Used by permission. All rights reserved.

As I keep hearing the Epistles of the blessed Paul read, and that twice every week, and often three or four times, whenever we are celebrating the memorials of the holy martyrs, gladly do I enjoy the spiritual trumpet, and get roused and warmed with desire at recognizing the voice so dear to me, and seem to fancy him all but present to my sight, and behold him conversing with me. But I grieve and am pained, that all people do not know this man, as much as they ought to know him; but some are so far ignorant of him, as not even to know for certainty the number of his Epistles. And this comes not of incapacity, but of their not having the wish to be continually conversing with this blessed man. For it is not through any natural readiness and sharpness of wit that even I am acquainted with as much as I do know, if I do know anything, but owing to a continual cleaving to the man, and an earnest affection towards him.[1]

2. Bishop Tom underlines the importance of Christian unity to Paul, who was determined that followers of Christ should resist pumping up their differences into church-dividing issues. Unfortunately, we are not as far ahead on accepting each other, being together, praying together or working together as one might have hoped by this stage of Christian history. I think those at the consultation were all aware that the Lausanne-Orthodox Initiative is a rare space for such conversations and collaboration. In both the Orthodox and Evangelical worlds there are still deep prejudices that prevent this kind of initiative in most places. Indeed, we risk being labelled 'ecumenists', a dreaded epithet in both our circles. And yet it is worthwhile remembering that the term 'Christian' was once an epithet. It still is in many parts of the world.

3. Bishop Tom recognizes that we still have our differences but is pretty certain that we can at least read the Bible together. Yet even on that point we may need to take a step back and first listen in on how we each read the Bible separately. There is a world of experience and assumptions that stand behind our simple act of reading the Bible, and I am not convinced that we are ready to read together with shared silent assumptions about *how* we are reading. But we can *be* together, be with each other as each worships and reads and expounds the Scriptures and be mutually illumined in this way, uncovering and explaining our assumptions and experience. That said, Bishop Tom's

---

[1] John Chrysostom, *Homilies on the Acts of the Apostles and the Epistle to the Romans* (Nicene and Post-Nicene Fathers, 1st series, 11: Edinburgh: T. & T. Clark, 1889), 543. Chrysostom goes on to say that in general the woeful state of Christianity arises from ignorance of the Scriptures. 'For from this it is that our countless evils have arisen – from ignorance of the Scriptures; from this it is that the plague of heresies has broken out; from this that there are negligent lives; from this labors without advantage. For as men deprived of daylight would not walk aright, so they that look not to the gleaming of the Holy Scriptures must needs be frequently and constantly sinning, in that they are walking in the worst darkness. And that this fall not out, let us hold our eyes open to the bright shining of the Apostle's words; for this man's tongue shone forth above the sun, and he abounded more than all the rest in the word of doctrine; for since he labored more abundantly than they, he also drew upon himself a large measure of the Spirit's grace'.

positive personal experience in Durham of inter-Christian Bible reading is hopeful, so perhaps I should be less cautious and join him in saying 'Let's just start and see what happens'.

4. Bishop Tom's lecture title is 'Learning from Paul Together: How New Insights into Paul's Teaching can help Move us Forward in Mission.' He focuses here on three key words: 'mission', 'teaching' and 'together'. But an Orthodox will also instinctively jump at the word 'new'. Perhaps we too often equate 'new' with another Orthodox taboo word, 'innovation'. As Jesus said, '[No] one after drinking old wine desires new; for he says, "The old is good"' (or, as some texts read, "the old is better"; Lk. 5.38-9). We Orthodox can be sympathetic to Paul's Jewish opponents who were perfectly satisfied with their faith and way of life built around written and oral Torah. But this is precisely the point where we also need to be challenged and unsettled by what Bishop Tom calls the 'shocking' newness of the gospel, the early church and Paul (although Bishop Tom noted that this newness did not come from nowhere: it was in fulfilment of all that came before). Creating a new covenant family, bringing Jews and Gentiles together in a single family, casting aside such basic identity markers as circumcision and kosher laws – this was radical newness for a pious Jew. And this innovation – which is how they saw it – was the reason relatively few Jews accepted Paul's gospel. Jewish faith, centred on the Torah and its communal memory of interpretation, was what devoted Jews had pledged to maintain, even in the face of persecution and suffering. The Maccabean martyrs were still a relatively fresh memory for Paul's contemporaries, so how could a pious Jew contemplate turning his back on the Torah to follow the rabbinic renegade Paul? The entire project of mission to the Gentiles was *new*, and despite Paul's biblically based arguments, this was seen as a dangerous challenge to Jewish tradition. And yet remarkably, Paul and the early Jewish church accepted this sacrifice of what had been essential identity markers of Jewish tradition in order to bring Christ to the wider family of the God of Israel, 'from whom every family in heaven and on earth is named' (Eph. 3.14).

Once this radical newness of Christianity is appreciated, then we Orthodox can take a more balanced view of discerning the times and discerning the spirits as we respond to current conditions in new ways as well as old. This applies especially to conditions in the so-called diaspora, beyond the Orthodox homelands in the Middle East and Europe. In fact, Paul's first-century churches have much more in common with the religious environment in North America than with the times and places where Orthodox churches are powerful national religious institutions closely aligned with the cultures and the states of Greece, Russia, Romania, Serbia and so forth. In these ethnic homelands of the national mother churches, Orthodoxy is the dominant tradition known by all. Orthodoxy in those lands, with their ancient churches, holy sites, monasteries, thousands of clergy and hundreds of bishops, represents the ancient, settled and completed patrimony of the Christian past which is to be delivered to the next generation as both a religious and national duty. This is totally unlike either the first century or the North American and western European scene today. Speaking about mission in North America, Archbishop Anastasios of Albania, perhaps the leading Orthodox missiologist, has said we need to rethink what we are doing: 'In North America especially, the Orthodox witness is offered within a dynamic society with universal interests. In such a society Orthodoxy is in a state of mission – and she cannot, certainly, be content with a museum-like preservation of the glorious Orthodox past of far-away homelands. Something substantially new and important ought to arise.'[2]

Something substantially new and important ought to arise. This is both a challenge and an episcopal blessing for the Orthodox, and we ought to take full advantage of it. Metropolitan Kallistos (Ware) of Diokleia expressed this same kind of bold openness when he was interviewed at the Anglican Lambeth Conference in 2008. He remarked that, when facing decisions on any new issue, the Church must be attentive to keeping a balance between 'catholic consensus' and 'prophetic action'. If the Orthodox have stressed consensus in the past, he said, they must nevertheless also remain open to the possibility of Spirit-inspired change coming from the most unexpected places. 'Will you ever have change unless some people are willing to stand up and say, this is what we ought to be doing? And even if their testimony is highly controversial, who will nonetheless stand by their position … Christ did not tell us that nothing should ever be done for the first time. The whole witness of the early Church points in a different direction.'[3]

5. Bishop Tom is correct that what he is presenting as Paul's holistic and transformative vision of the new creation may be controversial in some Protestant circles but is familiar to the Orthodox. Fr Sergius Bulgakov, one of the most prolific Orthodox theologians of the twentieth century, said that we Christians are put on earth not merely to be knowers of God, but to be transformers. No aspect of life in society was to be left untouched by Christ's sacrificial love, through members of the body of Christ. In this sense, as Bishop Tom says, the Church *is* Christ's mission in this world. 'God always purposed to work within creation *through his image-bearers,* so that saving people from sin and death was not simply for their own benefit but so that through renewed humans God would rescue creation itself.' The uniting of heaven and earth through the Church is a constant theme in Orthodox worship. The temple is seen as a microcosm of the new creation. Indeed, in the Russian tradition one hears regularly that the aim of mission is the 'churching' of the world, *votserkovlenie,* although this is often reduced to a kind of ecclesiasticalization. I shall say more about this later.

---

[2] Archbishop Anastasios, *Mission in Christ's Way* (Brookline, MA: Holy Cross & Geneva: World Council of Churches, 2010), 266-67.

[3] Fr George Westhaver, 'LAMBETH: Interview with the Most Rev. Kallistos Ware, Archbishop of Gt. Britain for the Ecumenical Patriarchate' [*sic*], online at: http://www.prayerbookatlambeth.org/interviews/2008/7/28/an-interview-with-the-most-revd-kallistos-ware-archbishop-of.html.

'God puts humans right so that they can then be part of his putting-right project for the world.' We Orthodox share with Bishop Tom a high anthropology, a high view of the role of human beings in creation and in the outworking of salvation. This is reflected in our understanding of the pivotal role of Mary, the Mother of God, for God was powerless to effect salvation without her. Divine-human synergy is also what Paul is speaking about in Colossians 1.24, which perhaps sounds blasphemous to Evangelical ears: 'Now I rejoice in my sufferings for your sake, and in my flesh I complete what is lacking in Christ's afflictions for the sake of his body, that is, the church.'

Practical application of this vision to transform society has not always been the Orthodox strong suit, often because of severe persecution or political constraints, but there is growing Orthodox involvement in practical action for the common good both in Orthodox homelands and around the world. Patriarch Bartholomew's ecological activism and International Orthodox Christian Charities are two prime examples. I think we can heartily agree with Bishop Tom that '[f]resh teaching in all these areas is urgently needed if we are to understand our shared mission as *both* the announcement of Jesus as the crucified and risen Lord, demanding the personal response of obedient faith, *and* the inauguration of new creation, with signs of healing and hope pointing forward to the eventual renewal of the whole cosmos.'

6. Bishop Tom emphasizes that mission and teaching go together. I could not agree more, but here too we face our own internal challenges. As Rod Dreher recently pointed out in *The Benedict Option*, Christians in general – and Orthodox are no exception – are losing touch with the historic Christian teaching and way of life, and replacing this rich inheritance with the pottage of 'Moralistic Therapeutic Deism':[4]

1. A god exists who created and ordered the world and watches over human life on earth.
2. God wants people to be good, nice, and fair to each other, as taught in the Bible and by most world religions.
3. The central goal of life is to be happy and to feel good about oneself.
4. God does not need to be particularly involved in one's life except when God is needed to resolve a problem.
5. Good people go to heaven when they die.

A Catholic priest in New Jersey recently told me, 'We are making consumers, not disciples.' To makes disciples, we urgently need liturgical preaching and biblical teaching inspired by the Fathers, saints and liturgy of the Church. We need to teach people how to read the Scriptures and build the practice into their daily routines. And all of this in the context of teaching people how to pray. Fr Thomas Hopko of blessed memory spoke of prayer as three commitments he learned from his mother at an early age: say your

---

[4] Rod Dreher, *The Benedict Option: A Strategy for Christians in a Post-Christian Nation* (New York: Sentinel, 2017), 10.

prayers, go to church, remember God. Meaning: commitment to a daily rule of prayer, to participation in liturgical life and constant remembrance of God during the day (using the Jesus Prayer, for example).

7. Bishop Tom underlines the centrality of holiness in Paul's thinking, and how it is intertwined with unity. He says, 'The world will take no notice of a divided church. The world will take no notice of an unholy church.' However, from an Orthodox perspective – and I would argue from Paul's as well – the two are not of equal weight. The unity of the Church is indeed 'one of Paul's overriding passions', but he refuses to purchase that unity at any price. Paul has a very high tolerance for differences and sins within the body of Christ, but we must not forget that he is willing to say 'anathema' and exclude from communion those who seriously threaten the holiness of the Church. This does not mean splitting lightly 'over every disagreement', and Paul dismissed as insignificant whatever nuances were driving Corinthian factionalism in 1 Corinthians 1.12. But the case of blatant public immorality in 1 Corinthians 5.1-13 was serious enough for Paul to expel the offender from communion, at least temporarily. Even more seriously, in Galatia the soul of the church was being threatened by a new imposition of Jewish law that cut the heart out of the universal gospel: this had to be forcefully resisted and the perpetrators excluded.

> I am astonished that you are so quickly deserting him who called you in the grace of Christ and turning to a different gospel – not that there is another gospel, but there are some who trouble you and want to pervert the gospel of Christ. But even if we, or an angel from heaven, should preach to you a gospel contrary to that which we preached to you, let him be *anathema*. As we have said before, so now I say again, If any one is preaching to you a gospel contrary to that which you received, let him be *anathema*. (Gal. 1.6-9)

Paul emphatically repeats his anathema against the 'circumcision party', who threatened the truth, grace, freedom and universality of the gospel message. It was not just that they threatened the unity of the new covenant family, they threatened the very heart of its message. This is why Paul was so disturbed by Peter's cowardly dissembling. Paul desires unity *almost* more than anything else, but when truth and justice are at stake, there can be no compromise. Consider John Chrysostom's commentary on Romans 12.18, '*If possible*, so far as it depends upon you, live peaceably with all.'

> For there are cases in which it is not possible [to live peaceably with all], as, for instance, when we have to argue about the faith, or to contend for those who are wronged. … And his meaning is nearly as follows: Do your own part, and to none give occasion for war or fighting, neither to Jew nor gentile. But if you see the cause of faith suffering anywhere do not prize concord above truth, but make a noble stand even to death. And even then be not at war in your soul, be not averse in temper, but fight with the things only. For this is the meaning of 'so far as it depends upon you, live peaceably with all.' But if the other will not

be at peace, do not fill your soul with tempest, but in mind be friendly as I said before, without giving up the truth on any occasion.[5]

8. Appreciation for Paul's Jewish background is one of the hallmarks of the New Perspective on Paul. However, we also have to admit that Paul's interpretation of Jewish faith was alien to most Jews, from his time down to the present day. Nor was Paul's love for Israel picked up by the later church. Speaking just for the Orthodox tradition, there are only rare voices rejecting the anti-Jewish feeling that found its way into church tradition and vilified, ghettoized, suppressed and persecuted Jews. This is not from Paul. We could benefit from familiarizing ourselves with the Jewish roots that shaped not only Paul but our Lord Jesus Christ. Just as importantly today we could learn to value the living tradition of contemporary Judaism that has withstood so much suffering. A pioneering Orthodox voice in this regard was Fr Lev Gillet whose far-sighted book *Communion in the Messiah*, published in 1942 during the Holocaust, goes 'beyond advocating Christian solidarity with persecuted Jews in Hitler's Europe' and 'sets out to identify points of convergence between Jewish and Christian theology, spirituality and religious practices'.[6]

9. Bishop Tom asks the question, '[Who] is really a member of the family of Abraham, the family promised in the foundation covenant of Genesis 15 which Paul expounds in Romans 4 and Galatians 3?' This is probably the biggest question facing the Orthodox in relation to other Christians and other religions, because we have difficulty affirming kinship outside the boundaries of the Orthodox nuclear family. We are not alone in this temptation to exclusivism, but I cannot help thinking of C. S. Lewis's *The Last Battle*, in which the dwarves refuse to find kinship or common cause with others. Their refrain is, 'The dwarves are for the dwarves.' This is where I think we could learn especially from the self-emptying, kenotic Christ of St Paul's letter to the Philippians.

> Let each of you look not to your own interests, but to the interests of others.

> Let the same mind be in you that was in Christ Jesus, who, though he was in the form of God, did not regard equality with God as something to be exploited but emptied himself [*heauton ekenōsen*], taking the form of a slave … (Phil. 2.4-7, NRSV)

Annually in Holy Week, we are forcefully reminded of Christ's self-emptying example, for instance in this hymn from Holy Thursday:

> Instructing Your disciples in the mystery, Lord,
> You said to them:

---

[5] *On Romans*, Homily 22 (NPNF-1, 508).

[6] See Paul Ladouceur, 'Religious Diversity in Modern Orthodox Thought', *Religions* 8.5 (2017), 77 [online journal], at: https://doi.org/10.3390/rel8050077; John Jillions, 'Review Essay: Lev Gillet, *Communion in the Messiah: Studies in the Relationship Between Judaism and Christianity*, London: Lutterworth, 2003 (1942)', *Logos: A Journal of Eastern Christian Studies* 47.3-4 (2006), 111-30.

'My beloved, see that no fear separates you from Me.
Though I suffer, it is for the sake of the world.
Let me not be a cause of scandal to you.
I came, not to be served, but to serve,
To give myself for the redemption of the world.
If you are my friends, then imitate Me.
Let the first among you be the last.
Let the master be like the servant.
Abide in Me and bear fruit, for I am the vine of life.'
(Holy Thursday, Matins Aposticha)

Christ's self-emptying generosity became the pattern for Paul and the early church, which was revolutionized by the inclusion of Gentile outsiders. But this new and generous ecclesiology was also the single greatest threat to the peace of the early church as traditionalists held on to a restrictive model. We see the results of that contest especially in Galatians.

The kenotic way of Christ points the Orthodox Church and the Church as a whole to an entirely new way of looking at others and to a new ecumenical method. Up to now the Orthodox have proceeded from the presupposition that ecumenical dialogue is successful when we Orthodox recognize in other churches the beauty, if only partial, of the Tradition we alone have retained in all its fullness. But Christ's self-emptying for the sake of the broken, sinful, rebellious world turns this on its head.

Metropolitan John Zizioulas underlines this essential point, saying that Christ's love – precisely as love of the ungodly and ugly – overturned the classic Greek formula of love for the good and beautiful. The more one is purified of 'self-affirmation', the more one will be willing to shed one's glory and love what is debased and ugly, even as Christ did.

[Freedom] from the self leads to a movement of finding one's identity not through self-affirmation, but through the other. This makes mysticism agapetic or erotic but in a way that distinguishes it from the Platonic eros of antiquity, for in the latter case love is not free; it is bound by the law of attraction exercised by the beautiful and the good. One cannot love the ugly or the sinner for one cannot be attracted except by the Good. In the ascetic experience, based on kenotic Christology, one loves precisely what is debased and ugly and this means that one loves free from all rational or moral necessity or causality … The ascetic loves first of all and above all the sinner, not out of condescension and compassion but out of a free existential involvement in the fallen human condition.[7]

'One loves precisely what is debased and ugly.' Perhaps this is not quite right. The Lord embraces the one who is ugly, weak and sinful, not just because he embraces the fallen human condition but because he sees past all of that to the beauty of the divine image that can never be eradicated. If the Orthodox have questions about the imperfection and 'ugliness' of others,

---

[7] John D. Zizioulas (ed. Paul McPartlan), *Communion and Otherness: Further Studies in Personhood and the Church* (New York: T. and T. Clark, 2006), 304.

then this ought to be motivation not to stand apart but to recognize that we are all the objects of Christ's generous self-emptying forgiveness and mercy. Paul understood this better than anyone.

Commenting on Romans 8, St John Chrysostom says:

> For full of affection is the whole race of the saints. Wherefore also St. Paul says, 'Put on therefore, as the elect saints of God, bowels of mercy [*splanchna oiktirmou*], kindness, humbleness of mind' (Col. iii. 12.) You see the strict propriety of the word, and how he would have us continually merciful. For he does not say, "show mercy" only, but put it on, that like as our garment is always with us, so may mercy be. And he does not say merely mercy, but 'bowels of mercy,' that we may imitate the natural affection of relations ... Let us not then be bitter judges of others lest we also get a strict account demanded of us. For we have sins that are too great to plead any excuse. And therefore let us show more mercy towards those who have committed inexcusable sins, that we also may lay up for ourselves the like mercy beforehand."[8]

10. The kenotic mercy of Philippians 2 might illumine our spiritual eyes to look out on the world (including other churches and faiths) as Paul did in Philippians 4.8: 'Finally, brethren, whatever is true, whatever is honorable, whatever is just, whatever is pure, whatever is lovely, whatever is gracious, if there is any excellence, if there is anything worthy of praise, think about these things.'

Fr Alexander Schmemann said 'The Christian is the one who wherever he looks, everywhere sees Christ and rejoices in him.'[9] Without tampering with our ecclesiological assumptions, I do not believe there is anything that prevents us from generously opening our eyes to recognize and bless whatever is good in the mission of our various churches, and collaborating. When the Institute for Orthodox Christian Studies was being founded in Cambridge as part of the Cambridge Theological Federation – a consortium of theological colleges representing Roman Catholic, Anglican, Reformed and Methodist traditions – at the first organizational meeting with representatives from Cambridge, the late Fr Sergei Hackel said, 'it's not about being less than Orthodox, but about being *generously* Orthodox'. That is the spirit – what we might call kenotic ecumenism – which ought to inspire us here as well.

11. Bishop Tom concludes by opening up the possibilities for just such collaboration in mission: Why should we not, 'together, engage in projects of generous and healing love and hope in the wider communities where we find ourselves? ... once we grasp the truth that our own justification by faith is part of God's larger project to put the whole world right – then there should be nothing to stop us'. And this is where the challenge will be for us as Orthodox: seeing ourselves – and other Christians, even other people of faith and good will – 'as *part* of God's larger project to put the whole world right'.

---

[8] Chrysostom, *On Romans*, Homily 14 (NPNF-1, 712).
[9] Quoted in Kallistos Ware, 'How to Read the Bible', online at: https://www.oca.org/scripture/how-to-read-the-bible [No source cited].

As I said earlier, we find it difficult to include others in the Church and in the family of God. But this is also where we need to keep coming back to Paul's most basic gospel message.

Time and again, throughout his letters, Paul brings his readers and listeners back to Christ as the new centre of their lives, boldly using his own example as a model. 'I decided to know among you, except Jesus Christ and him crucified' (1 Cor 2.2). 'Be imitators of me, as I am of Christ' (1 Cor. 11.1; cf. 1 Cor. 4.16; 1 Thess. 1.6). 'It is no longer I who live but Christ who lives in me' (Gal 2.20). In other words, everything else is secondary.

Here I would like to conclude my response to Bishop Tom's paper by citing Mother Maria Skobtsova, a twentieth-century Orthodox saint, because for her, as for St Paul, Christ is the centre and everything else comes second. She was an unconventional Orthodox nun who had been married, divorced, had children, served the poor and protected Jews in Nazi-occupied Paris. She was also a poet, philosopher and colleague of Nicholas Berdyaev. She died in Ravensbruck concentration camp near the end of World War II and was canonized in 2004.

While other Orthodox theologians in the early decades of the twentieth century spoke of 'churching' the world, Mother Maria preferred to focus on Christ and to speak of christifying' the world. She felt that an emphasis on 'churching' all too often obscures the heart of commitment to the evangelical path of Christ.

> What is most characteristic of this path? It is a desire to 'Christify' all of life. To a certain degree this notion can be contrasted to that which is understood not only by the term 'churching' but also the term 'Christianization'. 'Churching' is often taken to mean the placing of life within the framework of a certain rhythm of church piety, the subordination of one's personal life experience to the schedule of the cycle of divine services, the incorporation of certain specific elements of 'churchliness' into one's way of life, even elements of the Church's liturgical order [*ustav*]. 'Christianization', however, is generally understood as nothing more than the correction of the bestial cruelty of man's history through inoculation with a certain dose of Christian morality. And in addition to this it also includes the preaching of the Gospel to the whole world.

> 'Christification', however, is based on the words, 'It is no longer I who live, but Christ who lives in me' (Gal. 2:20). The image of God, the icon of Christ, which truly is my real and actual essence or being, is the only measure of all things, the only path or way which is given to me. Each movement of my soul, each approach to God, to other people, to the world, is determined by the suitability of that act for reflecting the image of God which is within me.

> If I am faced with two paths and I am in doubt, then even if all human wisdom, experience, and tradition point to one of these, but I feel that Christ would have followed the other – then all my doubts should immediately disappear and I

should choose to follow Christ in spite of all the experience, tradition and wisdom that are opposed to it.[10]

May we all be given the faith and courage to follow this evangelical path.

---

[10] Mother Maria Skobtsova, 'Types of Religious Lives', online at: http://incommunion.org/2005/01/20/types-of-religious-lives-5-the-evangelical-path/.

7. Discipleship between the Traditions

Dr David Lyons and Dr Ralph Lee*

This article reflects on the personal and ministry journeys of a few Christians from Western Evangelical Christian backgrounds which have included an encounter with Orthodox Christianity. David Lyons's journey is both personal and as a leader of the Navigator movement; Ralph and Sarah Lee's has come out of their personal encounter as representatives of The Navigators UK in the extraordinary nation of Ethiopia, and Taylor and Sally Hostetter's in a similar role in Serbia, working with the US Navigators.

David's Journey

My journey with the Orthodox Church began when my oldest daughter told us that she was becoming Orthodox. That led to many intense conversations! She was dissatisfied with what she called 'McDonald's Christianity'. She wanted something with deeper historical roots, and a greater sense of mystery and wonder. I respect my daughter, and I identified with her motives. So, although I felt allergic to liturgies and robes and religious forms, my love for her led me to look past those forms to learn of a part of the body of Christ that had been invisible and unattractive to me.

Soon she was about to marry an Orthodox young man. She had shared about me with the monk who was to give the homily at her wedding, and he asked to have lunch with me the day after her wedding. Before we even

---

* David and Ralph are staff of The Navigators, but do not claim to speak for all Navigators or for The Navigators organization. The Navigators are aware that, in pursuing the approaches to ministering to one another, understanding one another, and advancing the Gospel described or alluded to in this article, there is the possibility of significant misunderstanding and of being seen as compromising truth from either the Protestant or the Orthodox side of the debate. The Navigators are deeply committed to integrity, to the purity of the Gospel, to the glory of Christ in his Church, and to living and ministering under the authority of Scripture, as we wrestle with these vital matters of engaging deeply with those from Orthodox backgrounds and cultures.

ordered our meal, this monk told me that he had met Navigators when he was in college. He said that he had been quite impressed with them, but they did not know what to do with him. He said to me: 'I know something about discipling young men. That's what I do at the monastery. But we Orthodox are pathetic when it comes to reaching the unchurched. Do you think that The Navigators could help us?' That began a friendship and partnership which continues to bear fruit today. I have learned so much from my daughter and that monk, and it seems like I have been able to help them.

I want to highlight a couple of keys to Discipleship between the Traditions that are embedded in this story.

Humility

Each of us recognized and embraced the fact that we needed to learn from one another. A *disciple* is fundamentally a *learner*, and one must be humble to truly learn from another. We cannot have discipleship between the traditions without a humble desire to learn from someone in another tradition.

Where we cross paths with those from other traditions, pride tends to spring up with a vengeance. Rather than focusing on what we can learn from one another, we tend to mark out our territory and attempt to teach one another rather than to learn from one another. Jesus laid humility as the foundation of what he requires of his disciples. He began training the twelve with these words, 'Blessed are the poor in spirit' (Mt. 5.3). When pride cropped up among them, He impressed on them 'It shall not be this way among you' (Mt. 20:26).

I am learning so much from my Orthodox friends:

* Respect for tradition
* The beauty of multi-sensory worship
* The value of set prayers
* The power of communal faith
* The transforming power of *theosis*
* The long-term impact of God-parenting
* The importance of religious orders

I am less qualified to guess what my Orthodox friends might learn from Navigators and Evangelicals, but I notice that they are attracted to our:

* Practical mastery and use of the Scriptures
* Orthopraxy, or application of the Scriptures in everyday life
* Effectiveness in reaching the unchurched
* Mobilizing of everyday people (laymen) to do the ministry
* Effective tools and practices

Courage

It took courage for that monk to come to me. He and I have both been misunderstood and criticized by those from within our own traditions. There was a price tag for our collaboration. For me, part of that price tag was the US$700 a month that one of our supporting churches withdrew when they learned that I was collaborating with an Orthodox monk. I will not tell you the story of one of our most fruitful examples of a Navigator collaborating with an Orthodox priest because we believe that it would ruin his reputation among his Orthodox colleagues. I have been told that among some Orthodox, being accused of being a Protestant is worse than being accused of being an unbeliever. So from both sides it takes courage to pursue discipleship between the traditions.

It took courage for the apostle Peter to have fellowship with believers in the new Gentile churches that were springing up around the region. When he was criticized for being involved with them, 'he began to draw back and separate himself from the Gentiles because he was afraid of those who belonged to the circumcision group' (Gal. 2.12). Some of Paul's most severe critics were Christians from his own Jewish religious background, but he went back to Jerusalem more than once to be among his critics and to work out the implications of their unity in Christ.

It took courage for Navigator missionary Taylor Hostetter to seriously explore being discipled by Orthodox believers in Serbia. I am sure that he was afraid of being kicked out of The Navigators and losing support from those who were helping to fund his work there. It took courage for Orthodox leaders to endorse the discipleship materials that Taylor later published, materials that teach discipleship from the Orthodox liturgy.

One might wonder why conservative Evangelical Navigators would get involved with discipleship in the Orthodox Church. These aspects of our Navigators 'Core Calling & Values' naturally lead us to discipleship between the traditions:

The Kingdom

Our Navigator calling is 'to advance the Gospel of Jesus and His kingdom into the nations through spiritual generations of laborers who live and disciple among those who don't yet know Jesus'. The gospel of the Kingdom is bigger than any particular tradition, so although we are predominantly Evangelicals, we are non-denominational. Our founder, Dawson Trotman, generously promoted actively serving other works. From the beginning he gave away some of his best leaders and time to other groups in the body of Christ. That practice continues today.

One day, one of our Navigator fellow workers began exploring helping Catholic churches make disciples. This was controversial among us. But he pressed on, with the encouragement of key Navigator leaders. Eventually the Lord led him to sincerely become a Catholic Navigator; before that he launched a ministry called Emmaus Journey, a ministry of Catholic evangelization of, and discipleship in, many hundreds of Catholic parishes.

It is endorsed and promoted by Catholic bishops. Its purpose is 'to bring about in all Catholics such an enthusiasm for their faith that, in living their faith in Jesus, they freely share it with others'. We eventually encouraged Emmaus Journey to launch out on their own with our blessing, thoroughly embedded in the Catholic Church.

We did this because we are not called to advance the gospel of Protestant Evangelical Christianity, but rather we are called to advance the gospel of Jesus and his kingdom. One day, I was sitting with my monk friend in a meeting at St Vladimir's Seminary, and I asked: 'Explain to me again why we are here exploring partnering.' He came up out of his chair and pounded the table as he said 'We are here for the sake of the gospel!' That was all I needed to hear.

Spiritual Generations that Remain

Navigators are called to a distinct approach to advance the gospel of Jesus and his kingdom: 'through spiritual generations of laborers living and discipling among those who do not yet know Jesus'. We are called to birth and nurture long-term impact through movements of the gospel that continue generation after generation. More specifically, we are called to generations that live and disciple *among*. This is amplified in one of our core values, 'Families and relational networks in discipling the nations'.

This leads us to emphasize helping those we disciple to *remain* in their context. 1 Corinthians 7.17-24 says:

> Nevertheless, each one should retain the place in life that the Lord assigned to him and to which God has called him. This is the rule I lay down in all the churches. Was a man already circumcised when he was called? He should not become uncircumcised. Was a man uncircumcised when he was called? He should not be circumcised. Circumcision is nothing and uncircumcision is nothing. Keeping God's commands is what counts. Each one should remain in the situation which he was in when God called him. Were you a slave when you were called? Don't let it trouble you – although if you can gain your freedom, do so. For he who was a slave when he was called by the Lord is the Lord's freedman; similarly, he who was a free man when he was called is Christ's slave. You were bought at a price; do not become slaves of men. Brothers, each man, as responsible to God, should remain in the situation God called him to.

Why was this important? The previous context shows that it was important to the flow of the gospel through one's family and relational network.

For this reason, Navigators generally encourage Catholics to *remain* Catholic and Orthodox to *remain* Orthodox. One day, an Orthodox priest secretly asked a Navigator to disciple him, which he did for several years. As the priest grew, he became frustrated with his Orthodox fellow priests, and he decided to leave and start his own church. Our Navigator fellow worker urgently intervened and strongly persuaded him to remain in his context. As a result, the priest did remain and his discipleship ministry flourished there through generation after generation of Orthodox faithful.

Interdependent Relationships

Our final core value as Navigators is 'interdependent relationships in the body of Christ in advancing the Gospel'. 1 Corinthians 12.4-7 says: 'Now there are varieties of gifts, but the same Spirit. And there are varieties of ministries, and the same Lord. There are varieties of effects, but the same God who works all things in all persons. But to each one is given the manifestation of the Spirit for the common good.' We simply need one another.

Where would our Navigator ministry in Serbia be without being rooted in the Orthodox Church there? Perhaps dead. Where would our Navigator ministry in Ethiopia be without Ralph's integration into the Orthodox Church there? Much more limited and one-dimensional. Where would the fruit of our Navigator ministry in Russia be without our blessing as they return to their Orthodox roots? Less fruitful and uprooted.

I am much richer because of what I am learning from my Orthodox brothers and sisters. My prayer life is deeper. My faith is more deeply rooted. My experience of *theosis* is authenticated and strengthened. In short, I am a better disciple.

Discipleship between the traditions requires much of us, but it offers much more to us:

- Discipleship between the traditions must be built on a foundation of *humility* that opens us to learning from one another.
- Discipleship between the traditions will require *courage* that overcomes our fear of criticism and rejection.
- Discipleship between the traditions is a beautiful expression and manifestation of something much bigger than any tradition: the *Kingdom of God*.
- To pursue effective discipleship between the traditions, we need to agree to encourage those we help to *remain* where they are so that they are more likely to flourish into spiritual generations, whether Orthodox or Evangelical.
- Although we are disciples in quite different traditions, we truly do need to live in *interdependent relationships* to become all that God intends for us to be.

Discipleship between the traditions is a path less travelled. Robert Frost wrote:

Two roads diverged in a wood, and I –
I took the one less traveled by,
And that has made all the difference.[1]

---

[1] Robert Frost, *Mountain Interval* (New York: Henry Holt, 1916), 9.

Discipleship between the traditions is one of those paths described in Isaiah 42.16:

I will lead the blind by ways they have not known,
along unfamiliar paths I will guide them;
I will turn the darkness into light before them
and make the rough places smooth.
These are the things I will do; I will not forsake them.

Let us join hands and go down that path together, as Ralph Lee and Taylor Hostetter have done in Ethiopia and Serbia.

Ralph's Journey

The Navigators and the Orthodox Church in Ethiopia and Serbia

My encounter with Orthodoxy comes from Ethiopia, where I have worked for the Navigators since 1990, and since 1997 with my wife, Sarah. During my first two years in Addis Ababa, I attended the International Evangelical Church (IEC). This had been established to serve the needs of the international community, and particularly those without any knowledge of Ethiopian language, but it was also a place where, at least for Evangelicals, it was relatively free to worship God and study the Bible without interference from Communist authorities, which meant that many of the members of that church were Ethiopians.

In this context, observing Ethiopia, one thing was clear. The Ethiopian Orthodox Church has been the most profound influence on the formation of Ethiopia and its culture. Missionary effort in Ethiopia had started in areas of the south where the Orthodox Church was not very strong, and this had made it possible for missionaries naïvely to consider the Orthodox Church irrelevant, but in Addis Ababa and much of the north of the country, this simply was not possible.

I sought to find out more about the Orthodox Church, and in doing so, I think there are some important lessons to pass on to the LOI community, ones that are strongly reflected in many of the strong friendships that we can see.

I also speak on behalf of Taylor and Sally Hostetter. They joined the Navigator team in what was then Yugoslavia, considered to be one of the most secularized nations of Europe, particularly the part that is now Serbia. Under the layer of atheistic communism, Taylor and Sally affirm that with their Western eyes and mindset they could not see the Orthodox Christian heritage of Serbia reaching back more than a thousand years, and felt that they might have the opportunity to take the gospel there! They are connecting with many of the resources of Serbia's heritage, through teaching and serving in various ways, and through studying icon writing, to grow in their faith and in their personal commitment to share their faith with others.

Our goal in discipleship is expressed in many ways. The activity itself is rather simple, if we look at the life of St Paul: he spent time with people, and he prayed for them and shared the Scriptures with them; and if he could not, then he sent others to do the same, and wrote letters. One of our goals in discipleship is what St Paul tells us in Ephesians, that we should be renewed in the spirit of our minds, and clothe ourselves with the new self, created according to the likeness of God in true righteousness and holiness (Eph. 4.23-24).

Ephesians 4 provides a very helpful framework for some principles that God has taught us in through our fellowship with the Ethiopian Orthodox Church:

Our Common Ground

St Paul gives the most insightful advice on Ephesians 4.25: 'So then, putting away falsehood, let all of us speak the truth to our neighbours, for we are members of one another.' The instructions are given to believers. The starting point is that we are *members of one another*. It is obvious in the context of a LOI gathering that this is the case, but it needs to be stated clearly. With the different trajectories of history that Evangelicals and Orthodox Christians have, we have to make a fundamental commitment to the fact that we are *members of one another*.

This is the only way that we can proceed with integrity. When my wife Sarah and I joined the Ethiopian Orthodox Church, we felt compelled by our consciences to say to the monk who was accepting us that if our joining was understood to be a rejection of our Protestant past (as it would be understood by many) then we could not do it. His reply was: 'Why should you do that? You are on a path, and you are taking another step on that path.' He tacitly accepted that we were already *members of one another*. This leads to two aspects implicit in St Paul's instructions, generosity and honesty.

Generosity

Early on, I made one key friend, who through his great generosity made it possible for me to begin to understand the Ethiopian Orthodox Church. Yoseph Bereded, now the godfather to our son Sebastian, was a young architect who had joined the discipleship group based at the IEC but had never left the Orthodox Church. His Evangelical friends had been generous and had not pressed him to 'convert', probably because he showed so much maturity for a young man. Because of such generosity, he had been able to appreciate something about working together with others who sought to walk with the Lord Jesus Christ, a discipling community. Yoseph was also generous and was able to answer questions for me about the Orthodox Church that no one else I knew could. He took me to Orthodox churches. One of the marvels of Communist Ethiopia was that the city curfew in Addis Ababa, one of the longest in history, lasting eighteen years, was lifted (or was it just that it was impossible to impose it?) for the Nativity and Pascha vigil. I still remember going to Holy Trinity Cathedral in Addis late one night and encountering an Orthodox liturgy for the first time – sounds, smells, touch (not the least being jostled in the crowd), sights that I had never seen – and even taste, in the holy water. It was extraordinary, and perhaps even a little frightening; I had little idea of what was going on, apart from what Joseph could tell me.

Generosity also means taking some punches. It is a natural, if not fallen, tendency of humans to be suspicious, and in crossing cultures too it is hard to be sensitive always. I was talking with the head of an Evangelical mission agency, and he asked me: 'is Christ's sacrifice sufficient for the Orthodox?' It was a genuine question, that came from a strong desire to understand. It would have been easy to take offence, but not doing so gave an opportunity to build a relationship that may influence the strategy and outlook of some Christian missions.

Appreciation

Connected with generosity is a need to develop a genuine appreciation of the impact of Christian heritage. Whatever problems our Orthodox brethren may have with the Reformation, it had an undeniable impact on the lives of people, and on the ways that they could grow in their journey with God.

Cutting down the story of how I grew to appreciate the Ethiopian Orthodox Church over two years, through Joseph and his remarkable father, Ato Bereded, who had discipled his own son in the faith, they taught me something very important that is still imprinted on my memory. It became clear to me that Orthodox Christianity was not a passing interest, it was not just some anachronistic bureaucratic edifice waiting to fade out, it was more than what we might call a strong influence on the country: the only way that I could describe it was that it was the very heartbeat of the country. Whether Ethiopians are Orthodox, Protestant, Muslim, or perhaps something else, Orthodox Christianity has formed the way they think, the way they see the world, the way society functions.

It is easy to find negative things in most churches, and generally from the expatriate community I was bombarded with negative comments about the Ethiopian Orthodox Church. Things changed a little when the Communist government was overthrown by military force in May 1991. Following bloodbaths in Monrovia in Liberia in 1990, and in Mogadishu in Somalia in January 1991, many feared the same in Addis Ababa. A few voices who knew Ethiopia well said that it would not be like that, and they were right. Hundreds and thousands of defeated government troops fled the warfront, and came to Addis with all their weapons, and rather than looting and killing they sat on the streets with hands outstretched, begging for food. It is an unavoidable conclusion that the seventeen centuries of Christian witness in Ethiopia had made this possible.

Taylor's experience in Belgrade was similar. Starting not able to see, through studying Byzantine art and architectural history at the University of Belgrade he developed a virtual reality model of the frescoes at the Serbian Hilandar monastery on Mount Athos. Through many visits to Hilandar he developed deep relationships with the brotherhood there, and he and Sally began to look at other Orthodox churches, and learned to see the glory of the gospel of our Lord Jesus Christ as presented in their frescoes. They began to learn also the deep connection between architecture, iconography, theology and the sacraments. What was presented there was a beautifully joined-up view of life and worship, in which there was no dualistic separation of the physical and spiritual. Not only was this beautiful, but the approach, having been such a strong force in the formation of the Serbian nation, was expressed in ways that their Serbian friends could well understand.

Evangelicals are generally good at knowing what they are good at! Evangelicals take the Bible very seriously indeed, and this has often been a bridge to building relationships across complex boundaries. But this can lead to a certain arrogance. Many Evangelicals told me in Ethiopia, and Taylor in Serbia, that the Orthodox do not really take the Bible seriously, and they do not read it for themselves. I remember vividly the encounter that I had with a young twenty-three-year-old traditional scholar in Ethiopia, who pointed out to me that the beginning of his studies, Bible 101, was to memorize the whole Bible in Amharic, and in the classical language of Ge'ez! Taylor found the frescoes of Hilandar saturated with biblical allusions, theological connections and profound exposition. If we are to disciple across the traditions, we need to learn to see.

Honesty

Again, Ephesians 4 commends us to deal honestly. Shortly after my wife and I moved to Bahir Dar in the north of Ethiopia, where I was teaching in the university but also seeking, with the Navigators of Ethiopia, to find ways of connecting with the Orthodox Church. We wanted to see if we, as Navigators, could do what Navigators do in many universities around the world, to meet with Christian students to read the Bible together as a way to grow in our faith.

We started attending the Orthodox Church, and I am sure that pretty much every Ethiopian at that church wanted to know why, but being Ethiopians, they did not ask, or if they did, they were so indirect that we did not get it! After some months, we were introduced by a good friend to a monk, Abba Yibbabe. This remarkable man has given me more insight into the monastic tradition of the Orthodox Church than any textbook. Monks in Ethiopia are countercultural, and Abba Yibbabe expressed this by being very direct: 'Why are you coming to our church?' Struck by his directness, the only sensible option was to reply in the same way, and I replied: 'My wife and I seek to help young people become strong in their faith and to reach out to others to make them strong, making the Church strong.' There was what seemed like an interminable pause. 'This is what God has brought you here to do' was the reply, and 'from today you are to be called Abraham, because Abraham and Sarah lived by faith in a foreign land, and that is what you must do to achieve this goal (and by the way, your wife already has the right name)'.

There has been a history in Ethiopia of Protestant churches developing 'Orthodox-friendly' approaches, a term for which I have come to have an intense dislike. The fundamental objective of many such ministries is 'to teach the Orthodox the true gospel'. We must be clear that there is nothing whatsoever 'Orthodox-friendly' about such approaches. In practice, such ministries promote conformity to Protestant ways of worship and of reading the Scriptures that fundamentally undermine a person's ability to thrive within the Orthodox Church. In many cases in Ethiopia the result is people joining Protestant churches, or even forming their own churches. For me, this approach is fundamentally dishonest; many Orthodox Christians in Ethiopia consider missionaries to be 'wolves in sheep's clothing' for this very reason.

Another aspect of this is seeking deep understanding of each other. Generosity and honesty are hard things. In our journeys together, we need to understand that moving forward in relationship is difficult. We need to be tender-hearted in our relationships, forgiving one another as we have been forgiven. When we moved to Bahir Dar, we prayed for a cultural counsellor, one who would forgive our questioning and mistakes, who could help us to understand the Orthodox faith more deeply. The good Lord provided that for us in our dear friend Fasikaw. Taylor found this through his studies and being welcomed by the Hilandar community. Taylor was honest about the things that he did not understand, or even struggled with, and the generous-hearted community took those questions, they saw his heart and they taught him.

Genuine Enquiry

I can remember after a short time in Bahir Dar thinking that I could have done with a long period of study to prepare me for the encounter with the Orthodox Church. After eight years in Bahir Dar we returned to the UK to do just that, and I did a further four years of study, which has turned into a significant part of my work. The natural outcome of seeking to be generous and honest is a desire to develop deep understanding. This will not resolve all issues. As I have studied Orthodox Christianity (and I know that Taylor would echo these sentiments), and Ethiopian Orthodox Christianity in particular, I have found:

- things that I have found difficult to understand;
- things that I have found it difficult to embrace;
- things that just make a lot of sense;
- things that have been transformational in my spiritual journey.

One of the characteristics that many of us Westerners struggle with is the need to resolve things quickly, and this can create problems. We ask questions like 'Are they saved?' My Orthodox friends do not always understand this, and have a very different outlook. They are content to live with paradox, and they are content to live with things unresolved, seeking to move towards resolution.

Reflection

One of the Fathers of the Church who has inspired me the most is Ephrem the Syrian. In his commentary on the *Diatessaron* (1.18), he says that understanding the word of God is like drinking water from a fountain: we can be fully satisfied and yet leave behind much more than we take out, leaving plenty more to return to.[2] This expresses our need to be humble as we approach the Scriptures, not sensing that we have worked it all out. This seems to me to be the way we need to approach each other as we seek to be generous towards one another and work together in discipleship.

Conclusion

Our purpose in writing this article has been to share our journeys as an encouragement to others to take steps of faith to experience, and enjoy fellowship with Orthodox Christianity. We would all testify to the immense enrichment which our encounters have given, but also to the need for this to be done in community and fellowship with others. The reflection, guidance, and leadership that David has given is invaluable, and long conversations between Taylor and Ralph were essential. This fellowship and reflection has, we hope, fostered the development of new minds, enabling us to test and approve God's will.

---

[2] C. McCarthy, *Saint Ephrem's Commentary on Tatian's Diatessaron: An English Translation of Chester Beatty Syriac MS 709 with Introduction and Notes* (Oxford: Oxford University Press, 1993), 49.

8. Why Discipleship,
or Making Disciples, Matters*

Dr Joshua Bogunjoko

(With Dr Ken Baker, SIM Ministry Training Facilitator, &
Dr Tom Lunsford, SIM Africa Discipleship Coaching Movement)

In the last several decades, a stream of books and programmes, along with wholesale methodologies and even movements, have alerted us to the importance of disciple-making, discipleship and mentoring in the Church. These endeavours highlight a core component of kingdom mission and its primacy in the Church, yet they also reveal how far we have drifted from a Church-wide and mission-wide commitment towards everything it means to be, and to make, disciples.

On one level, it is somewhat disconcerting that we are having a conversation about the criticality and necessity of prioritizing discipleship or disciple-making in the Church and in global mission. It is disconcerting that a confusion exists regarding what disciple-making means; that some in the Church and even in missions do not feel called to (or have an idea of) disciple-making; and that some in the Church and in missions do not believe they have ever been 'discipled'. These realities demonstrate that being and making disciples is not as integral to the Church's ministry and ethos as we had thought and affirmed in our often-quoted Great Commission passages. On the other hand, exposing such deficiencies also frees us to address them. We have the open opportunity now to embrace our role as disciples who are making disciples both within the Church and among those who live and die without hearing God's good news.

The redeemed persons in Jesus Christ are disciple-pilgrims on a journey together. As we journey together, we mutually receive and assist others on their journey towards Christ. Being and making disciples are inseparable realities for our life in Christ. This is the defining identity of God's people and the central organizing ethos of the ministry of the Church. As such, our new SIM Purpose statements choose to make explicit what has always been the enduring calling of God's people:

Convinced that no one should live and die without hearing God's good news, we believe that He has called us *to make disciples* of the Lord Jesus Christ in communities where He is least known.

Terminology

Perhaps one of the greatest challenges in a discussion like this is how imprecise the language has become over time. Any conversation hinges upon shared meanings and understandings of key words. We generally assume in the Church that we understand disciple-making – a deeply biblical calling – yet our understandings vary dramatically. Some see 'disciple-making' and 'discipleship' as synonymous; others see one as dominant; still others view them in sequence, in which disciple-making describes the start of a process which discipleship completes. Furthermore, most of us tend to think that discipleship is what we *do* to other people, perhaps through leading a Bible study or one of the programmes in our church. These impressions and opinions reveal a variety of interpretations within the Church which is at once useful and bewildering.

In *The Complete Book of Discipleship*, Bill Hull gives the following definition of a disciple which I have found very helpful: 'A disciple, *mathetes*, is a learner or follower – usually someone committed to a significant matter.'[1] He quotes Michael Wilkins, Professor of New Testament Language and Literature at Talbot School of Theology, who further describes the term this way:

> Disciples is a primary term used in the Gospel to refer to Jesus' followers and is a common reference for those known in the early church as believers, Christians, brothers/sisters, those of the way, or saint, although each term focuses upon different aspects of the individual's relationships with Jesus and others of the faith. The term was used most frequently in this specific sense: at least 230 times in the Gospels and 28 times in Acts.[2]

The term 'disciple-making' comes from the verb *matheteusate*, which means to 'make disciples' (Mt. 28.19). Hull describes the process of becoming and being a disciple as: Deliverance, the first step into following Christ (Repentance: turning from darkness to light: Acts 26.17-18); followed by Development (Equipping: Eph. 4.11-13) and Deployment (Participation in works of service: Eph. 4.12). He continues:

> 'Discipleship', the widely accepted term that describes the ongoing life of the disciple, also describes the broader Christian experience. This word is not a pure biblical term, but a derivative. Yet most Christians generally accept discipleship as the process of following Jesus. The addition of '-ship' to the end denotes the state of' or 'contained in'. So discipleship means 'the state of

---

[1] Bill Hull, *The Complete Book of Discipleship: On Being and Making Followers of Christ* (Colorado Springs, CO: NavPress, 2006), 32.
[2] Michael Wilkins, *Following the Master* (Grand Rapids, MI: Zondervan, 1992), 40.

being disciples'. In fact, the term discipleship has a nice ongoing feel: a sense of journey, the idea of *becoming* rather than *having been made* a disciple.[3]

What We Can Affirm

In the pursuit of this conversation about why discipleship matters or the importance of making disciples, let us identify certain aspects of the current reality to affirm and promote, and other aspects which we ought not to affirm. This will lead us towards a core concept that we can understand and embrace collectively, as well as a clarification of why disciple-making matters (or should matter) in the Church and in missions.

In his much-appreciated book, *The Master Plan of Discipleship*, Robert Coleman writes: 'Discipling men and women is the priority around which our lives should be oriented.'[4] If indeed this should be the orientation and priority of our lives, then we have definitely wandered off into the weeds today. It was Mike Breen who said: 'If you make disciples, you always get the church. But if you make a church, you rarely get disciples.'[5] This statement is borne out by the story of Willow Creek Community Church in Chicago, Illinois. Making church, not making disciples, had been their focus prior to a very helpful review in 2007. The results were published in a book, *Reveal: Where Are You?*, co-authored by Greg Hawkins, executive pastor of Willow Creek. Bill Hybels called the findings 'earthshaking', 'ground breaking' and 'mind blowing'.[6] I believe most of the church community in the United States as well as around the world were as surprised by the result as Willow Creek leaders themselves. We have embraced something utterly different than what our Saviour modelled and commanded. In some parts of the world today, churches are described as 'a mile wide and an inch deep'. My experience has convinced me that this description is true, even in those parts of the world that coined this saying! The root of this shallowness is a lack of disciple-making in the church.

In my own opinion, there are many reasons why discipleship or, preferably, disciple-making matters so much in the church and in the global mission. Here are ten:

   1. *It is the model that the Lord left us.* Our Saviour did not try to preach to the whole world in his time. Instead, while he did not neglect preaching,

---

[3] Hull, *Complete Book of Discipleship*, 35.

[4] Robert E. Coleman, *The Master Plan of Discipleship* (Grand Rapids, MI: Fleming H. Revell, 1997), 9.

[5] Mike Breen, *Building a Discipling Culture*, 2nd ed. (Greenville, SC: 3DM Publishing, 2011), 9.

[6] 'Willow Creek repents?', *Christianity Today*, 18 October 2007, online at: https://www.christianitytoday.com/pastors/2007/october-online-only/willow-creek-repents.html.

teaching and healing (Mt. 4.23), he devoted most of his ministry life to investing in a few people who would, in turn, invest in others.

2. *It is the command of the Master.* Our Lord has many commands regarding his Great Commission: he asked us to preach the gospel to all creation; he commanded that as the Father sent him, so he was sending us. But perhaps the clearest understanding of his manner of our sending, which will produce the kind of witnesses that he anticipates in Acts 1.8, was the command in Matthew 28 to *make disciples as we go.* This was not advice, it was a command. And it is understood by the Church as the commission of the Saviour himself.[7]

3. *It is the example of the early church.* The early church took the work of disciple-making seriously, in Jerusalem and everywhere the gospel went. Teaching new believers (sharing fellowship and breaking bread), instructing them in the way of the new faith (the Jerusalem council), or travelling with a young believer (Paul and Timothy in Acts 16.3-4) gave a rich foundation to the new believers.

4. *It is the connection by which God's Kingdom is spread and established.* Whether through individuals or groups, disciple-making is about people connecting with people in the faith community. It is interesting to note what one commentator had to say about the failure of Willow Creek Community Church:

> The one thing that immediately struck me about Willow Creek circa 1991 was that I could walk in and walk out without anyone caring that I had been there. No one needed to say one word to me. I could just go, sit in my seat, have a quasi-spiritual experience and then drift back into the crowd and be forgotten. And people went to that church and hundreds of other CGM [Church Growth Movement] churches like it just for that reason: anonymity. But that's not how you make disciples.[8]

By contrast, believers who are authentically being made into disciples of Jesus Christ can hardly help but feel motivated to make other disciples. They want to share what they have received and to see the Kingdom of God expand, irrespective of where the Lord has placed them.

5. It leads to growth, maturity and effective participation in gospel work through
   a. Reproduction
   b. Maturity
   c. Godly foundation in the word
   d. Establishing believers in the faith.

---

[7] See, for example, Darryl Wilson, 'Three Reasons Why Discipleship Is Important', 2 Oct 2013, at: http://28nineteen.com/three-reasons-why-discipleship-is-important.
[8] Cerulean Sanctum,' Church Growth Movement Fall Down and Go Boom!', 25 October 2007, at: http://ceruleansanctum.com/2007/10/church-growth-movement-fall-down-and-go-boom.html.

6. *It prepares believers to express biblical compassion towards the needs of the world.* A disciple lives a dynamic life of learning and growing. It is within this flourishing relationship with Jesus, relationship with the word of God and relationship with others that believers learn to appreciate, discern and engage with the tremendous needs of the surrounding world in ways that are biblical and effective.

7. *It prepares God's people to confront the works of darkness.* Like the apostle Paul, we are called to bring others 'from darkness to light, and from the dominion of Satan to God, that they may receive forgiveness of sin and an inheritance among those who are sanctified by faith in me' (Acts 26.18, NAS). Only true disciples of Jesus are equipped to identify and confront the forces and the works of darkness.

8. *It encourages fellowship and endurance in faith.* None of us is an island and no human being is truly self-sufficient. This is as true in the Church as it is in the world. Disciple-making is the journey that draws us into true fellowship with one another and enables us to support and encourage one another in the journey. A disciple who has been assisted in his or her journey is more often able to find courage and strength in times of difficulty and persecution than those who have not experienced this journey of being and becoming disciples in Christ.

9. *It is the only way to truly plant and build the Church of Jesus Christ.* Many church planting methodologies exist today, and many people are busily 'making church'. But disciple-making is the only time-tested and Spirit-attested way to plant and build the Church of Jesus Christ that is founded on, and secured in, his teaching and demonstrates his kingdom's character amidst our hostile and broken world. If discipleship plants and builds the Church, then it stands that forsaking discipleship diminishes and ultimately extinguishes the Church. Richard J. Krejcir points out:

> Growing in Christ is the key to growing a church. This is all about being a good and effective witness of who Christ is and what He has called your church to be and do. Following up, teaching, and mentoring new as well as seasoned Christians are the keys to spiritual growth and the replication of the witness. When a church forsakes discipleship, its people will not grow and thus will not reach out. Many will give up on Christianity while others become confused, calloused, or complacent. Alternatively, they will be swept away by false doctrines and cults because they do not know the difference. When we forsake discipleship, we end up just living for and unto ourselves. We miss out on opportunities, learning experiences, growth, and will exchange an

eternity of rewards for a limited time of fun. This will turn into anger and bitterness later on in our lives.[9]

10.   *It brings glory to our Saviour.* Mature believers live lives of such integrity and witness that they glorify the Lord and shed light into the world around them. Mature people of God express his love, communicate truth, and ultimately reveal the glory of the Lord.

There are many benefits to disciple-making. Three such benefits are outlined by Trillia Newbell in her article 'Three Benefits of Discipleship':

Discipleship builds humility: Our temptation might be to think we know what is best for ourselves. As you've heard, and maybe said before, "we know ourselves better than anyone." Scripture says that we might be more confused than we think. The heart is deceitful and so to trust yourself at *all* times is probably not the best route to take (Jeremiah 17:9). Wise counsel from a friend, pastor, or spouse could be just the thing God uses for our protection. It *unites us with fellow believers*: The body of Christ isn't meant to simply exist for us to gather together on Sundays and then move along with our lives the rest of the week. God's word paints a picture of believers doing life together (Acts 2:44-47). Seeking counsel and discipleship is one way to invite others into your life. And finally it *equips us for faithfulness and (faithful service)*: Paul tells us in Titus 2:3 that the older women in the church should teach what is good and train the younger women. They are to equip other women in how to walk in step with the truth of the gospel. And this isn't a suggestion – it is God's instruction for how we should relate to one another.[10]

Intent

What is the intent of this conversation about why discipleship matters?

- to increase engagement and intentionality about being and making disciples;
- to prioritize and catalyse a lasting change in ethos regarding the key role of being and making disciples in the Church and in global missions;
- to highlight being and making disciples within the larger necessity for spiritual vitality in the Church;
- to demonstrate the personal, corporate and evangelistic aspects of being and making disciples;
- to communicate the broad spectrum of what it means to be and make disciples, beyond programmes, curricula and events;
- to dispel incorrect ideas about discipleship and disciple-making;

---

[9] Richard J. Krejcir, 'The Importance of Discipleship and Growth', at: http://www.churchleadership.org/apps/articles/default.asp?articleid=42814&column id=4543, accessed 24 April 2018.

[10] See, for example, Trillia Newbell, 'Three Benefits of Discipleship', at: https://www.desiringgod.org/articles/three-benefits-of-discipleship, accessed 24 April 2018.

- to foster unity around the principle that 'making disciples' is the community identity of Christ's followers.

Challenges

Such an undertaking naturally poses some significant challenges:

- there is the daunting task of developing, across many cultures and Christian traditions, a common understanding and prioritization of what it means to be and make disciples. This means rejuvenating our vocabulary as well as removing errant ideas, jargon and fads in popular Christian culture;
- there is the perceived interchangeable nature of 'discipleship' and disciple-making';
- a definition of discipleship rooted in relationship and journey means that discipleship will not be as simple to measure or package as the event- and programme-based discipleship many have known.

Key Issues for Further Discussion

1. Is there a difference between a convert and a disciple? In other words, is it possible to be 'born again in the Spirit' but not to follow Christ as a disciple?
2. When does one become a disciple? Does this occur the moment one is 'born again' or does the disciple journey begin upon initial captivation with Christ and his teaching?
3. What defines maturity as a disciple?
4. What changes do we need to make in the Church and in global missions to become more effective in being and making disciples?
5. What is the difference between disciple-making, evangelism and church-planting?
6. What do we mean by 'discipling' or 'to disciple' others?
7. Should we distinguish between "discipleship" and "disciple-making"?
8. Should we emphasize 'disciple-making' (as the more biblical usage) over 'discipleship' (which often does not translate well or carries the sense of a programme rather than a life-on-life relational journey)?

May I call us, therefore, to certain affirmations[11] as we recognize the importance of disciple-making in the Church:

A Commitment

- To being [made] disciples, as recipients of the Holy Spirit's ministry (Mk 8).

---

[11] The commitment and affirmations that conclude this chapter are adapted from a SIM document edited and co-authored by Ken Baker and Tom Lunsford.

- To be a disciple means to 'follow' Christ – to learn the character and ways of Jesus and walk in them toward maturity, trusting and obeying with faith in action.
- To be a disciple means lifelong growth as followers of the Master, intentionally emphasizing both being disciples and making disciples.
- To disciple-making, as workers with Christ on mission (Mt. 28).
  - All believers have received the mandate from Christ to make disciples. Thus, making disciples is not just one category of activity for some, but the central purpose for all.
- To understanding that making disciples is inherently *relational.*
  - No matter what our role, we enter into relationship with others in the hope that they too may experience all that God intends for them as his image-bearers and join us on the journey as his disciples making disciples.

These affirmations dispel the ideas that
- being and making disciples is an exceptional or optional endeavour;
- meeting physical need alone is a sufficient basis for ministry.

- To the fact that the Church exists to worship God and make new disciples. Thus our role as churches and mission practitioners is to undertake disciple-making in the context of a faith community. This may mean helping to establish a faith community or ensuring that new disciples are connected to a faith community.

This affirmation dispels the idea that
- disciple-making within ministries is an end in itself and can operate apart from the wider faith community.

- An understanding that:
  - Being and making disciples brings God's blessing to communities and the nations and is a foundational role of the people of God on mission together in the community of faith. (All mission work of the Church is shaped by our lives as faithful disciples of Christ in community.)
  - The life of a disciple and disciple-making requires a growing, learning community of believers characterized by mutually edifying relationships and corporate prayer.

Being and making disciples involves growing in spiritual and theological understanding, but it is also about *humbly applying and living* that knowledge in our daily relationships.

- The purpose of being a disciple is to faithfully reflect Christ in the world, through the Church, and make more disciples. Therefore, the journey of being and making disciples involves two roles, as both follower and mutual learner of Christ in the community of believers, as well as being an intentional helper to others who are learning to follow Christ.

> *This dispels the ideas that the purpose of being and making disciples*
> - is simply a static programme or a series of spiritual stages;
> - is only about acquired spiritual and theological knowledge;
> - is only a response to spiritual needs.

The contexts and dynamics through which the Holy Spirit chooses to develop us as disciples are varied, both corporate (such as the instructive environment of a local assembly or small group) and individual (personal mentoring). The recorded dynamic of being and making disciples in the gospels was almost exclusively in community with other disciples, and the context of spiritual growth throughout Scripture is the community of the faithful.

- The life of a disciple is not merely a personal journey but also a collective journey. Character and ethics are lived out in the Church and before the world (Mt. 10.40-42; Lk. 9-10).
  - Disciples of Christ are sent from the Church in the authority of Christ as co-workers in the mission of Christ (Mt. 10, 28; Lk. 9-10).
  - Disciples in community must accurately reflect the character of the Master in their lives and relationships (Mt. 5-7, 18).
  - Disciples in community share all aspects of the Master's mission, including participating in the sufferings of Christ, while standing in the authority of Christ (Mt. 16).

Furthermore, being and making disciples is an opportunity for the body of Christ to function as intended, by members mutually building each other up.

> *This dispels the ideas that*
> - its primary expression is one-on-one, mentor to learner;
> - it is only a personal, individualistic journey.

- Being and making disciples of Christ involves:
  - Gospel – the starting place of all disciples;
  - Relationship – loving God, one another and all others;
  - Learning and communicating truth – through relationships;
  - Ethics – manifesting the character and justice of, and obedience to, our King Jesus;
  - Mission – to make disciples as workers together in Christ's mission in the world;
  - Kingdom vision – to be captivated by our King Jesus and his restorative purpose.

Summary of Affirmations

- Being and making disciples is the *biblical mandate* for every believer and is *a foundational role* of the people of God on mission with Christ.
- Growing as a disciple is a *lifelong process*.
- Disciple-making is about both *evangelism* and *helping believers grow* to maturity, not one or the other.
- Disciple-making is a *relational* process and the foundational intent of all relationships in every ministry.
- Helping believers grow extends *beyond initial establishing* in the faith to increasing maturity and fruitfulness at *all levels* of growth.
- Maturity as a disciple of Christ is not just about knowledge, but also about *abiding* in Christ, *obeying* in all areas of life and moving out in *mission*.
- Making disciples includes *sharing the truth* of the gospel together while authentically *modelling* Christ.
- Being and making disciples includes living and communicating God's good news in the context of *relationship*, the broader *community* of faith, *smaller groups* and *person-to-person*.
- Disciple-making in missions should be an *extension of the Church* at some level (sending, local, etc.) and the aim should be to *connect disciples into churches*.
- Being and making disciples is both a *collective pilgrimage* of believers and an *intentional process* where a person or community helps others come to faith and grow in Christ.

While the decades ahead may continue to bring us programmes and methodologies, may they be marked even more deeply by an earnest return to a Church-wide and mission-wide commitment to everything it means to be and to make disciples. This will necessarily include a grassroots hunger and devotion to learning, prayer, fellowship and abiding together in Christ, in the same spirit as the early church (Acts 2.42). The fabric of such a Spirit-filled community reproduces as maturing disciples go out in power and love to serve their neighbours and proclaim the good news.

9. Why Discipleship Matters:
A Response to Joshua Bogunjoko

Deacon James Nicholas

Discipleship Matters to Christ

Discipleship is not a one-dimensional spiritual enterprise that makes people into Christians. Rather, it is a diamond with many brilliant facets that together make it a very beautiful and priceless gem in the spiritual life of the Church. As we share between our two traditions, this is one of the things that we recognize.

In the previous chapter, Joshua Bogunjoko has described many, if not most, of the facets of this diamond for you already and so I will reflect on some of those that he has pointed out. But in the process, I may also step around to the other side of that diamond and highlight some other facets as well: facets that we as Orthodox Christians recognize.

The lead question for us to answer here is: Why does discipleship matter?' Why does it really matter? Well, the simplest answer, which has been referenced in other chapters, is this: it matters because it matters to Christ! When Christ said: 'Go, make disciples of all nations', he did not say: 'Do this, if you feel like doing it', or: 'If you feel this is your personal calling, then you should do it.' He did not say those things. He said: 'Go, do it!' It is a command. You can either choose to obey Christ's command in this, or you can choose to disobey him: it is really up to you. This is so simple, and it is where it begins. So when Joshua says in the first of his concluding affirmations, '[b]eing and making disciples is the biblical mandate for every believer', he is absolutely correct. But it is not just a biblical mandate, for that matter, because in historical terms it is pre-biblical: Christ said this before it was recorded in what we refer to as the Bible today. It drove the apostles from the beginning to 'Go, do this.'

Perpetual Discipleship

Joshua has also pointed out that growing as a disciple is a life-long process. I am so glad that he has made this point, I really am, because far too many times in my life I have heard discipleship described in much more finite terms than that, like, if we do this and that and cover these subjects by such and such a date then by spring you should be good to go, you'll be there. It reminds me in a way of baking a pie. If we put the pie into the oven at 375°F for an hour and ten minutes then it should be ready to serve. Discipleship does not happen this way, it is an ongoing process. It is like Paul said, 'Being confident in this very thing, that He which hath begun a good work in you will perform it until the day of Jesus Christ' (Phil. 1.6).[1] Until the day of Christ Jesus, maybe not just for my lifetime, but 'until the day of Christ Jesus'; but that is another topic for another time.

In the Orthodox Christian faith, as many readers know, we have the term *theosis*. In very simple terms (if that is possible), *theosis* is a dynamic process. Just as that scripture says, it is a dynamic process of becoming increasingly Christ-like, increasingly formed by him, increasingly moving forward and receiving the fullness of God's life. We do not believe that we instantly become Christ-like – we do not. We see that as a process, a perpetual process. Discipleship is one of the ways in which *theosis* is accomplished. As Joshua notes, it extends beyond the initial stage to increasing maturity and fruitfulness. Here he is referencing the perpetual nature of discipleship as well. He says: 'disciple-making is about both evangelism and helping believers to grow in maturity, not one or the other' (his third affirmation). You see, evangelism is evangelism and discipleship is discipleship. However, there is (I am not going to attempt to describe it fully) a convergence between these two things, because it is not simply a fact that evangelism produces a person who can then be discipled; rather, there is an overlap. Just think about the times when you may have begun to evangelize someone, and what you are doing as you evangelize them. Within the context of the very words and communication that you are using for evangelism, you are already beginning to teach and catechize and speak that faith into them, even before they may have accepted Christ as their Saviour. You are already doing it. So there is some sort of convergence there. I am already transmitting the knowledge of my faith.

Relational Intent

Two of Joshua's affirmations in his concluding summary deal primarily with relationship, so I am going to put those two together and address them together. In the first of these (the fourth), he states: 'Discipleship is a relational process and a foundational intent of all relationships in every ministry'. In the second (the eighth), he says: 'Being and making disciples includes living and communicating God's good news in the context of relationship,' and then continues, 'in the broader community of faith, smaller groups and person to person'. There are a number of points and sub-points he is making there but I will highlight a couple of things that really stand out to me. The first is this: discipleship is indeed relational. After all, we are created by God for relationship with him and with one another; we are reconciled to God through Christ for eternal relationship. There is really nothing that occurs in the Christian life that is not relational in some form or manner, or else it would be incompatible with the nature of God. Therefore, one could say that discipleship is instrumental in this holy process of reconciliation, under God, to God.

---

[1] Scripture quotations in this chapter are taken from the King James Version.

Joshua states that 'discipleship is the foundational intent of all relationships in every ministry'. I honestly have to think about that statement, and I might have worded it a little differently. I am not disagreeing with it, but let me give a different perspective. The word 'intention' to me implies a determined objective, and I do not disagree with that objective, but there is an incarnational side to it as well, which is the point I am going to make here. If I am being a minister of God, whether I am lay or clergy, and I am incarnating the gospel, then do you know what is going to happen? John 7.38 suggests that rivers of living water will then flow out of me. And as this happens, discipleship occurs. It has to, because discipleship is one of the products of this incarnation of the gospel. So, do I think we should be intentional about discipleship? Absolutely, I am totally convinced, but I think another facet of that is the incarnational nature of discipleship.

Mutual Abiding

I now move on to Joshua's sixth affirmation, in which he says: 'Maturity as a disciple of Christ is not just about knowledge, but also about abiding in Christ'. Very true, amen! I am reminded here, obviously, of John 15.4, where Jesus is saying to the apostles: 'Abide in me and I in you. Just as the branch cannot bear fruit of itself unless it abides in the vine, neither can you, unless you abide in me, for without me you can do nothing.' Now I have to confess here that during my Evangelical upbringing (and this may not be the case for every Evangelical), I viewed discipleship as a personal action, almost entirely as a personal action, I think. It was something that I did to help make someone into a Christian. In modern vernacular, I saw it as my effort to download Christ into somebody, and although there is truth to that, as an Orthodox Christian I came to see that discipleship is not just downloading Christ into someone but (just as importantly) downloading someone into Christ. It is both. The Scriptures to which we have just referred say, 'he who abides in me, and I in him'; there is a two-way download going on here. (I hope this vernacular language is not offensive to anyone.)

Let me give you another analogy, an image that came to mind as I was thinking about this passage. I saw an image of a deep spring, and I can imagine myself walking up to that spring with a glass and bending over and dipping this glass into that spring of clean water and taking it and drinking it, taking it inside myself – refreshing, helpful, quenching, life-giving. And then I imagine myself walking out to that water, entering in the water, into this spring until I am totally submerged. It is no longer just in me, it is covering me, it is in every pore of my body and I am consumed by it totally. So I believe, that although it is wonderful to have Christ abide in me, how much more wonderful it is for me to abide in Christ, to be submerged in him.

Reciprocal Discipling

Another important point is that discipleship is never one-way; rather, it is reciprocal. True discipleship is not one-way any more than true relationship is one-way, especially if discipleship is based on relationship, as Joshua has suggested. Anyone who has been involved regularly in discipleship has noticed this at some point. As I am discipling someone, I discover that I am being discipled too. There is this holy thing going on: 'oh, my goodness, what is happening to me?' I can feel myself growing too as I engage in this. This is holy stuff! This is the spiritual dividend you receive when you invest yourself in discipleship.

I have found that those who are most ignorant of Christianity, but then come to know and accept Christ, are often those from whom I learn the most. This is because they came to Christ as a child, a true spiritual child, as Jesus says in Matthew 18.3: 'Unless you turn to become like little children, you will never enter the Kingdom of Heaven.' You see, the faith of such people is sometimes so simple and uncomplicated that it convinces me that I might have moved away too far from this child-like spirituality. It is very convicting! I also learnt this lesson through my children and now my grandchildren, when in a moment of parental or grandparental instruction or explanation of some sort they catch me totally off-guard and overwhelm me with some simple but profound word or gesture of love, or a touch or a look that so obviously is Christ making myself known to me through my children and my grandchildren. It's precious and humbling. That happens in discipleship too. As you share Christ with someone else, he shares more of himself with you. It is a beautiful reciprocity that goes on there.

Encountering Christ in the Sacraments

My final point is very important. For Orthodox Christians, the road of discipleship leads through the sacraments. Am I talking about the seven sacraments, or the dominical sacraments or the Orthodox Church's broad view of the sacraments? The quick answer to this is yes, yes and yes, but a fuller explanation of this is for another time. Rather, let me touch on just two important points. Firstly, let me talk about baptism. From the Orthodox point of view, I have to begin by saying that the chief purpose of sacraments, and I am willing to be corrected on this by my superiors, is to impart to the believer the very life of Christ. And is that not the objective of discipleship? Through baptism the door is opened, if you will, to full and complete communion with God. Is this not also the goal of discipleship? In the Orthodox Church, following the service of baptism a procession takes place around the font while singing these words: 'As many as have been baptized into Christ, have put on Christ', a direct reference to Galatians 3.27. Is putting on Christ not the goal of discipleship?

This procession is actually, theologically speaking, a procession to the eucharist, to participate in Christ's Pascha, his crucifixion, his burial, his resurrection and (living through him) his kingdom. Is this not the ultimate intention of discipleship? So with regard to the Eucharist, the Lord's supper, the mass, whatever you want to call it, in John 6.53 we read: 'Jesus said unto them: Unless you eat of the flesh of the Son of Man, and drink his blood, you have no life in you.' If you want to make sure that the one you disciple has full life, make sure they partake of the Eucharist, because by doing so they take Christ into themselves, the divine nature. That is discipleship. So in an Orthodox view, discipleship is not complete without the journey through the sacraments, without the appropriation of the sacraments, because each sacrament is a personal encounter with Christ.

Restoring the Image of God

I conclude with one more thought. I think we all understand discipleship to be transformational, but it is also restorative to a degree. Sometimes we speak of transformation as changing something or someone into something else, generally for the first time. But what if it used to be that way at the beginning? Remember, we were created in the image of God and, from an Orthodox perspective, we do not believe that the image of God in us was destroyed in the Fall. It may have become obscured, or whatever proper term is best for that, but it was not destroyed. Think, just for just a moment, of the beautiful work that Michelangelo did, not only with his painting but with his sculptures, and think of what he is supposed to have said about his sculpting: 'I saw the angel in the marble and I carved until I set him free.' In the same way, you need to look deep into this newly illumined Christian that you are discipling, you need to see the image of Christ there. You need to teach and catechize and guide and mentor and let them journey through the sacraments. Carve and carve until the image of God comes forth. That is why discipleship matters.

10. Re-Centring the Bible in the Missional Goal of Theological Education[*]

Revd Dr Chris Wright

Introduction

The church of today stands in spiritual continuity with the people of God throughout the Bible, as those whom God has called into existence in the great moments of election, redemption and covenant, to glorify and enjoy God for all eternity, and to participate with God in God's mission within history – God's mission of redemption and reconciliation for all nations and all creation. And in order to *be* such a missional community, God's people must *live* worthy of their calling (Eph. 4.1). The Church's missional calling demands an ethical response. There is a message to be proclaimed *and* a life to be lived and they must go together. God's people need to be 'fit for purpose', God's purpose.

How are God's people to be thus shaped for mission? One clear answer that the Bible itself gives is – through teaching by those whom God has given to his people for that purpose. In both Testaments, God's people need godly teaching and godly teachers, and disaster strikes when both are lacking. And the primary focus of such teaching is the word of God in the Scriptures.

Now, the phenomenon which we call 'theological education' did not exist in Old Testament Israel or the New Testament church in the kind of formal structures and institutions we have developed in the history of Christianity. Nevertheless, inasmuch as theological education is one significant (and rather expensive!) dimension of the teaching ministry of the Church, we are including it under that wider generic term. So then, when I use the phrase 'the ministry of teaching' in this article, I intend it to have a broad meaning. It includes the regular preaching of pastors in churches, the long-term impact of scriptural liturgy, church-based courses of study and training, and also the formal world of theological education in Bible colleges and seminaries. These are all ways – formal and non-formal, short and long-term – in which the teaching ministry can take shape within the Church.

In this chapter, we shall attempt to answer three questions:

---

[*] This a revised and condensed version of an earlier and fuller essay that was published as 'The Missional Nature and the Role of Theological Education', in Dirk R. Buursma, Katya Covrett, and Verlyn D. Verbrugge (eds), *Evangelical Scholarship, Retrospects and Prospects: Essays in Honor of Stanley N. Gundry* (Grand Rapids, MI: Zondervan, 2017), 225-54.

Scripture quotations in this chapter are from the Holy Bible, New International Version®, NIV® Copyright ©1973, 1978, 1984, 2011 by Biblica, Inc.® Used by permission. All rights reserved worldwide.

1. Why is the ministry of Bible teaching so important in relation to the mission of the Church?
2. What are the goals of the ministry of teaching in the Bible itself and how do they relate to our mission, particularly in relation to the goals of theological education?
3. And, finally, how can we re-centre the Bible in our theological education?

Why is the Teaching Ministry Important for the Mission of the Church?

Because the Bible Says So

The teaching of God's word is integral to the growth and mission of God's people. The Bible provides robust support for this conviction.

i. The Old Testament

The work of teachers and teaching is deeply rooted in Old Testament Israel. It was an essential part of the way God called, shaped, and educated his people. 'The Old Testament is the oldest and longest programme of theological education': this remarkable affirmation was made by Professor Andrew Walls.[1] Throughout the whole Old Testament, for a millennium or more, God was shaping his people, insisting that they should remember *and teach to every generation* the things God had *done* ('what your eyes have seen) and the things God had *said* ('what your ears have heard'). This is stressed again and again in Deuteronomy. God gave his people the Levitical priests as teachers of the Torah, the prophets to call them back to the ways of God, and Psalmists and wise men and women to teach them how to worship God and walk in godly ways in ordinary life. When reformations happened in Old Testament times (e.g. under Jehoshaphat, Hezekiah, Josiah, Nehemiah and Ezra), there was often a return to the teaching of God's word by the Levites (e.g. Neh. 8). God's people were to be a community of teachers and learners, shaped by the word of God, as we see so emphatically in the longings of the author of Psalm 119. Israel's mission was not to *go* to the nations (yet), but to *so live among the nations* that the name and character of Yahweh would become known among the nations. And teaching was necessary for that mission.

ii. Jesus

It is not surprising, then, that when Jesus came, he spent years doing exactly the same: teaching, teaching, teaching his disciples as the nucleus of the new community of the Kingdom of God. Even as a twelve-year-old boy he showed

---

[1] In an unpublished paper, 'Two Thousand Years of Theological Education: Constants and Contexts', given at the Mission Leaders' Forum at the Overseas Ministries Study Centre, New Haven, CT, in April 2012.

that he was rooted in the Scriptures and able to engage with the rabbis in the temple.

And in the Great Commission, he mandates his apostles to teach new disciples to observe all that he had taught them (Mt. 28.20) – which was a lot! Teaching was at the heart of Jesus' own mission and ministry, and he makes himself the model for his mandate. We are to make disciples the way Jesus made disciples – with patient teaching over time. It is no good just bringing people to conversion and leaving it at that. The seed needs deep soil and good roots in order to bear fruit. Churches need not only to be planted through evangelism, but also to be watered through teaching. Both evangelism and teaching are Great Commission mandates. And both are clearly also God's will for his people. God is at work not only bringing people to faith in Christ, but also bringing them to maturity in Christ, through the work of the Holy Spirit within them, with his gifts, power and fruit in their lives. The ministry of teaching within the Church is a participating in the process by which God himself brings his people to the fullness of maturity and Christlikeness. It is one way in which our mission shares in the mission of God. Theological education, then, as the Cape Town Commitment says, is *intrinsically* missional, and should therefore be *intentionally* missional.

iii. Paul

When we look at Paul, we notice that teaching was integral to his whole life as a missionary church planter. Often he had to leave a newly planted church quickly, under threat, but even then he would write to them to encourage and teach them. And when Paul had the opportunity, as in Ephesus, he stayed for nearly three years, during which he transformed a group of twelve disciples into a city church with several households and functioning elders. He later tells them that he had taught them not only all that was helpful for them, but 'the whole counsel of God', i.e. the whole scriptural revelation of God's great plan and purpose (Acts 20.20, 27).

And when Paul could not personally do the teaching, he ensured that it was done by others who were part of his missionary team, such as Timothy and Titus, or Apollos (from Africa), who was learned in the Scriptures (i.e. the Old Testament) and a gifted teacher. Apollos gained further theological education at the home of Priscilla and Aquila (in Asia), and then went to Corinth (in Europe), where he engaged systematically in teaching that included Old Testament hermeneutics, Christology and apologetics (Acts 18.24-28). Later, when the Christians in Corinth divided into factions boasting loyalty to Paul or Apollos, Paul would not allow it. True, Paul and Apollos had had different parts to play. Paul was the evangelist church-planter. Apollos was a theological church-teacher. But they shared a *common mission*. Paul insists that the evangelist (planter) and the teacher (waterer) have 'one purpose', or a single mission (in Greek, 'they are one'; 1 Cor. 3.5-9). The apostolic understanding and practice of mission clearly included systematic teaching of new believers, and the bulk of that teaching seems to have been a Christ-focused understanding of the mission of God as revealed in the Old Testament, leading to the inclusion of the Gentile nations and the vision and hope of Christ's return and the restoration, reconciliation and redemption of all creation.

So Bible teaching within the Church in all its forms, including what we would now call theological education, is an intrinsic part of mission. It is not an extra. It is not merely ancillary to 'real mission'. The ministry of teaching has to be included within our obedience to the Great Commission. The Bible itself commands it.

Because the Church Needs It

The Lausanne Movement's Cape Town Commitment (CTC) identifies several ways in which we, as Christians, have failed to live up to our calling. There is confession of *failure* (in repentance) as well as confession of *faith* (in affirmation). We have to confess that we Christians are not always particularly attractive in the way we live and behave, and that we simply do not look like the Jesus we proclaim.

> When there is no distinction in conduct between Christians and non-Christians – for example in the practice of corruption and greed, or sexual promiscuity, or rate of divorce, or relapse to pre-Christian religious practice, or attitudes towards people of other races, or consumerist lifestyles, or social prejudice – then the world is right to wonder if our Christianity makes any difference at all. Our message carries no authenticity to a watching world.[2]

But what lies behind these areas of failure? Surely the moral confusion and laxity of the global church is a product of a 'famine of hearing the words of the LORD' (Amos 8.11), that is, a lack of biblical knowledge, teaching and thinking, from the leadership downwards. As in Hosea's day, there are many of God's people who are left with 'no knowledge of God' – at least, no adequate and life-transforming knowledge. And this is so for the same reason as Hosea identified, namely the failure of those appointed to teach God's word (the priests in his day) to do so (Hos. 4.1-9).

Without good biblical teaching rooted in a missional hermeneutic (that is, biblical teaching that is conscious of its own purpose, namely to shape God's people for their mission in the world), people forget the story they are in, or never knew it in the first place. They may know that their sins are forgiven and they are 'on the way to heaven'. But as for how they should be living now, engaging with God in God's mission in today's world – of that story and its demands and implications, they know nothing. Lack of missional teaching inevitably results in absence of missional interest or engagement.

---

[2] Cape Town Commitment IIE.1. This document is accessible online at: https://www.lausanne.org/content/ctcommitment.

Decades ago, John Stott believed that it was this lack of biblical teaching, more than anything else, that was to blame for the ethical and missional weakness of the contemporary church. And he believed that the key remedy, 'the more potent medicine', as he called it, was to raise the standards of biblical preaching and teaching, from the seminaries to the grass-roots of the churches. He wrote:

> If God reforms his people by his Word, precisely *how* does his Word reach and transform them? In a variety of ways, no doubt, including their daily personal meditation in the Scripture. But the principal way God has chosen is to bring his Word to his people through his appointed pastors and teachers. For he has not only given us his Word; he has also given us pastors to teach the people out of his Word (e.g. Jn. 21.15-17; Acts 20.28; Eph. 4.11-12; 1 Tim. 4.13). We can hardly exaggerate the importance of pastor-preachers for the health and maturity of the church.

> *My vision, as I look out over the world, is to see every pulpit in every church occupied by a conscientious, Bible-believing, Bible-studying, Bible-expounding pastor. I see with my mind's eye multitudes of people in every country world-wide converging on their church every Sunday, hungry for more of God's Word. I also see every pastor mounting his pulpit with the Word of God in his mind (for he has studied it), in his heart (for he has prayed over it), and on his lips (for he is intent on communicating it).*

> *What a vision! The people assemble with hunger, and the pastor satisfies their hunger with God's Word! And as he ministers to them week after week, I see people changing under the influence of God's Word, and so becoming more like the kind of people God wants them to be, in understanding and obedience, in faith and love, in worship, holiness, unity, service and mission.*[3]

That was John Stott's vision, which lies behind his foundation of the Langham Partnership and one of its three key programmes, Langham Preaching, establishing movements for hands-on, face-to-face training in biblical preaching in more than sixty countries around the world. Such a vision seems also to be very close to how the apostle Paul also saw the primary task of those who were appointed as elders and pastors within the churches. And that brings us to the third reason why the teaching ministry is important for the mission of the Church:

Because It Is the Priority for Pastors and Those Who Train Them

What should a pastor be *able to do*? What should a pastor-in-training in a seminary be trained and equipped to do? We can start to answer that question by consulting the list of qualifications that Paul gives for elders / overseers in the churches he had founded which were now being supervised by Timothy and Titus. We find extensive lists of qualities and criteria in 1 Timothy 3.1-10 and Titus 1.6-9.

---

[3] John Stott, 'The Langham Trust's Strategic Vision' (1992), online at: http:// https://hk.langham.org/why-langham/our-founders-vision/.

What is striking is that almost all the items Paul mentions are matters of character and behaviour – how they should live and conduct themselves and their families. Pastors should be *examples* of godliness and faithful discipleship. Only *one* thing could be described as a competence, ability or skill: 'able to teach'. Above all, the pastor should be *a teacher of God's word*, able to understand, interpret and apply it effectively (as Paul further describes in 1 Tim. 4.11-13; 5.17; 2 Tim. 2.2, 15; 3.15–4.2). The pastor's personal godliness and exemplary life is what will give power and authenticity to this single fundamental task. The pastor must *live* what he or she *preaches* from the Scriptures. But preaching and teaching the Scriptures is the fundamental task and competence for those who are called into pastoral leadership in the Church. That is very clear.

So then, if seminaries are to prioritize in their training what Paul prioritizes for pastors, they ought to concentrate on two primary things: a) *personal godliness* and b) *ability to teach the Bible.*

Now of course there are many other things that pastors have to do in the demanding tasks of church leadership. They will need basic competence in pastoral counselling, in leading God's people in worship and prayer, in management and administration of funds and people, in articulating vision and direction, in relating to their particular cultural context, and so on. But above all else, Paul emphasizes what they must *be* (godly and upright in their personal life), and what they must commit themselves to *do* (effectively preach and teach God's word).

Yet equipping future pastors with that skill of careful, diligent, imaginative and relevant preaching of the Bible seems sadly neglected in many seminaries. Or so it seems from the response I often get when, at a Langham Preaching seminar somewhere, I ask participants who I know have already been to a seminary, 'Did you not learn how to preach from Bible passages at seminary?' 'Well', comes the answer many a time, 'we did have a course called "Homiletics", but it was just ten lectures on different kinds of preaching. We were never taught *how* to move from a Bible text to a biblical sermon, or given any practice and assessment in doing it.' When I hear that, it points to a tragic abdication of what ought to be a primary responsibility, both for pastors themselves and for institutions that train them.

So, to be very frank at this point, whenever theological education neglects or marginalizes the teaching of the Bible, or squeezes it to the edges of a curriculum that has become crammed with other things, then that form of theological education has itself become unbiblical and disobedient to the clear mandate that we find taught and modelled in both Testaments. Theological education which does not produce men and women who *know* their Bibles thoroughly, who know how to *teach and preach* the Scriptures, who are able to *think biblically* through any and every issue they confront, and who are able to *feed and strengthen* God's people with God's word for God's mission in God's world – whatever else such theological education may do, or claim, or be accredited for, it is failing the Church by failing to equip the Church and its leaders to fulfil their calling and mission in the world. That kind of theological education is failing to fulfil the very biblical mandate for which it exists.

To conclude this first section, then, I am arguing that we must give greater priority to the ministry of scriptural teaching (a) because of the biblical mandate and examples, (b) because of the dire need of the Church, and (c) because of the clear instruction of Paul that preaching and teaching the Scriptures should be a primary calling and competence of those who exercise pastoral leadership in churches.

What are the Goals of the Ministry of Scriptural Teaching?

As we have seen, the Bible affirms from very early on, and repeatedly in both Testaments, that God's people need teaching and teachers, and that God's people are vulnerable and endangered when teachers are either absent or false and unfaithful. But we need to take a step further and ask what the ultimate goals of such teaching are.

What, then, are the *intended outcomes* of faithful and effective teaching, according to the Bible? What goals are we aiming at? What results should we want to achieve through the ministry of teaching? And since theological education is an integral part of the wider concept of teaching within the Church, what should be the outcomes of theological education if it is truly going to reflect the goals of teaching that the Bible itself envisages?[4]

I suggest three focal points. Each of the following sections is connected with a Bible character who was either commissioned to teach, or commissioned others to do so – *Abraham, Moses and Paul*. And in each case, there is a strong reason given for why such teaching matters in the context of our world.

Here, then, are three biblical outcomes of teaching:

a) *Mission*: in a world of many nations, the Abrahamic outcome.

b) *Monotheism*: in a world of many gods, the Mosaic outcome

c) *Maturity*: in a world of many falsehoods, the Pauline outcome

Mission, in a World of Many Nations – the Abrahamic Outcome

Abraham will surely become a great and powerful nation, and all nations on earth will be blessed through him. For I have chosen him, so that he will direct his children and his household after him to keep the way of the Lord by doing

---

[4] These questions were very much to the fore at the Triennial Conference of the International Council for Evangelical Theological Education (ICETE), in Antalya, Turkey, in 2015: see http://www.icete-edu.org/antalya/index.htm. The materials from the conference are available at:
http://theologicaleducation.net/articles/index.htm?category_id=77.

what is right and just, so that the Lord will bring about for Abraham what he
has promised him. (Gen. 18.18-19)

In a world going the way of Sodom and Gomorrah (18.20-21; 19; Isa.1.9-23;
Ezek. 16.49-50), God wanted to create a community that would be different: not
just religiously different, but *morally and socially distinctive* (committed to
righteousness and justice). That is the reason God chose and called Abraham and
commissioned him to teach his own household and descendants (says Gen.
18.19).

But then, *why* did God want such a community to exist in the world? Why
did God plan to create a nation chosen in Abraham and taught by him? God
reminds us of God's own purpose in verse 18. It was in order to fulfil God's
promise to Abraham, that through him and his descendants *all nations on
earth would find blessing* (echoing, of course, Gen. 12.3). That is God's
ultimate purpose.

There is, then, a *universal and missional context* here to the teaching
mandate given to Abraham. And significantly, this instruction to Abraham
comes in Genesis, long before the giving of the law in Exodus. Already,
however, the *ethical* content of the law ('way of the LORD', 'righteousness
and justice') is anticipated in the kind of teaching that Abraham was to give
to his household after him. Abraham was to teach his people not only *about*
God, but also about the ethical character of God, and how God wants people
to *live*. In other words, this is missionally focused ethical teaching to shape
a people through whom God can fulfil his mission among the nations, a long-
term eschatological vision no doubt, but clearly expressed in the syntax and
logic of the verse. Notice the three statements in verse 19: 'I have chosen
him ... he will direct ... the LORD will bring about what he has promised',
joined together by two 'so that's'. God's election flows through human
teaching within God's people towards God's ultimate mission of blessing all
nations.

This in itself shows that teaching (whether in church or in institutions of
theological education) is never merely the imparting of cognitive knowledge,
but the *shaping of character and behaviour*. The language of 'walking in the
way of the LORD' is common across the Torah, the prophets, the Psalms and
wisdom literature.

So the *ethical purpose* of teaching in Old Testament Israel is governed by
the missional purpose behind Israel's existence in the first place. In the midst
of the nations, *this* nation is to be *taught* how to live as the redeemed people
of God, ultimately for the sake of the nations, and as part of the mission of
God for the nations.

The ministry of teaching within God's people, including theological
education, is, as the Cape Town Commitment puts it, *intrinsically* missional.
Its whole purpose is to serve the mission of the Church. Therefore it ought
also to be *intentionally* missional, since it seeks to train the people of God
for their mission of life and work in the midst of the nations.

Monotheism, in a World of Many Gods – the Mosaic Outcome

There is a strong emphasis on teaching in Deuteronomy. God's word in its broadest sense (the knowledge of God's mighty acts along with understanding of God's law), must be *constantly taught to the people*, the whole people, and every generation of the people.

Moses himself is repeatedly presented in the book as the one who teaches Israel the requirements of their covenant God (to be followed by the Levitical priests: Deut. 33.10). And the primary content of Moses' teaching was that YHWH, God of Israel, was *the one and only, unique and universal God, beside whom there is no other* (Deut. 4.35, 39). For that reason, the first and greatest commandment, as Jesus said, is to love that one whole single God with your one whole single self, with heart and soul and strength (Deut. 6.4-5).

And that primary love command is immediately followed by *the necessity of teaching*, teaching that is to apply to the personal realm (hands and foreheads), the family realm (the doorposts of the home) and the public arena (the 'gate').

> Hear, O Israel: The Lord our God, the Lord is one. Love the Lord your God with all your heart and with all your soul and with all your strength. These commandments that I give you today are to be on your hearts. Impress them on your children. Talk about them when you sit at home and when you walk along the road, when you lie down and when you get up. Tie them as symbols on your hands and bind them on your foreheads. Write them on the doorframes of your houses and on your gates. (Deut. 6.4-9).

Such teaching was necessary because of the polytheistic culture that surrounded the Israelites. Monotheism, in its proper biblical sense (i.e. not just the arithmetical conviction that there is only one God, but the specific affirmation of the identity and universality of YHWH, God of Israel), is *not* an easy faith to inculcate or sustain (as the rest of the Old Testament shows). But since this crucial affirmation is both the primary *truth about God,* and the primary *obligation and blessing for God's people* (the privilege of knowing, loving and worshipping the one true creator and redeemer God), then whatever threatens that biblical monotheistic faith must be vigorously resisted at any cost. Idolatry is the greatest threat to biblical mission, for God's people cannot bear witness to the true and living God if they are obsessed with the worship of the gods of the cultures around them (whether in Old Testament Israel or in today's church).

So, the whole of Deuteronomy 4 is a sustained challenge to *avoid idolatry*, and the emphasis on *teaching* within the chapter is strong and repeated. It is worth reading the chapter carefully noting how the two themes (idolatry and teaching) are interwoven, since each is integral to the other. The way to avoid idolatry is to pay attention to the teaching; and the purpose of the teaching is to keep future generations from idolatry. The intention, goal and outcome of the teaching that God wanted for Israel was to keep people from idolatry and preserve their monotheistic faith and covenant obedience.

If Israel were to be true to their mission among the nations, in such a way that the nations would ultimately come to worship the one true living God, then they – Israel – must preserve the knowledge and worship of YHWH alone. For that reason, there must be *teaching* from generation to generation of all that the God of Israel had *done* and all that the God of Israel had *said*. Teaching was essential to preserving their monotheistic stewardship, the knowledge of God that God had entrusted to Israel. The 'theological education' of Israel had the missional intention of preserving their monotheistic faith for the sake of the nations who had yet to come to know this truth about the living God.

Maturity, in a World of Many Falsehoods – the Pauline Outcome

When we talk about church growth, we usually mean numerical growth through successful evangelism and church planting. But if you had asked *the apostle Paul*, 'Are your churches growing?', I think he would not have understood the question in that way. For Paul, evangelistic growth was simply 'gospel growth'. So he could write: '*the gospel is bearing fruit and growing* throughout the whole world – just as it has been doing among you since the day you heard it and truly understood God's grace' (Col. 1.6).

The kind of church growth Paul prayed for was *growth in maturity*. Here is how Paul described the kind of qualitative church growth that he prayed for in his churches.

> We continually ask God to fill you with the knowledge of his will through all the wisdom and understanding that the Spirit gives, so that you may live a life worthy of the Lord and please him in every way: bearing fruit in every good work, growing in the knowledge of God, being strengthened with all power according to his glorious might so that you may have great endurance and patience … (Col. 1.9-11)

In those few verses, Paul prays for three kinds of maturity:

- Paul wants the believers in Colossae *to know God's story* (v.9; the will and purpose of God). That involves 'head knowledge' of the whole great narrative of God's plan revealed in the Scriptures.
- Paul wants them *to live by God's standards* (v.10). That involves their practical lives and moral choices and behaviour.
- Paul wants them *to prove God's strength* (v.11). That involves their spiritual commitment to Christ and perseverance in spite of suffering.

So for Paul, growth in maturity could be measured, firstly, by increasing knowledge and understanding of the faith; secondly, by a quality of living that was ethically consistent with the gospel and pleasing to God; and thirdly, by perseverance under suffering and persecution. And all of those would be necessary if the believers in Colossae were to participate in God's mission in the surrounding pagan culture of their region.

But how will such Christian maturity be attained? Not surprisingly, through sound teaching by those whom Christ has gifted to the Church. We could go to the Pastoral Epistles and prove this point repeatedly through the many places where Paul instructs Timothy and Titus to be teachers themselves, and trainers of teachers, all with a view to *opposing false teachings and practices* of all kinds. Then, as today, Christian believers were surrounded by competing worldviews and seductive alternatives to the true confession of faith. All kinds of false teaching were around. Then, as today, the apostolic remedy and protection against false teaching was sound teaching rooted in the Scriptures.

Paul is even more clear about this in Ephesians. There he affirms that the teaching ministry within the Church (within which we could now include the work of theological education), is *a Christ-ordained gifting*. Theological education is not an end in itself (that is the temptation of academia, which can easily become an idolatrous seduction), but rather *a means to an end*, namely the goal of equipping God's own people for *spiritual maturity* and effective mission in the world.

> So Christ himself gave the apostles, the prophets, the evangelists, the pastors and teachers, to equip his people for works of service, so that the body of Christ may be built up until we all reach unity in the faith and in the knowledge of the Son of God and become mature, attaining to the whole measure of the fullness of Christ.
>
> Then we will no longer be infants, tossed back and forth by the waves, and blown here and there by every wind of teaching and by the cunning and craftiness of people in their deceitful scheming. Instead, speaking the truth in love, we will grow to become in every respect the mature body of him who is the head, that is, Christ. From him the whole body, joined and held together by every supporting ligament, grows and builds itself up in love, as each part does its work. (Eph. 4.11-16)

Let us apply that text for a moment to the world of theological education, where future pastors are trained.

Doubtless some young graduates come out of seminary thinking they are God's gift to the Church! Well, they are right – but not in the sense they may imagine! They are not so much the gifted ones, as *the given ones*. God has not given *to* them all the gifts to do all *the* ministry themselves; rather God has given *them* as people (with their particular gifts) *to equip others for their ministry*.

So, the job of pastor-teachers, according to Paul (their unique ministry gifting, in other words), is precisely to equip the rest of the people of God (the saints) for *their* ministries – their many ways of serving God in the Church and in the world. In theological education, we do not train people for a clerical ministry that is an end in itself, but for a *servant* ministry that has learned how to train disciples to *be* disciples in every context in which they live and move.

I sometimes say to congregations: 'I hope you do not think that you come to church every Sunday to support the pastor in his or her ministry. It is precisely the other way round. The pastor comes to church every Sunday to support *you in your ministry*, which is out there in the world, in the front line of your everyday life and work. *You* have the ministry, *you* have the mission, where it really counts. You need to be fed and taught and equipped for whole-life discipleship out there in the world, and it is the pastor's job to do that. Make sure he or she does, and pray for them until they do!'

Are we teaching future pastors to think like that? Do we give them the missional task of training others for ministry and mission? Do we encourage and equip them to shape their preaching and teaching and pastoral ministry for that goal – to be equippers of the saints for *their* ministry? Do we inculcate in them the understanding that *their* mission is not to *do* all the mission or ministry, but to train and equip the rest of God's people for mission and ministry in the world?

John Stott: A Neglected Challenge

This is a perspective that John Stott repeatedly pointed out through fifty years of writing (sadly, it is probably the most neglected element of his understanding of the nature of Christian ministry and mission). He insisted that, in biblical terms, pastoral ministry is not *the* ministry (certainly not the only one), nor are pastors the only people who 'do ministry'.

> We do a great disservice to the Christian cause whenever we refer to the pastorate as 'the ministry', for by our use of the definite article we give the impression that the pastorate is the only ministry there is ... The fact is that the word 'ministry' is a generic term; it lacks specificity until we add an adjective.
> ...
>
> There is a wide variety of Christian ministries. This is because 'ministry' means 'service', and there are many different ways in which we can serve God and people. [There follows a discussion of the events in Acts 6]. ... It is essential to note that both distributing food and teaching the word were referred to as ministry (*diakonia*). Indeed, both were Christian ministry, could be full-time ministry, and required Spirit-filled people to perform them. The only difference between them was that one was pastoral ministry, and the other social. It was not that one was 'ministry' and the other not; nor that one was spiritual and the other secular; nor that one was superior and the other inferior. It was simply that Christ had called the Twelve to the ministry of the word and the Seven to the ministry of tables. ...
>
> It is a wonderful privilege to be a missionary or a pastor, *if God calls us to it.* But it is equally wonderful to be a Christian lawyer, industrialist, politician, manager, social worker, television script-writer, journalist, or home-maker, *if God calls us to it.* According to Romans 13.4 an official of the state (whether legislator, magistrate, policeman or policewoman) is just as much a 'minister of God' (*diakonos theou*) as a pastor. ...

There is a crying need for Christian men and women who see their daily work as their primary Christian ministry and who determine to penetrate their secular environment for Christ.[5]

Consequently, there is also a crying need for institutions of theological education to train future pastors to be *equippers*, pastors who have a high view of the calling and ministries of *all* God's people, including the vast majority (98 per cent) who are *not* pastors etc., but who are out there as salt and light in the world.

To summarize, then, God has ordained that there should be teachers and teaching within the people of God:

a) so that God's people as a whole should be a community fit for participation in *God's own mission* to bring blessing to the nations (the Abrahamic goal);

b) so that God's people as a whole should remain committed to *the one true God* revealed in the Bible (as YHWH in Old Testament Israel, and incarnate in Jesus of Nazareth in the New Testament), and resist all the surrounding idolatries of their cultures (the Mosaic goal);

c) so that God's people as a whole should *grow to maturity* in the understanding, the obedience and the endurance of faith, and in effective mission in the world (the Pauline goal).

Now, if we think particularly of the world of theological education, and the work of Bible colleges and seminaries, the question we have to ask at this point is this: What kind of graduates would we need to be producing from our programmes if we wished to show that our theological education is being effective and fulfilling its biblical purpose? What should be our goal in our theological training, if we want to be faithful to the purposes for which God has ordained and provided for the teaching ministry among his people? What 'outcomes' should we want to see emerging from our theological education investments?

Surely, it means that we ought to be seeing men and women who graduate and go out into their own preaching and teaching ministry in the churches, who are:

a) *committed to mission* (in all its multiple biblical dimensions): eager to participate with God in his mission and to lead the communities they serve in the mission entrusted to the Church.

b) *faithful to biblical monotheism*: totally committed to the God of the Bible alone, and able to discern and resist the false gods that surround us. This includes not only the ability to understand and defend the uniqueness of Christ in contexts of religious plurality (and where necessary to bear costly witness to that faith), but also the spiritual insight to discern many idolatries that are more subtle in all cultures (e.g. consumerism or ethnocentrism).

c) *marked by maturity*, in understanding, ethics and perseverance: able to do the things Paul urges Timothy and Titus to do; people who are taking care

---

[5] John Stott, *The Contemporary Christian* (Nottingham: IVP, 1992), 140-42; italics original.

of their life and their doctrine, and building up others in maturity, by godly example and steady biblical teaching.

So, I ask, is that actually the kind of *goal* we have in mind as we shape our curricula and construct our syllabi, and develop our lecture courses and hold our seminars and workshops – across the whole range of our theological disciplines and departments? Is that what we are trying to achieve?

Are we aiming to produce people who are *biblically mission-minded, biblically monotheistic and biblically mature*?

If that is our aim, then one necessary component of achieving it will be to bring the Bible back to its central place both in the regular teaching and preaching ministry of local churches, and in the world of theological education in seminaries. And that leads us to our final question and answer.

How Can We Re-Centre the Bible in Our Theological Education?

If our theological education is to be effective in achieving the goals the Bible itself sets for it, then I believe that we need a re-centring of the Bible itself in all our ministry of teaching, and we need a more missionally integrated way of teaching it. The Cape Town Commitment calls for this, quite emphatically, twice.

> We long to see a fresh conviction, gripping all God's Church, of the central necessity of Bible teaching for the Church's growth in ministry, unity and maturity. We rejoice in the gifting of all those whom Christ has given to the Church as pastor-teachers. We will make every effort to identify, encourage, train and support them in the preaching and teaching of God's Word. (CTC IID.1.d.1)

> We long that all church planters and theological educators should place the Bible at the centre of their partnership, not just in doctrinal statements but in practice. Evangelists must use the Bible as the supreme source of the content and authority of their message. Theological educators must re-centre the study of the Bible as the core discipline in Christian theology, integrating and permeating all other fields of study and application. Above all theological education must serve to equip pastor-teachers for their prime responsibility of preaching and teaching the Bible. (CTC IIF.4.d).

So the *Cape Town Commitment*, like the Great Commission itself, brings theological education into the sphere of Christian mission, and then urges that it should be biblically rooted and centred.

In calling for a re-centring and re-integrating of the Bible, I mean two things:

- an integrated way of reading, studying, preaching and teaching the Bible itself;
- *and* integrating a biblical perspective into all other areas of study.

Missional Integration of Biblical Studies

The discipline of Biblical Studies has become very fragmented in many seminaries. First of all, into Old Testament and New Testament, but then also into further canonical sections of those, then further into a whole range of critical disciplines, languages, etc. As a result, it is sadly possible for students to gain great expertise in various parts of the Bible, without having a thorough and integrated understanding of *what the Bible is as a whole.*

We need to help theological students – and ordinary Christians in our churches – to know that the Bible is

- *not* just a book full of *doctrines*, for systematic theologians to rearrange and order properly;
- *not* just a book full of *promises*, for Christians to gain some comfort and 'blessed thoughts' each day;
- *not* just a book full of *rules*, for some kind of ethical applications to the problems of life around us, by whatever system of hermeneutics we use to get our ethics from the Bible.

Rather, God has given us his word as a whole canon of Scripture that is, fundamentally, *a story* – the grand narrative of God, creation and the history of the world. The Bible has a coherent plot: a beginning, a problem, a promise of a solution, a climax and resolution, and a final ending (which is a new beginning). The Bible is like a great 'drama' – in six 'acts' or stages.[6]

1. Creation – 2. Rebellion – 3. OT Promise – 4. Gospel – 5. NT Mission – 6. New Creation

Reading and studying the Bible with this overarching framework in view at all times keeps us working with the direction of the text itself, and *aligned with the mission of God* (which is why this narrative approach has been broadly adopted by those seeking a missional hermeneutic).

So while, of course, it is necessary to get down deep into the exegesis of biblical texts from every part of the canon (with all the very specific and detailed work that requires, and all the disciplines we can bring to bear on the task), we must bring students back to the surface often, to survey their particular text within the wider flow of the whole narrative. What has already come before this text, where is it leading, where does it fit in the canonical framework, how is it integrated into the whole Bible story? I would love to see all seminaries teaching a required preliminary course on what it means to take the Bible as a whole, for what it is – the grand narrative of God's mission – before getting down to the more narrowly focused work of exegetical and critical studies.

What does this integrated reading of the Bible as a whole story do?

---

[6] See Craig G. Bartholomew and Michael W. Goheen, *The Drama of Scripture: Finding our Place in the Biblical Story* (Grand Rapids, MI: Baker, 2004).

It tells us the Story we are in

We are *in* the story of the Bible – participating in act 5. We must live in the light of all the Bible tells us in its first four stages (acts 1 to 4), and in anticipation of what God will do in act 6. We live 'within the story', which means participating in the mission of God that the story is telling.

So living as a Christian is not just a matter of 'applying this verse to my life' (as if my life was the central reality and the Bible must be applied in an adjectival way), but rather asking: Where does my life fit into this great drama in a way which is consistent with the story of what God has done and plans to do? How am I implicated in this text, as a participant in the story of which it is part and to which I belong? These are fundamentally missional questions to ask.

It shapes our Worldview

Worldviews are basically shaped by narrative. That is true of all religions and philosophies. They have a 'narrative', by which they seek to answer questions about ourselves and the world in the past and present and what they expect in the future. The Christian faith, as a coherent worldview, answers all the fundamental worldview questions *from within the Bible story – as a whole*, from creation to new creation, with Christ at the heart of it. Once again, the Cape Town Commitment emphasizes this narrative nature of biblical revelation and theology.

> *The story the Bible tells.* The Bible tells the universal story of creation, fall, redemption in history, and new creation. This overarching narrative provides our coherent biblical worldview and shapes our theology. At the centre of this story are the climactic saving events of the cross and resurrection of Christ which constitute the heart of the gospel. It is this story (in the Old and New Testaments) that tells us who we are, what we are here for, and where we are going. This story of God's mission defines our identity, drives *our* mission, and assures us the ending is in God's hands. This story must shape the memory and hope of God's people and govern the content of their evangelistic witness, as it is passed on from generation to generation. (CTC I.6B)

So then, the task of re-centring the Bible in the ministry of teaching, including theological education, means that we help our congregations and our students

- to inhabit the Bible story, and see it as *The Story* within which we live. We have to live in the world, but we do not live by the world's story;
- to adopt the Bible's worldview, in marked contrast to the worldview of whatever cultures surround us.

Biblical Centring of the Whole Curriculum

This may seem the more challenging task, since it is inviting those who are not biblical specialists, but teachers of systematic theology, ethics, church history, pastoral studies, and so on, *to see the overall biblical narrative as the governing paradigm* for their disciplines.[7]

This does not mean that the Biblical Studies department simply takes over the whole curriculum, any more than a missional integration means that the Mission Department takes over the whole faculty. Rather, it takes seriously our Evangelical affirmation that the Bible is our sole authority for all our life and doctrine, including all that we teach.

I think this means, for example, that the teaching of *Christian doctrine* should show how the grand house of Christian theology in fact reflects the implications of every part of the revelation contained within the great Bible story. Systematic theology simply draws out the systems and themes and their implications that are built upon the whole story of what God has done and will do, according to the whole Bible. Doctrines express the truth revealed and the life required by that story, but the story has pre-eminence. That's why it is the 'canon' of Scripture.

It means, for example, that *church history* should be seen as the outworking of God's mission in act 5 of the Bible story. The Church has been living in act 5 since the day of Pentecost. So we can study and evaluate the subsequent history of the Church in terms of its faithfulness or otherwise to the patterns already set in acts 1 to 4 and the expectation of act 6. We need constantly to assess the story of the Church in the light of the story of the Bible, which is uncomfortable but necessary.

It means, for example, that in *ethics*, we help our congregations and students to bring every ethical issue into the light of every part of the Bible story, asking what light is shed on the issue by the implications of the great facts and truths of each section – all six acts. That is, we help them to *think biblically* about any issue, rather than be given answers to every issue.

The problem is that, in theological education, we are tempted to multiply the number of bolt-on courses on this or that new social or ethical issue that has just arisen in the world. Something else becomes 'a big issue' in our context, and we feel we must add a lecture course on it to our already over-burdened curriculum, often squeezing out the biblical courses to make room. But of course, as soon as the students graduate and leave college some other 'big issue' will hit them. Now they are stumped because they did not 'take a course on that subject at seminary'.

Rather, we need to teach people how to *think biblically* about any and every issue that will arise. They need to have learned how to bring every issue into the light of all the key points along the Bible narrative and how to hear the major 'voices' of the biblical canon. The Bible may not have a direct answer (chapter and verse) to the new problem, but by systematically shining the light of biblical revelation along the whole sweep of the canon onto the

---

[7] On this point see, for much more thorough analysis, Michael W. Goheen, 'A Missional Reading of Scripture for Theological Education and Curriculum', in Michael W. Goheen (ed), *Reading the Bible Missionally* (Grand Rapids, MI: Eerdmans, 2016), 299-329.

issue, they can generate an informed ethical response that can have some claim to being 'biblical'.

I would love to see such a 'whole-Bible approach' become characteristic of all theological education – across all disciplines, and indeed, of all biblical preaching and teaching that is planned over time in our churches. We should be learning together to read the Bible as a whole and to root our theology and our practice deeply in 'the whole counsel of God' (Acts 20.27). We need to help our students and congregations see that the Bible is not just an *object* of their study (limited to when they are doing 'Biblical Studies', but rather that the Bible becomes the *subject* of their thinking – about everything. That is to say, the Bible is not just something we '*think about*', but rather something we '*think with*'. The Bible informs and guides the way we think about everything else, whether in the class-room or in all the rest of life in the world.

I would like to finish by saying 'I have a dream'. At least, I once *had* a dream, which I used to muse upon when I was the principal of All Nations Christian College in the UK. I dreamt of a 'Bible College' which would be exactly and only that: a place where we would teach and study *only the Bible* together in depth, sequentially from the very beginning, and let everything else flow out of the exegesis, interpretation and application of the biblical text – inviting the experts in other disciplines to contribute as appropriate. And immediately you would be forced not only to be rooted in what the Bible says, but also to engage with all the issues that the Bible itself engages with. You would have to deal with monotheism and cosmology, issues of science and faith, the nature of humanity, the meaning and purpose of sex and marriage, the problem of evil, gender relations and disorder, creation care and ecological challenges, violence and corruption, ethnic diversity and conflict, urban development and cultural progress …

… and that is before you even get past Genesis 1-11!

11. Teaching the Bible: How Can We Do This Better Together?[*]

Very Revd Dr Eric George Tosi

> It is the Traditional teaching of the Orthodox Church that the Bible is the Scripture of the Church, that it has its proper meaning only within the life and experience of the people of God, that it is not a thing-in-itself which can be isolated from its organic context within the church community, in which and for which and from which it exists …[1]

When I was a parish priest teaching a catechism class, a student asked me a startling, but simple, question. 'Father, we read the Bible and we hear so many different interpretations, how do we know if it is really true or just something made up?' Of course, we know that people have been asking that same question for thousands of years, but this question from a sincere and educated believer gave me pause. What are we really teaching about the Bible and can we teach more effectively?

It is the Orthodox contention that the Bible does not exist in a vacuum as a text or as a product of men or culture. It is *the* Scripture of the Church. It came from the Church and through the Church. To be sure, various people of a certain time and context wrote it, but it arose from their experience of the Church. It came from the Church and thus it must be within the Church that truly effective teaching and reception happens. If not, if it is something that we read as a book of history, of culture, or even (as some think) of science, then we cannot really understand the Bible and cannot teach it to others. We must be immersed in the Church to be able to teach the Bible, and those who seek to learn the Bible must likewise be immersed in the Church in order understand it. As Archimandrite Vasileios wrote in his well-known book *Hymn of Entry*, 'For this reason, the Gospel cannot be understood outside the Church nor dogma outside worship.'[2]

So, in order for us as pastors to teach the Bible effectively together, I am presenting an Orthodox view on the Bible and I make suggestions on how we can work together based on what we can do in common. Certainly there will be differences between Orthodox and Evangelical perspectives on the Bible. The history of the differences is well documented and has caused some

---

[*] Scripture quotations in this chapter are taken from the Orthodox Study Bible, © 1993 by St Athanasius Orthodox Academy. Special Helps © 1997 by Conciliar Press. Used by permission. All rights reserved.

[1] Thomas Hopko, *All the Fulness of God* (Crestwood, NY: SVS Press, 1982), 49.

[2] Archimandrite Vasileios, *Hymn of Entry: Liturgy and Life in the Orthodox Church* (Crestwood, NY: SVS Press, 1984), 18.

level of conflict through the years. However, in order to work together, perhaps we need to place those differences aside for the moment and discover the common ground between us. While this may be difficult and controversial, such dialogue may dispel some of the more controversial differences while allowing the common factors to emerge. In these days, when we see Christianity attacked from many sides, it is more important than ever to focus on what unites us as Christians.

An Orthodox Understanding

The Bible is a Liturgical Book

When I was in Jerusalem, I discussed the Orthodox Liturgy with an Anglican bishop. He proclaimed: 'The Orthodox Liturgy is one profound meditation on the Scriptures.' His insight into the nature of Liturgy is probably a good starting place when teaching the Bible. First and foremost, we must encourage our people to attend the liturgical services of the Church. It is there that they will encounter the Scriptures in their fullness. In Orthodox worship, there are few words in the text and the hymns that are not scripturally based. Over the course of the service, one encounters the Old and New Testaments, as well as the hymns of the Church Fathers. All three are inextricably linked and form a logical progression. The services are replete with passages from the Psalms and Proverbs and the cycle of epistle and gospel readings completes the entire New Testament in every year. We bring alive the words of Christ through the feasts, and the very life of the Church through the saints and other celebrations. For that reason, the faithful know the Scriptures because they constantly hear them. I have a Liturgy book which has the words of the service on one side and the scriptural reference for every single line on the opposite page. This is a remarkable tool for education – and we are just talking about the Divine Liturgy. There are the regular cycle of services, the special services, and of course, the height of the liturgical year, Holy Week. During this time, we read the entire gospel and the services follow the procession from Jerusalem to Golgotha to the empty tomb. Therefore, for Orthodox Christians, to attend the services is to learn the Scriptures.

When one enters an Orthodox church, the most noticeable features are the icons. These are the painted word of God and convey the gospel in pictures as the Bible does in words. For this reason, one cannot separate the icons of the Church from the worship service. This allows the communicants to experience the gospel through multiple senses. I once showed a busy icon of Christ surrounded by a number of images to one of my friends, a Protestant minister, and asked him if he could identify what he saw. He could not, so I explained that it illustrated the passage from Ezekiel 1 in which the image of God, the evangelists, in fact all of heaven is revealed, with Christ on the throne. It was a revelation to him that one could see such a passage in one icon. So it is important to remember that the iconography is not merely 'decoration' but rather the entire gospel message being shown to the faithful. One is literally immersed in the gospel.

In order to teach the Bible better, then, we must learn how to make it come alive liturgically for the faithful. Not just through the readings and sermons but through our very participation in the Liturgy itself. We must not only hear the word of God but also see the word of God contextually revealed to us through the Liturgy. While Orthodox and Evangelical services have differing liturgical traditions, perhaps the starting point is to identify how those traditions, through worship, bring the Bible alive. By respecting and utilizing these wonderful 'tools' through worship, we will find a more effective means of transmitting the truth of Jesus Christ. In other words, immerse the people from every angle available through worship. And just as Isaiah had the glory of God revealed to him when his tongue touched the burning coal, so must we, when we too have the Bible revealed to us through our life in the services of the Church.

The Bible is a Communal Book

Just as the Bible is *the* book of the Liturgy, it is also *the* book of the church community. It cannot and should not ever be read or taught in a vacuum. The history of the Church is replete with examples of individual interpretations of the Scriptures: sometimes with success and sometimes (sadly, all too often) with failure. As such the Bible should be read, interpreted and taught within a context of the community. In Metropolitan Kallistos Ware's short article in the *Orthodox Study Bible*, 'How to Read the Bible', he writes:

> We read the Bible personally, but not as isolated individuals. We say not 'I' but 'we'. We read as the members of a family, the family of the Orthodox Catholic Church. We read in communion with all the other members of the Body of Christ in all parts of the world and in all generations of time. This communal or *catholic* approach to the Bible is underlined in one of the questions asked of a convert at the reception service used in the Russian Church: 'Do you acknowledge that the Holy Scripture must be accepted and interpreted in accordance with the belief which has been handed down by the Holy Fathers, and which the Holy Orthodox Church, our Mother, has always held and still does hold?' The decisive criterion of our understanding of what Scripture means is *the mind of the Church*. The Bible is the book of the Church.[3]

This does not mean that it cannot or should not be studied individually, for this is the life-blood of the Christian spiritual life (more on this later). But it does mean that relying on self-interpretation is fraught with possible misuse. One can justify almost any position with the Bible if one looks hard enough and is creative enough. Only look at the current diversity of faith traditions which have split from one another over 'correct' interpretation of

---

[3] Kallistos Ware, 'How to Read the Bible', in *The Orthodox Study Bible* (Nashville, TN: Thomas Nelson, 1993), 765-66.

the Scriptures. So the challenge we have here is this: despite the split between the Orthodox and Evangelical traditions, how can we teach the Bible as a Christian community?

Perhaps the answer lies in the fact that when the Church gathers to hear and teach the Bible, it is doing so in order that all of the members can immerse themselves into the context of the communal understanding of the Scriptures. Think of the many sermons, Bible studies, *ad hoc* discussions and church schools that gather to study and learn the Scriptures. There is power and depth in many hearing and receiving the word of God together. The Bible was written as a book of faith *by* the community and as such must remain as a book of faith *for* the community. So by gathering in community, we can together immerse ourselves in the word of God, not relying on our own, often flawed interpretation, but rather relying on the Holy Spirit to come and rest upon us all (Mt. 18.20).

The Scriptures also calls for communal, as well as personal, action. In Matthew 25, we are called, as a community, to put into action our faith towards those around us. We are called to feed the hungry, clothe the naked, visit the sick and those in prison as a personal action, but also as a communal activity. The Scripture becomes intensely personal while calling a community to action. As an Early Church writer, Tertullian stated, 'It is mainly the deeds of a love so noble that lead many to put a brand upon us. See how they love one another, they say, for they themselves are animated by mutual hatred; how they are ready even to die for one another, they say, for they themselves will sooner put to death.'[4] The Scriptures become more than just words but an actual reality. How we love one another is the most powerful manner of teaching the Bible more effectively. As one of the great Desert Fathers wrote, 'Understand the words of Holy Scripture by putting them into practice, and do not fill yourself with conceit by elaborating on theoretical ideas.'[5] By gathering as communities together *in action* we can not only hear the Scriptures but live them out. Nothing is more powerful and more effective than not merely talking about the gospel of Jesus Christ, but by actually incarnating the gospel of Jesus Christ by our actions. The Lausanne-Orthodox Initiative has a history of doing such actions together, far apart from the doctrinal differences, by simply and prayerfully being the gospel of Christ.

The Bible is the Book of the Church

Before the Scriptures are read in church during the Divine Liturgy, the priest says this prayer on behalf of the faithful:

> Illuminate our hearts, O God who loves mankind, with the pure life of Thy Divine knowledge, and open the eyes of our mind to understand Thy Message

---

[4] Tertullian, *Apology* 39.

[5] Mark the Ascetic, 'On the Spiritual Law: Two Hundred Texts', in *The Philokalia.*

of Good Tidings. Implant in us the fear of Thy Blessed Commandments; that, trampling down all carnal desires, we may pursue a godly life, both thinking and performing such things as are well pleasing to Thee. For Thou art the Light of our souls and bodies, Christ our God, and to Thee we ascribe glory, together with Thy Eternal Father and Thine All Holy, Blessed and Life-Giving Spirit, now and ever, and unto ages of ages. Amen.

It is a powerful prayer in which we ask for a better understanding of what we are about to hear, but it also impels us to a more godly life. This life is found and developed within the Church so that we as a gathering of individuals become something more: a church. Fr Thomas Hopko, one of the major Orthodox theologians of the twentieth century, wrote:

> Once the Bible has been constituted as the scripture of the Church, it becomes its main written authority, within the Church and not over or apart from it. Everything in the Church is judged by the Bible. Nothing in the Church may contradict it. Everything in the Church must be Biblical; for the Church, in order to be the Church, must be wholly expressive of the Bible. More accurately, it must be wholly faithful to and expressive of that reality to which the Bible is itself is the scriptural witness.[6]

If we think back on the differences that separate the Orthodox from the Evangelicals, there was always, from both sides, a real desire to be biblically based. From the Protestant Reformation to the patristic witness, both sides have claimed to have a Church based on the Bible. The approaches and conclusions may have been different but the goal has always seemed the same.

So, therefore, everything that the Church does and is needs to be based on the Bible. If it strays from that then it ceases to be a book of the Church, and becomes rather a book with some interesting ideas and concepts. But when it is within the Church and the Church is within the Bible, then the Bible itself comes alive. It becomes the witness of the Church. So we should always look at our own church and ask that basic question: is this of the Bible? Is our church being a witness to the Scriptures? If we cannot present the Church as being of the Bible then we will continue to lose to the secularism that is encompassing our world. Fr Alexander Schmemann, one the most prominent Orthodox theologians of modern times, warned us on this in 1963:

> There exists – such is the assumption – a basic religion, some of basic 'religious' and 'spiritual values,' and they must be defended against atheism, materialism, and other forms of irreligion. Not only 'liberal' and 'nondenominational,' but also the most conservative Christians are ready to give up the old idea of mission as preaching of the one, true universal religion, opposed as such to all other religions against the enemy: secularism. Since all religions are threatened by its victorious growth, since religion and the

---

[6] Hopko, *Fulness*, 49-50.

'spiritual values' are on the decline, religious men of all faiths must forget their quarrels and unite in defending these values.[7]

So we must unite in order to defend the Church, but also to present the Church as a witness to what is good and right and holy. We can easily forget this as we teach the Bible, that we are witnessing to something bigger. Our actions must match our words. Our words must be true. And truth can only be found in Jesus Christ. What we can do together is to present this to the world. We know that those outside of it will misrepresent the Church and so we must present the Church as being based on biblical principles that we live out daily. People will recognize hypocrisy immediately, so we must be true to who we are and what we are: a church based on the Bible.

The Bible is Personal

St Tikhon of Zadonsk, writing in eighteenth-century Russia, has this to say about our Orthodox attitude towards the Holy Scriptures: 'If an earthly king, our emperor, wrote you a letter, would you not read it with joy? Certainly, with great rejoicing and careful attention. You have been sent a letter, not by any earthly emperor, but by the King of Heaven. And yet you almost despise such a gift, so priceless a treasure.' He goes on to say: 'Whenever you read the Gospel, Christ Himself is speaking to you. And while you read, you are praying and talking to Him.'[8]

Daily personal Scripture reading is essential. It feeds the soul and enlightens your life. As St. Tikhon reminded us, when we read the Scriptures we are praying and talking to God. This affects us in a personal way. We are not the same after we read a passage. New thoughts come to us, we see problems and issues in a different way, and we are enlightened and enlivened by the word of God. We can all recount the many times we have witnessed people reading the Scriptures on their break from work, on the plane, in the quiet corners of their rooms. We have seen small Bibles marked with passages that touched the person's heart, gave meaning to a problem, or comfort through a crisis. The words of God become our words, our foundation, our comfort and our strength. As St Justin Popovich wrote in the twentieth century, 'By reading the Bible you are adding yeast to the dough of your soul and body, which gradually expands and fills the soul until it has thoroughly permeated it and makes it rise with the truth and righteousness of the Gospel.'[9]

---

[7] Alexander Schmemann, *For the Life of the World* (Crestwood, NY: SVS Press, 1973), 108.

[8] St Tikhon of Zadonsk, *Journeys to Heaven: Counsels on Particular Duties of every Christian* (Jordanville, NY: St Job of Pochaev Press, 1991), Part I, ch. 4, 'The Law of God'.

[9] Justin Popovich, *How to Read the Bible and Why*, quoted on: http://www.orthodoxchurchquotes.com/2013/12/11/st-justin-popvich-by-reading-the-bible-you-are-adding-yeast/.

Part of such reading is to also immerse yourself in prayer. One should never read the Scriptures without praying first. It opens our minds and our hearts to the understanding of the Scriptures. Only when we are open to this does meaning come through the word of God. Therefore teaching people to pray is essential to teaching them to read the Bible more effectively. St Isaac the Syrian, a seventh-century saint, wrote: 'In all things that you find in the Holy Scriptures, seek out the purpose of the words, that you may enter into the depth of the thoughts of the saints and understand them with greater exactness. Do not approach the reading of the Divine Scriptures without prayer and asking the help of God. Consider prayer to be the key to the true understanding of that which is said in the Holy Scriptures.'[10] (I would also add reading the Church Fathers' commentaries, which are an incredible source of interpretation and analysis.)

The irony is that the Bible has never been more available than it is today in the many formats and languages. There really is no excuse for us not to, as the ordination exhortation to newly ordained clergy states, 'peruse the Scriptures daily'.[11] Yet with all this availability, it is easy to fall away from reading the Bible. We are bombarded from all sides with a variety of media, and the quiet refuge of the Scriptures gets lost in the noise. We must seek together a way to reintroduce the reading and study of the Bible to our people, not as an intellectual or perfunctory exercise but rather as a way to seek refuge and to feed our soul. This requires teaching people to read again. It requires relearning the discipline of spending time each day with the Scriptures. It *requires* us to make sure that our church members actually have a Bible in their possession and it is used for something other than a paperweight or decoration. I personally used to give an Orthodox Study Bible to every one of my catechumens at the beginning of their study for reception into the Church and told them to start to actually read the Bible in conjunction with their studies. If they followed the lectionary of the Church readings then they would actually cover the entire New Testament in one year. What better way to introduce someone to the Church then have them actually read the preeminent text of the Church?

So the co-operative project we can actually do together with great effectiveness is to get Bibles into the hands of the people. Teach them how to read the Scriptures in conjunction with their developing prayer life. Ensure that they are following the readings of the Church on a daily basis and even introduce them to the writings of the Church Fathers who are, in the Orthodox Church, the penultimate interpreters of the Scriptures. Keep away from controversies and differing interpretations as they only introduce conflict and frustration. We do not need people arguing about what the Bible *really* says; we should rather have them just read the Bible. As St John

---

[10] Isaac the Syrian, *Sermon* 1.85.
[11] *Book of Needs, Vol. 1* (South Canaan, PA: STS Press, 1998), 243.

Chrysostom writes, 'It is not possible, I say *not possible*, ever to exhaust the mind of the Scriptures. It is a well which has no bottom.'[12]

Conclusion: The Bible is the Book of Faith

So what is the point of all of this? Why read the Bible, why teach the Bible, why even concern ourselves with the Bible? We are spending hours and hours discussing this topic and we must make sure we recognize the purpose of this investment. We do not read or teach the Bible as an end but rather as a means to that end. It is not just the Bible but rather growth in faith in our Lord and Saviour Jesus Christ that is our goal. It is not just knowledge of the Scriptures but rather growth in communion with God himself that is our goal. As Fr Hopko wrote,

> … it is the witness of the Church that the whole Bible reveals God and makes Him known in His Word; that in and through the Bible – as it lives in the community of God's people through Christ, the enfleshed Word, and through the Spirit – man can come to a genuine knowledge of God Himself in communion with Him. In this perspective, the final meaning of the Bible, therefore, is seen not to lie within it as a text or collection of texts. Its final significance and purpose lies in reality itself, the reality to which it itself bears witness, the reality of God and all things in Him. The purpose of the Bible is to reveal God, to point beyond itself to Him, to indicate Him, to disclose Him, to lead man into a living communion with Him, to lead man into true knowledge. Through the Bible man should see, hear, taste and even touch the Word of Life, who is God Himself, the ground and the goal of all that exists.[13]

In other words, we read and teach the Scriptures to come to know God incarnate and ever-existing. We welcome God into our lives, our thoughts and our very actions. Through this we change and become more human or, better yet, *real* humans as God intends. Humans are created for the very purpose of being in communion with God by knowing God. We know God through his word. So if we are to teach the Bible together more effectively we must recognize together that the ultimate goal is know God and grow in communion with him. The Bible is the tool *par excellence* for growing in communion with God, but only if it is used in conjunction with the liturgical life, the life in the Church and the community, and if we ourselves are personally immersed in the Scriptures, as we cannot give that which we do not possess. Fr Hopko exhorted those who would teach and preach the word of God:

> … prayer, fasting, silence, acts of mercy, and ascetical efforts which provide for the preachers are the dispassion, discernment, humility and love that allow him to truly hear, listen, see, perceive and so to speak. Those who say true words, and surely those who preach God's Word, must know God, themselves,

---

[12] John Chrysostom, *Homily* 19, 'On Acts'.
[13] Hopko, *Fulness*, 62-3.

and others as they really are. This accomplishment, say the saints, is an achievement greater than raising the dead.[14]

So, in the final reflection, the Bible is the book of faith. How we grow together in that faith is the ultimate test as to whether we are teaching the Bible effectively. If our people are growing in faith through the ways outlined here, then we are moving in the correct direction.

---

[14] Thomas Hopko, *Speaking the Truth in Love* (Crestwood, NY: SVS Press, 2004), 51.

12. Educating Ecumenically:
How Does Appreciation of a
Broader Ecumenical Context Help Us?

Dr Sergey Koryakin and Vladimir Strelov

Dr Sergey Koryakin

When we talk about Russian Christianity, we have to deal with two major denominations. In a recent poll, around 41 per cent of Russians identified themselves with the Russian Orthodox Church, although only 5 per cent claimed to have read the Gospels, and only 2 per cent went regularly to confession.[1] Protestants amounted to less than 1 per cent of the respondents to the poll.[2] More accurate figures show that there are around three million Protestants in Russia,[3] slightly more than 2 per cent of the population.

It would not be an overstatement to say that, in general, each tradition shows considerable prejudice toward the other. Although there have been examples of collaboration in the area of Bible translation and interdenominational dialogues about religious freedom and persecution, there is a shared feeling that they are not ready to work towards rapprochement. Occasionally, one can hear about Orthodox getting together with Protestants to drink tea and discuss their differences,[4] or a Protestant community studying Orthodox theology and preaching about the *Theotokos*.[5] Overall, however, these moments of openness are few and far between.

From my own experience as a faculty member at a Protestant seminary, although limited, I would say that 99 per cent of my students are ignorant of

---

[1] The Arena Project, by the Research Service 'Sreda', online at: http://sreda.org/opros/arena-reliz. The survey was done in 2012 and embraced 59,900 respondents.

[2] According to the survey, Protestants (Baptists, Evangelicals, Anglicans, and Lutheran) and Pentecostals formed two different groups, totalling less than 0.5% each.

[3] Roman Lunkin, 'Russian Protestantism: Evangelical Christians as a New Social Phenomenon', *Contemporary Europe* 59.3 (July-September 2014), 133-43, online at: http://www.sov-europe.ru/2014/3/Lun1.pdf, accessed 25 August 2017.

[4] The Baptist church 'Evangelie' (the Gospel) in the Moscow suburbs is a frequent participant in such meetings, which are hosted by the Holy Trinity Orthodox Church in Elektrougli.

[5] A charismatic church 'Kraeugolny Kamen' (the Cornerstone) is a good example of this; see K. Antonenko, '"Selah" – The Time of Silence and Attending the God's Voice', *The Transfiguration Brotherhood*, online at: https://psmb.ru/a/selah-vremya-tishiny-i-vslushivaniya-v-golos-bozhiy.html, accessed 25 August 2017.

real Orthodox faith and practice. Their opinion is based mostly on their encounters with so-called 'folk' Orthodoxy (a pagan mentality wrapped in religious piety), or the news media, which are quick to expose bribery, nepotism and abuse of power among Orthodox clergy. Sometimes their judgements are based on personal experience, when local officials or even neighbours (many of whom consider themselves to be Orthodox just because they are Russian) make the lives of Protestant believers difficult by claiming to defend Orthodox Russia.

Needless to say, the Orthodox perception of Protestants ranges from total ignorance to open hostility. Some years ago, when I mentioned to a group of Orthodox that I was a Protestant working at a Protestant seminary, they were astonished: 'Oh, really? Do we have many Protestants? And they even have seminaries!' Many of those who have actually heard about Russian Protestants have a rather narrow and prejudiced view, such as 'Protestants are sectarians and pro-Western sympathizers.' So there is a sense that each tradition has its long-standing bias towards the other and is not ready to recognize others as genuine Christians. I believe that this situation must be changed. It is time that Russian Protestants and Orthodox both realized that they are not the only Christians on the planet, or even in Russia, and started taking into account a broader ecumenical context. It is high time they became curious and learned *about* and *from* each other. Iron sharpens iron, and I am convinced that such engagement would serve mutual rapprochement. Let me offer four reasons for this.

First of all, if Russian Christians really care about being faithful witnesses of God to the world, both Protestants and Orthodox should study each other's traditions and work towards unity. Jesus prayed that his disciples 'may all be one' as he and the Father are one, '*so that* the world may believe' that he was sent from the Father (Jn 17.21). Earlier in the gospel, Jesus put it differently by saying that his disciples will be known as such if they have 'love for one another' (Jn 13.35). In other words, the world will have a very limited picture of Christ if it does not see unity and love among his followers. I do not want to be misinterpreted, but there was a certain point at which I stopped believing in the pious Protestant talk about the 'invisible Church' and therefore the 'invisible unity' among Christians. This very old Augustinian idea, developed among the Reformers, now allows many Protestants to justify their disunity (even among themselves) and their unwillingness to change the situation. I believe that unity among Christians should be tangible, so that it may be perceived, appreciated and accepted as the way to learn about God's love. Of course, seeking this unity would require serious theological dialogue and readiness to change some ecclesiological definitions; I believe this should also prompt Orthodox theologians to revisit such concepts as the boundaries of the Church, canonical territory and proselytism.

The second reason for seeking rapprochement is in mutual enrichment and edification. On the one hand, Russian culture is saturated with Orthodox ideas and imagery. The Orthodox faith has shaped Russia in many ways: Russian history, literature, art, philosophy and folk customs – all have been markedly influenced by this faith. It would not be an overstatement to claim that it is virtually impossible to fully appreciate the works of Dostoyevsky, Tolstoy or Leskov, or read the works of Soloviev, Berdyaev or Bulgakov, without taking into consideration their Orthodox convictions. Unfortunately, many Western missionaries in the 1990s proved to be ignorant of the vast Christian heritage of Russia and quite often claimed to be the ones who would 'bring Christ' or 'bring the gospel' to Russia, as if for the first time in history. Yet it is even sadder to see Russian Protestants who are unaware of their own culture. In Russian, we call these people 'Ivans who do not know their kin'. With a better understanding of Orthodoxy, Russian Protestants could rediscover their heritage. By the same token, Russian Orthodox are utterly unaware of the riches of Western theological thought. Many have never heard of Barth, Moltmann, Rahner or Pannenberg ... the list goes on. And even though they have heard of Luther, Calvin and Wesley, and are ready to criticize them, they are very unlikely to have read their works or to understand the origins of the Reformation. The Protestant focus on personal conversion and life in Christ could be appreciated; it could be used to awaken Russian believers to real (rather than folk) spirituality, to a Christian ethic and lifestyle that is suited to everyday life rather than a monastic community. This leads me to the third point.

The third reason for rapprochement would be a better understanding of the nature of spiritual life. On the one hand, Russian Protestants are well known for holding high moral standards, for being very zealous about practising what they preach. Once I heard an Orthodox priest saying to his congregation in a sermon: 'We should all be like, God forbid, Baptists. They do not drink, they do not smoke, they do not swear. They have to drop these habits when they join the church, while we Orthodox priests have to constantly remind our parishioners that these things are bad and not to be practised.' It is very true. By stressing personal conversion and commitment, Protestants advocate an exclusivist approach: 'You cannot be a member of our church and live in sin.' At the same time, the Russian Orthodox Church in general tends to be more inclusive, and thus more tolerant to human weaknesses. One can easily find examples of priests baptizing people without teaching them the basics of faith or having them read the gospels.

In spite of holding high moral standards, however, Russian Protestants seem to know little about the mechanics of spiritual life. They can hardly demonstrate any consistent teaching about asceticism or spiritual disciplines. That is why often moral behaviour or emotional experiences serve them as a measure of spirituality, especially among charismatics. Here, I believe, Russian Protestants may draw extensively from the Orthodox tradition, while their way of life could arouse jealousy among the Orthodox believers and lead them to strive for better moral standards.

Finally, the fourth reason for rapprochement is related to the Bible and theology. Although the *Sola Scriptura* principle is believed and proclaimed by Protestants, there is considerable theological diversity among them. Some believe in speaking in tongues, while others consider it a devilish delusion; some practice infant baptism, while others think it is unbiblical; some think penal substitution is at the heart of the gospel, while others think it is a culturally conditioned interpretation of the atonement, and so on. It shows that there is no such thing as an objective reading of the Scripture. As William Blake put it, 'Both read the Bible day and night, but thou read'st black where I read white.'[6] Our interpretation is always shaped by small denominational traditions, reason and experience. Sometimes it seems that it would be much better to have one tradition, one mind, one experience that would inform our reading of the sacred texts and save us from doctrinal innovations. Here, I believe, Protestants may learn a great deal from the Orthodox. At the same time, the average Russian Orthodox believer is scarcely familiar with the Bible and is not acquainted with methods of biblical interpretation. I think that the Protestant example of being daily shaped and guided by the word may be a good model to follow. Thus I see at least four areas where both traditions could benefit from each other.

If we speak about educating ecumenically, our primary goal would be to broaden the horizons of our students and, to some extent, changing – or at least challenging – their paradigm of thinking. The school where I teach does not have a particular vision for ecumenical education as far as the Orthodox tradition is concerned. We accept students from all Protestant traditions and try to foster an atmosphere of openness, mutual understanding and respect. As our motto puts it, 'We accept everybody but graduate Evangelical Christians.' The atmosphere we create allows students to come out of their denominational ghettos, so to speak, and to understand other fellow Protestants. If, in spite of the differences, they learn to treat other Protestant traditions and theologies with due respect, I believe this could be a good starting point in understanding and appreciating the Orthodox tradition.

As for the Orthodox tradition, every three years we have a course entitled 'The Russian Orthodox Church', in which an Orthodox professor teaches about history and liturgy of the Russian Orthodox Church. Furthermore, when we discuss theology in my class, I always try to reach beyond the classic Millard Erickson or Wayne Grudem volumes on theology. We talk a lot about the tradition of the early church. Following William Abraham's 'Canonical Theism' proposal,[7] I try to present the heritage of the Church as a result of the work of the Holy Spirit. In other words, we learn to regard episcopacy, liturgy, sacraments, saints, icons and other parts of tradition not as human inventions added to clear biblical teaching (as Protestants typically

---

[6] William Blake, 'The Everlasting Gospel', in *Blake: The Complete Poems*, ed. W. H. Stevenson, 3rd ed. (London & New York: Routledge, 2007), 900.
[7] W. J. Abraham, J. E. Vickers, and N. B. van Kirk (eds), *Canonical Theism: A Proposal for Theology and the Church* (Grand Rapids, MI: Eerdmans, 2008).

do), but as God's gifts to the Church in order to guide the believers into the fullness of salvation and truth.

Of course, this approach requires changing typical ways of thinking. First, one needs to understand that the Bible is itself part of the tradition; therefore it cannot alone validate or invalidate certain theological beliefs and practices. In other words, we cannot say, for example, that baptizing infants is wrong because the Bible does not teach about it. The Bible itself speaks a lot about taking oral tradition seriously (Jude 3, see also 2 Tim. 2.15; 1 Cor. 11.2).

Secondly, one needs to adopt epistemological humility: we should not start any intellectual, let alone theological, pursuit by assuming that we know it all. I keep telling my students: 'Before you have your own opinion about another tradition you should, first, hear what it says, then understand it, then examine it, and then make your own judgement.' Do not judge prematurely, based on what you have heard from your pastor or read in a brochure. This understanding will help you to approach another tradition as a learner but not as a teacher, or rather, as explorer but not as executor.

Historical facts, theological rationale and personal experience – all are important when we learn about another Christian tradition. However, I believe that if we pursue ecumenical education, first and foremost we should be attentive to the voice of the Holy Spirit. He alone can reveal our biases and strongholds. He alone can humble us when we become aware of our lack of love for other Christians, and he alone can guide us into all truth.

Vladimir Strelov

Let me begin with the official documents which regulate Orthodox practice and give guidelines for Orthodox ecumenical dialogue and ecumenical education. The first, 'Basic Principles of Attitude to the Non-Orthodox',[8] is well known, whilst the second, 'WCC International Inter-Orthodox Consultation on the Ecumenical Movement in Theological Education and in the Life of Orthodox Churches',[9] is less well known and unfortunately is not translated into Russian.

The first, rather conservative, document regards non-Orthodox Christians as belonging to communities which are not the Church but which enjoy a measure of grace. It states the necessity of ecumenical dialogue, but it sees this only in the form of testimony to non-Orthodox Christians. It also notes the importance of collaboration in the field of public morality and social service, and opposes proselytism in Russia. Nothing is said about the exploration of the spirituality of others or the possible benefits of studying

---

[8] Department for External Church Relations of the Russian Orthodox Church, 'Basic Principles of Attitude to the Non-Orthodox', online at: https://mospat.ru/en/documents/attitude-to-the-non-orthodox/ and http://www.patriarchia.ru/db/text/418840 in Russian, accessed 25 August 2017.
[9] 'The Ecumenical Movement in Theological Education and in the Life of Orthodox Churches', WCC International Inter-Orthodox Consultation, Sibiu, Romania, 9-12 November 2010.

other traditions, nor is there anything about joint testimony of faith in Christ Jesus or prayer together.

The second document, from Romania, is more interesting because of its awareness of possible sectarianism in Orthodoxy, so it offers some observations and suggestions regarding education in ecumenism, for instance:

1. Broad discussion not only in church structures but also in academic circles and in seminaries about the nature of participation in the ecumenical movement, and the involvement of opposing parties in this dialogue (if possible);
2. A self-critical approach to Orthodox ecclesial life, in the spirit of humility;
3. The recognition of the impact of dialogue with other Christians, both on their thinking and in understanding our own roots;
4. A new approach to depicting other Christians, free from apologetics and polemics;
5. Academic exchanges for students and researchers.

I find this document very encouraging, but the problem is that these points were proclaimed in an international forum for a prepared audience.

At the same time, ecumenical dialogue is viewed as unnecessary and false by the majority of Russian Orthodox Christians. They maintain that the Orthodox Church already has all the truth and ecumenical involvement demands more tolerance than they can afford.

For example, there was a priest, Daniil Sysoev, who was killed in 2009 for his anti-Islamic speeches. He is viewed by some as a martyr and one can find his books in every Moscow church book shop. In one of his sermons, he says: 'We don't want somebody to perish in Hell, so we pray for the non-Orthodox, in order that they might become Orthodox.' Then he equates all non-Orthodox with Satanists, and treats them in the same way as he does Islam and Christian sects. He states: 'We can be proud of our Orthodoxy because our truth is grounded in the Trinity, so we can boastfully demonstrate the superiority of our faith and preach that all others will perish if they stay as they are'.[10] The movement founded by him engages passionate young Christians and finds semi-official support in Orthodox Church circles. One of his spiritual descendants is a priest, Georgy Maksimov, who is responsible for mission among non-Orthodox Christians in Moscow and abroad. He finds ecumenical dialogue funny and despises those who are involved in it,[11] and his method of mission is to convert Catholics and Protestants to Orthodoxy. He teaches at the Moscow seminary and academy, publishes books with the permission of the Church and is a member of different church institutions. He finds support from a wide audience because most Orthodox Russians outside Moscow or St Petersburg do not know the

---

[10] Interview online at: https://youtu.be/tphAoO3TOEU, accessed 24 August 2017.

[11] See his social network posts on Vkontakte.com, online at: https://vk.com/id293099986?w=wall293099986_14904, accessed 24 August 2017.

difference between Protestants and sects, and are fearful that 'ecumenists want to destroy the Church'. His position is an extreme one, of course, but it is publicly and loudly declared.

At the other end of the spectrum, we have spontaneous super-ecumenism represented by the veneration of Vassula Ryden, a very ambiguous figure with her message of the unification of all humanity under the Lordship of the Trinity, or by those who do not know their own Orthodox tradition, and even despise it, but want to practise something new and exotic borrowed from others.

The most common form of normal ecumenism for Russia is now visits to Taizé for youth and participation in Catholic ecumenical movements, such as Chemin Neuf, with its Cana division for families, or simple friendships and marriages between Orthodox and non-Orthodox Christians.

A positive sign of the new face of Orthodox Christianity, which is more open to brothers and sisters in Christ, is slowly becoming apparent in academic circles. Since 2018, we have seen annual international conferences dedicated to the study of the gospels convened in Russia by the Society of Biblical Literature (SBL) in partnership with the Saints Cyril and Methodius Theological Institute for post-graduate studies, which is chaired by Metropolitan Hilarion Alfeev. Sometimes these include public lectures by experts in global issues (such as online communications or volunteering) from other churches. Even so, such events are not widely announced in order to avoid unnecessary scandal. Seminaries are changing, too, due to educational reforms and the invitation of lecturers from secular institutions who are not so confessionally oriented.

This is the current landscape of Russian attitudes towards ecumenism and ecumenical contacts. I am not sure that all Christians, or even all Christian teachers, are called to special efforts on the path of ecumenism. It must be a special call, I suppose. But we can work on overcoming prejudices and building trust and respect between Orthodox and non-Orthodox. For this I would make several proposals:

- *to start as early as possible through informal meetings.* In Russia and Ukraine, all Scripture Union teams are made up of both Orthodox and Protestants. They read the Bible together with adolescents and it is a great witness to church unity for teenagers. Some of these teens and group leaders have since become our students, and there is no need to educate them about ecumenism. On the contrary, they themselves can educate their colleagues.

- *to read the Bible more than any other books during catechesis and throughout the educational process.* In the Bible, we see an amazing variety of devotional styles or types of spirituality: the devotion of the patriarchs is different from that of the prophets or scribes, yet they are all God's people. In the Bible, we see the unity of the ancient church, although the differences between Pauline Christianity and the Jerusalem centre may have been much more serious than those between modern Christians. And it is in the Bible that, most importantly of all, we find the Lord's plea and command to his disciples to love one another and to be one as he is one with the Father.

- *to explore the different traditions of Bible interpretation.* When we see that some interpretations from the Reformed tradition are as relevant for us as the Church Fathers' interpretation, we start to appreciate these traditions without even putting on special ecumenical courses. It is the love of God that motivated Matthew Henry, William Barclay or N. T. Wright to work on their commentaries (I mention especially commentaries originating from the UK and translated into Russian), and we feel it. And as we feel it, we feel fraternal love. Even Hebrew interpretations of Scripture can play their role in this: we see that the treasure of Scripture belongs not only to Orthodox Christians, and so we learn humility. In Russia, there is a particular question posed by Bible translations. Our official Synodal Translation dates back to the middle of the nineteenth century. In the past thirty years, the Seventh-Day Adventists managed to bring together a well-qualified team of scholars and produced a new translation, the best among several others. We use it as a supplementary text in our college, and I am pretty sure the students are grateful to the Adventists for this work.

- *to promote information about well-known ecumenically minded figures and to notice ecumenical incidents in the lives of present-day saints.* A good example of a faithful servant of God is better than a thousand words. We do not push the ecumenical agenda: that can have the opposite effect. But when we talk about biblical studies and pastoral care, we cannot avoid Fr Alexander Men (1935-91), who was an outstanding scholar and missionary. He was ecumenically open and borrowed from other traditions in order to improve the community life of his parish. We can see some peculiar examples of ecumenism in the most conservative Orthodox circles; for example, in the prayer book of the last universally acknowledged Russian starets, Ioann Krestyankin, we find a prayer of St Francis, and this also makes an impression.

- *to encourage the participation of students from other denominations in the educational process.* When we do not know anybody from other traditions, we can be fearful and full of prejudices. When we see that other Christians also love Christ and try to live according to God's commandments, and when we find that we can learn from them, it changes things. We have had Pentecostals, Catholics and Methodists in our institution, and it was a blessing. This experience is not ours alone: there are mixed groups in the Biblical-Theological Institute of St Andrey and the Theological Institute of St Thomas Aquinas.

- *to teach courses on the religious thought of the twentieth century* – Barth, Bultmann, Tillich, Maritain, Bonhoeffer and others. My own personal experience was that when I was reading these theologians, I found the ideas of some of these thinkers more congenial than those of some third-class traditionalist Orthodox. I see how this course now transforms the minds of our students, making them more interested in other Christians.

- *to study the culture of other traditions and to see whether they provide answers for present-day problems.* A well-known Russian monk, Petr Mescherinov, began with J. S. Bach. He researched his heritage, translated his works and introduced Bach to Russian Orthodox audiences as a great composer and also as a great man of faith. At the same time, he taught youth courses and saw the growing number of young Christians who no longer attend Church but still say that they believe. After years of studying Orthodox ascetic authors, he started to read early Protestants such as Weigel, Arndt and Tersteegen; he found that they observed the same phenomenon, and did not see it as a catastrophe but as a step towards more mature Christianity. The translations and public activity of Fr Petr now encourage interest in the Protestant tradition among educated Orthodox Christians in Russia.

- *to send students abroad or invite lecturers with ecumenical experience.* This needs no comment.

These ideas have proved to be effective in building trust and love in the hearts of our Orthodox students towards Protestants. At the same time, there is one obstacle which could destroy all these efforts and which we Orthodox cannot overcome ourselves, because it does not depend on us. I mean this: we are more or less in agreement regarding fundamental teaching concerning salvation, the Lord Jesus and the Trinity. But if Protestants continue to change moral teaching, to reinterpret commandments, soon these measures will not work because the Orthodox majority simply would not be able to regard them as Christians.

So I see an open door of opportunities, but also obstacles. I pray to my Lord Jesus Christ to help us to read the signs of the times, not to be conformed to this world but to be transformed by the renewal of our mind to discern the will of God, what is good and acceptable and perfect (Rom. 12.2). I hope that educating ecumenically, which seeks to fulfil the Lord's prayer and command to love one another and to be united together, is part of that.

13. Learning from Three Centuries of Orthodox-Evangelical Encounter in the Middle East*

Dr Tim Grass

Previous chapters have reflected on how we handle and witness to our differences. I want to offer a historical perspective on that topic. As a civil servant friend of mine once commented, the best way to understand where we should go involves working out how we got to where we are. This chapter will look at what has happened over the three centuries that Orthodox and Evangelicals have been encountering one another in the Middle East and North Africa. In chronological order, it will outline and illustrate four patterns which that encounter has taken: curiosity, assistance, confrontation, and dialogue and co-operation. All four of these patterns may be seen today, which shows that there is no one way to characterize relations between the Orthodox and Evangelical traditions. Each specific encounter should be looked at in its own terms and context.

The focus here is primarily on Western Evangelical mission to this region. A full treatment of the subject would require investigation of relevant Arabic and Orthodox sources, as Westerners were not the only actors in this drama. It would also need to be alert to potential differences between the what are known as the Eastern Orthodox, the Oriental Orthodox, and the Church of the East. Nevertheless, I hope this outline will help us to reflect on the state of relationships in our own contexts. What follows may appear critical of Western mission, but I do not wish to deny or belittle the undoubted achievements of many mission workers and national Christian leaders. Our service for Christ is always imperfect, sometimes very much so; yet the Holy Spirit is pleased to use it.

During the three centuries of Evangelicalism's existence, the initiative in contacts between the two traditions has usually been taken by Western Evangelicals. Partly because of this, Eastern churches have often been on the defensive against what were seen as attempts to bring them under foreign domination or to draw away their members, or else as the recipients of external help in education, Bible translation and distribution, social work and diplomatic advocacy. Yet Orthodox self-understanding as the church(es) of the Fathers and of the Ecumenical Councils makes it logically impossible for

---

* This is a considerably shortened and somewhat amended version of my chapter on 'Evangelicals and Eastern Christianity', in Andrew Atherstone and David Ceri Jones (eds), *The Routledge Research Companion to the History of Evangelicalism* (Abingdon: Routledge, 2019), 110-26. The argument there is similar but more nuanced and with reference to the wider Orthodox world.

them to regard Protestant churches (with which most Evangelicals have been found) as equal partners. Westerners have often found that difficult to accept.

A complicating factor has been Roman Catholic missionary activity. Since the late medieval period, a key missionary objective had been to bring Eastern churches under Roman jurisdiction, usually allowing them to keep their Eastern liturgy. In several cases, these churches split, part remaining outside Roman authority, and part – the so-called 'Uniate' churches – entering into communion with Rome. These should not be confused with Western-rite Catholics, who are often present too, and they often see themselves as Orthodox, in spite of their allegiance to Rome, but space precludes their discussion here. This history has sometimes made leaders of Eastern churches wary lest Protestant missionaries should likewise be seeking to bring them under a foreign jurisdiction; it has allowed Protestants and Orthodox to regard each other either as potential allies against Rome or as potential collaborators with it.

Furthermore, Evangelical mission during the 1830s and 1840s stimulated increased Catholic activity in parts of the Middle East.[1] And Western Evangelicals have often interpreted Orthodoxy in terms of what they know of Catholicism, or else contrasted it favourably with Catholicism on issues such as Bible translation and distribution, especially during the first half of the nineteenth century. Often, then, Catholicism (as perceived by Evangelicals) set the agenda, making it more difficult for them to understand Eastern Christianity on its own terms.

Curiosity

Before Westerners could engage with Eastern Christianity, they had to be curious about it. This curiosity really developed during the early nineteenth century. This was an age of exploration and of Western Protestant mission. Overlapping the academic interest, which was motivated at least in part by missionary concern, was an outlook which portrayed the East as degenerate and corrupt, contrasting it with Western commercial and political efficiency and Evangelical uprightness. The West so often looked down on the East, and this extended to Western attitudes towards Eastern Christianity. Such attitudes were reinforced where Evangelicals belonged to Western nations seeking to make their presence felt politically in the region.

Curiosity also helped stimulate the growth of Evangelical pilgrimage to the Holy Land (pilgrimage also became popular among Russian Orthodox). However, such visits usually confirmed Evangelicals in their negative attitude towards Eastern Christianity. Protestant sensibilities rejected the

---

[1] Heleen Murre-van den Berg, 'The Middle East: Western Missions and the Eastern Churches, Islam and Judaism', in Sheridan Gilley and Brian Stanley (eds), *Cambridge History of Christianity*, vol. 8: *World Christianities, c. 1815 – c. 1914* (Cambridge: Cambridge University Press, 2006), 461.

ritualized worship and were horrified at the infighting between different jurisdictions. Evangelicals tended to regard nineteenth-century Palestine as poor and underdeveloped, due to its rejection of God's grace. Only when the inhabitants turned to a pure form of Christianity would divine judgement be reversed, and economic and political reform become possible.[2]

This curiosity about Eastern Christianity still exists. In the 1960s, it was the result of reports of Communist persecution of Orthodox as well as Evangelical believers (although this sometimes led to a negative estimate of Orthodox as well as Evangelical Christians deemed to have compromised with Communist authorities). More recently, interest in patristic theology has deepened as part of a paradigm shift in Evangelical self-understanding and a move to greater sophistication in Evangelical theology. As Evangelicals have engaged in sustained missiological reflection, they have investigated Orthodox missiology. Finally, some have become Orthodox, the best known being those who followed Peter Gillquist in joining the Antiochian Orthodox Church in the late 1990s. The late Fr Michael Harper once told me that he saw this as the logical end of the Evangelical and charismatic quest for New Testament church life. The primary significance of these 'conversions' lies in the awareness of Orthodoxy which they have generated, rather than any changes in the ethos of Evangelicalism which might have resulted. Indeed, we should not overstate the level or extent of Evangelical interest in Orthodoxy; sadly, ignorance is widespread, even in some Orthodox countries. Some know little of their neighbours, perhaps because what they see does not motivate them to find out more, perhaps because they are unwilling to accept that anything good can come out of, or rather be found in, Orthodoxy.

Assistance

Western Evangelicals developed a concern for the whole Christian world, motivated by their expectation of an end-time ingathering of souls. This would lead into the millennium, which was expected to culminate in Christ's return. The emerging Protestant missionary movement appeared to be taking the first steps towards such a harvest, and by 1800 the beginning of the millennium seemed imminent. With the French Revolution and Napoleon's rise to power, one Antichrist – the papacy – was tottering; the other – Islam – was seen as likely to fall soon after, given the weakness of the contemporary Ottoman Empire. Missionaries could then expect conversions on a scale hitherto unknown, notably among Jews (whose ingathering was seen in the light of Romans 11 as precipitating a global turn to Christ) and Muslims. In this context the first Evangelical missionary societies came into being. The two main English-

---

[2] Ruth and Thomas Hummel, *Patterns of the Sacred: English Protestant and Russian Orthodox Pilgrims in the Nineteenth Century* (London: Scorpion Cavendish, 1995), 35, 37.

speaking societies which began work in Orthodox areas were the Anglican Church Missionary Society (CMS; from 1815) and the Presbyterian and Congregationalist American Board of Commissioners for Foreign Missions (ABCFM; from 1819).

An initial objective of the ABCFM mission to the Middle East was that of reaching Jewish people.[3] They and their land were seen as holding a key place in God's purposes. The establishment of the joint British and Prussian Jerusalem bishopric in 1841 demonstrates the strategic spiritual value which Jerusalem was thought to possess, not only for reaching Jews or Eastern Christians but also for reaching Muslims. The desire to take the good news to Muslims shaped nineteenth-century mission strategy decisively. It was thought that the ancient local churches would be the best agents to achieve this. But (it was argued) they were corrupt and sunk in despair, as the result of centuries of oppression. Their condition was seen as the result of divine judgement through Islam on account of their fall into error and corruption, an argument with a pedigree almost as old as Islam itself. Before they could reach anybody, they would need to be renewed; it was argued that such renewal must take place along Evangelical lines. But some also hoped that these churches would turn out to be remnants of an early, purer form of Christianity, and that they might have preserved early biblical manuscripts.

The importance accorded by Evangelicals to Bible translation and circulation meant that the British and Foreign Bible Society (founded in 1804) and its local counterparts became central to engagement with Eastern Christianity. A number of similar societies were set up around the Near East. Fundamental to their strategy was the belief that circulation of vernacular Scriptures would lead to spiritual renewal; this was an expression of the Reformation-era conviction that faith comes by hearing, and hearing by the word of God (Rom. 10.17). (Orthodox missionary strategy, too, had historically stressed vernacular translation of the Scriptures, but Evangelicals would have been unaware of this.[4]) The CMS established a base in Malta in 1815, which printed and distributed Bibles and Scripture portions in various languages. Some co-operation did take place with Eastern churches and local Bible societies.

Likewise, translation of liturgical texts (also a key component of historic Orthodox mission strategy) became an Evangelical priority, although it resulted from a sense of the superiority of Evangelicalism to other forms of Christianity, rather than the superiority of Christianity to other forms of religion. Thus the Anglican Book of Common Prayer was translated into various languages.[5]

---

[3] Clifton J. Phillips, *Protestant America and the Pagan World: The First Half Century of the American Board of Commissioners for Foreign Missions, 1810-1860* (Cambridge, MA: Harvard University East Asian Research Center, 1969), 135.

[4] James J. Stamoolis, *Eastern Orthodox Mission Theology Today* (Maryknoll, NY: Orbis, 1986).

[5] *Missionary Register* 8 (1820), 486; 29 (1841), 333.

Let me give some examples of this approach. The first is provided by Claudius Buchanan (1766-1815) and the CMS in India. In 1806 Buchanan visited the Syrian Orthodox in the Travancore region, and reported positively on their relative freedom from error. He even advocated a full union between the Syrian Orthodox Church and the Church of England, which would strengthen both parties to resist Roman activity, although he later admitted that this was impracticable.[6] In 1811 the CMS portrayed the Syrian Orthodox as a communion for which sympathy should be felt due to its oppression by Rome:

> … they have maintained a regular Episcopal Succession from the earliest ages, and in all important points accord with the faith of the Primitive Church; and have not departed into those errors, which have infected the Syrian Roman Catholics. … A few learned, prudent, and zealous clergymen would be received, as there is ground to hope, with open arms by this venerable Church. Their labours would tend, under the divine blessing, to revive and confirm the influence of the faith in that oppressed community; and might lead, ultimately, to a union between our Churches.[7]

Here were 'the Protestants of the East', a communion present in several countries which could be a source of missionaries to Muslims and pagans.[8] The Syrians were apprehensive that Protestants would try to subjugate their church, as the Catholics had done in 1599, but they were won over and the CMS set about educating children, training clergy and translating the Bible into Malayalam. In 1818 a synod of the church instructed priests to conform their rites and doctrines to the teaching of the missionaries. However, the moral state of the clergy was low, their educational level was no better, and from 1825 the church's leadership grew increasingly hostile. When Bishop Daniel Wilson insisted on its submission, memories were stirred of earlier Roman actions, and his demand was rejected. In 1836 relations were formally severed, and a CMS-supported church was set up, as well as the larger Mar Thoma Church, which wished to undertake reform independently of the missionaries but which was also forced to separate from the parent body.[9]

A second example is the work among Armenians and 'Nestorians' (now known as the Church of the East) of Turkey and north-west Persia. These

---

[6] Hugh Pearson, *Memoirs of the Life and Writings of the Rev. Claudius Buchanan, D.D., late Vice-Provost of the College of Fort William in Bengal*, 2 vols (Oxford: University Press, 1817), 2.328, 336, 453, 455.

[7] *Proceedings of the CMS* 12 (1811-12), 413.

[8] Pearson, *Claudius Buchanan*, 2.457.

[9] Eugene Stock, *The History of the Church Missionary Society: Its Environment, its Men and its Work*, 3 vols (London: Church Missionary Society, 1899), 1.231-5; W. H. Taylor, *Antioch and Canterbury: The Syrian Orthodox Church and the Church of England 1874-1928* (Piscataway, NJ: Gorgias Press, 2005), 5, 7-8; Robert Eric Frykenberg, *Christianity in India: From Beginnings to the Present*, Oxford History of the Christian Church (Oxford: Oxford University Press, 2008), 246-48.

churches were presented in ways which resonated with Protestants – free of what were regarded as the iconographic excesses of other Eastern churches, and needing to be strengthened and protected against Roman attempts to subjugate them. Moreover, whilst Evangelicals disapproved of their non-Chalcedonian Christologies, it was argued that their early separation from Rome and Byzantium had preserved them from many other errors. Armenians in particular were regarded as noble, hard-working and enterprising, and they were present throughout the Middle East. This, and their church's relative freedom from error, marked them out for Evangelicals as potential sowers of the gospel.[10] Furthermore, there was already a reform movement in the Armenian Apostolic Church, which welcomed the missionaries when they arrived in Constantinople.[11]

The Nestorians, rediscovered around 1830, were seen as 'a living fossil, which it was necessary to study, to preserve and finally to convert'.[12] The ABCFM deemed it worth sending missionaries to them because of 'their extreme liberality towards other sects, their ideas of open communion, and their entire rejection of auricular confession'.[13] Their problem was 'spiritual death, rather than theological error'.[14] They were, however, in a situation of political weakness, and their openness to Western mission, whether Protestant or Catholic, was motivated in considerable measure by their need for political support. All the same, when Perkins arrived among them in 1834, his main objective was to enable their church to play a part in reaching Asia, as it had done centuries before. Initially it appeared that efforts to stir the ancient church to new life were being blessed.[15] But the failure of the missionaries to come to the aid of the Nestorians when they were attacked in the early 1840s, coupled with increasing opposition to aspects of Nestorian religious practice and what were perceived by the American Evangelicals as high Anglican machinations, soured relations. Nevertheless, Perkins continued to oppose the creation of separate congregations; unlike other

---

[10] Eli Smith and H. G. O. Dwight, *Missionary Researches in Armenia: Including a Journey through Asia Minor, and into Georgia and Persia, with a visit to the Nestorian and Chaldean Christians of Oormiah and Salmas* (London: George Wightman, 1834), Advertisement; Samir Khalaf, *Protestant Missionaries in the Levant: Ungodly Puritans, 1820-60* (Abingdon: Routledge, 2012), 144.

[11] Avedis Boynerian, 'The Importance of the Armenian Evangelical Churches for Christian Witness in the Middle East', *International Review of Mission* 89 (2000), 76-7.

[12] Christoph Baumer, *The Church of the East: An Illustrated History of Assyrian Christianity* (London: I. B. Tauris, 2008), p. 254.

[13] Rufus Anderson, *History of the Missions of the American Board of Commissioners for Foreign Missions to the Oriental Churches*, 2 vols (Boston, MA: Congregational Publishing Society, 1872), 1.86.

[14] Justin Perkins, *A Residence of Eight Years in Persia, among the Nestorian Christians; with Notices of the Muhammedans* (Andover, MA: Allen, Morrill & Wardwell, 1843), 3, 417.

[15] Perkins, *Residence*, 499.

ABCFM fields, it was only after his final departure in 1869 that a separate Assyrian Protestant Church assumed formal existence.[16] Missionaries had been able to justify their strategy on the basis that conversions were occurring and they were being allowed to preach in Nestorian churches.[17]

In Ethiopia, the third example of this approach, the CMS was active from 1829. The country was seen as a bridgehead for reaching the heathen of Central Africa, and the Ethiopian Orthodox Church was commended for resisting the attacks of Romanism as well as Islam.[18] Here too, the missionaries stressed the production and distribution of vernacular Scriptures as the main stimulus to Church reform; one result was the formation in Eritrea from the 1860s of a renewal movement which was eventually forced to separate from Orthodoxy. This developed into the Evangelical Church Mekane Yesus.

A significant part of the assistance offered by nineteenth-century Evangelicals was education. Confidence in all things Western was evident in the advocacy of Western-style education. This was a key component of regional mission strategy. Some ABCFM institutions proved highly successful, such as the Syrian Protestant College (1863), which developed into the American University of Beirut. Whilst such institutions might prove fruitful in terms of the development of the nations in which they were located, we may question whether the efforts devoted to education ever bore much fruit in terms of converts to Christianity or reawakened Eastern Christians.

Eastern Churches tended at first to welcome Western Evangelicals coming alongside them. The assistance offered included education and medical care, and often came from nations deemed to have sufficient political and military weight to secure an improvement in the fortunes of Christians under Ottoman rule. Often, however, missionaries felt it necessary to create separate churches for their converts. There were three main reasons for this action: mission policy formulated from the home base, the need to provide for converts excommunicated from their own churches, and the desire to provide a spiritual refuge for Muslims converting to Christ.

By the 1860s, the emphasis on assisting the ancient Eastern churches was lessening. One problem was the idea that you could seek individual converts who would then reform their churches from within. This rested on a separation of salvation from the Church which was foreign to Eastern Christianity.[19] Even where the Scriptures circulated freely, that alone did not

---

[16] Anderson, *History*, 1.216; Murre-van den Berg, 'Why Protestant Churches?', 108-9; Baumer, *Church of the East*, 254-56.

[17] Murre-van den Berg, 'Why Protestant Churches?', 112, following Habib Badr.

[18] [Samuel Lee], 'A Brief History of the Church of Abyssinia', *Proceedings of the CMS* 18 (1817-18), 208.

[19] Habib Badr, 'American Protestant Missionary Beginnings in Beirut and Istanbul: Politics, Practice and Response', in Heleen Murre-van den Berg (ed), *New Faiths in Ancient Lands* (Leiden: Brill, 2006), 225.

produce the rethinking that missionaries had hoped for. Many of them therefore concluded that it was impossible for the message of the gospel ever to be heard within those churches, and that it was impossible to work with them.

Another problem was that the Ottoman *millet* system made it difficult for a Muslim to convert to Christianity, because it treated religion as intertwined with all aspects of life. Evangelical converts tended to come from the Christian community, which provoked antagonism from the existing churches. In Turkey, for instance, after 1846, converts excommunicated by the Armenian Church needed a separate church, but excommunication also entailed exclusion from the Armenian *millet* and so it brought civil as well as religious disadvantages. British officials therefore lobbied successfully for recognition of Protestantism as a *millet* in its own right.[20] In time, however, antagonism against Evangelicals wore off and a measure of contact with the Armenian Church was resumed. Missionaries discouraged converts from seceding, and the original vision was partially fulfilled.[21]

Some Evangelicals still advocate coming alongside ancient churches with a view to equipping them to reach Muslims.[22] Others advocate coming alongside spiritually alive Orthodox individuals as the best way of seeking renewal of the Eastern churches. The Lausanne Movement has on occasion expressed this view. A Lausanne discussion paper issued in 1980 hoped for the time when members of both traditions would be able to co-operate in outreach. It regarded what it saw as the born-again minority within Orthodoxy as key to reaching others: they needed help to grow and encouragement to witness so that 'the way may be prepared for a mighty Reformation and spiritual renewal within the Orthodox Church'.[23] However, Lausanne Evangelicals, like Orthodox, do not all have the same approach to contacts with the other tradition.

Opinions differ regarding the effectiveness of this approach. It has been argued that '[r]ather than strengthening the Christian presence in the Middle East, ... missionaries contributed to the fragmentation, dispersion and even decimation through massacre of the Christian communities'.[24] But there has

---

[20] Anderson, *History*, 1.424; H. L. Murre-van den Berg, 'Why Protestant Churches? The American Board and the Eastern Churches: Mission among "Nominal" Christians (1820-70)', in Pieter N. Holtrop and Hugh McLeod (eds), *Missions and Missionaries*, Studies in Church History, Subsidia 13 (Woodbridge: Boydell and Brewer, 2000), 105.

[21] Kenneth Scott Latourette, *A History of the Expansion of Christianity*, vol. 6: *The Great Century in Northern Africa and Asia A.D.1800 – A.D.1914* (Exeter: Paternoster, 1971), 50.

[22] Joyce Napper, *Christianity in the Middle East*, revised ed. (Larnaca: Middle East Christian Outreach, 1996), 5-6.

[23] 'Christian Witness to Nominal Christians among the Orthodox', Lausanne Occasional Paper 19 (1980), 4c(v), 4e(iii), at: http://www.lausanne.org/content/lop/lop-19.

[24] Murre-van den Berg, 'The Middle East', 470.

also been considerable renewal in parts of the Orthodox world, one example being the Coptic Orthodox Sunday School movement; some observers have argued that this has been due partly to Western input. And the CMS has adopted this sort of approach to good effect during the last three decades in the post-Communist world and elsewhere.

Confrontation

Before too long, those who accepted the Evangelical message began to experience persecution. During the 1860s and 1870s the Evangelical Alliance in Britain led the way in lobbying for religious liberty in Turkey and elsewhere, often on behalf of fellow Evangelicals, but not always: in 1861, it made representations on behalf of the Nestorians in Persia.[25] However, lobbying on behalf of Evangelical converts was liable to bring Evangelicalism into confrontation with Orthodoxy.

Confrontation with Eastern churches could also be provoked by Western religious disagreements. For instance, around 1850, the CMS found itself having to counter the charge of proselytism from high-church Anglicans who wanted to establish good relations with the Eastern churches. Its defence was that its mission was to make available the Scriptures and win Easterners for Christ, even at the risk of their leaving the ancient communions.[26] One CMS writer asserted that these communions 'must be led to see that what they consider Christianity is not Christianity, and that what they regard as truth is not truth'. The missionary's aim was not to detach people from their church, but to preach the gospel; if that led to people separating, he was not to be held responsible.[27] Increasingly, the expectation was that it would.

A key thinker in the shift to a church planting strategy by the ABCFM was its secretary, Rufus Anderson (1796–1880). In 1872 he produced a history of the ABCFM's work among the Eastern churches, arguing that they were a legitimate object of mission. A key criterion for his assessment was the doctrine of justification: 'Of the doctrine of a justifying faith of the heart, – the distinguishing doctrine of the Gospel, – the people of the Oriental Churches are believed to have been wholly ignorant, before the arrival of Protestant missionaries among them'.[28] He considered that even the Nestorian field, where missionaries had been late in forming separate churches, showed that 'the dead Church could not be galvanized into spiritual life. There was no way for the truly enlightened but to leave it, and form reunions on the Apostolic basis.'[29]

---

[25] Ian Randall and David Hilborn, *One Body in Christ: The History and Significance of the Evangelical Alliance* (Carlisle: Paternoster, 2001), 98.
[26] Stock, *Church Missionary Society*, 2.144-5.
[27] 'The Oriental Churches', *CMS Intelligencer* 2 (1851), 194-5.
[28] Anderson, *History*, 1.viii, 3.
[29] Anderson, *History*, 2.312.

The second half of the nineteenth century also saw a subtle shift in the dominant Evangelical missionary outlook, from *idealism* inspired by end-time hope to a more *pragmatic* focus on the need to create spiritual homes for evangelical converts. The new faith missions did not usually have strong connections with Protestant denominations. Their outlook was pessimistic, whereas the earlier outlook had been optimistic. They focused on rescuing as many individuals as possible, at the expense of longer-term objectives such as church reform or education. They often saw 'Christendom' as apostate and doomed, calling on converts to leave it and join the churches which they tried to form.

Some of the confrontation was rooted in Orthodox perceptions of Evangelicalism as something foreign and threatening.[30] This could lead to a rejection of what Evangelicals had to offer. But some resulted from Evangelical attitudes, whether we describe them as insensitive or imperialistic. If coming alongside the ancient churches was not going to work, and missionaries longed to see Evangelical conversions, converts must be provided with a spiritual home. From saying that separate congregations were necessary in *practice*, they came to be seen as desirable in *principle*, because the ancient churches were thought to be no place for anyone who came to a living faith and wished to worship in a scriptural manner. This approach was widely adopted. American Presbyterians aimed at creating a separate church from the beginning of their work in Egypt in 1854. By contrast, the CMS sought to encourage renewal in the Coptic Orthodox Church. Whilst a separate Anglican church came into being in 1921, the missionary Temple Gairdner (1873-1928) refused to proselytize other Christian traditions; the Anglican church was seen as a bridge between Orthodox and Evangelicals.[31] Not surprisingly, the Presbyterian work produced a much larger church than the Anglican one; the two Protestant traditions have not related to Orthodoxy in quite the same way, although both do so positively.

However, a church planting strategy did not necessarily rule out the earlier practice of seeking to assist the ancient churches. Even after the formation of a separate Assyrian Protestant Church, for example, W. A. Shedd of the ABCFM continued to hope for the renewal of the communion from which it had separated: 'The reformation of the old churches themselves may be hastened by the presence alongside of bodies of Christians practising a simpler and more active faith.'[32]

---

[30] Tibebe Eshete, *The Evangelical Movement in Ethiopia* (Waco, TX: Baylor University Press, 2009), 4.

[31] Norman Horner, *A Guide to Christian Churches in the Middle East* (Elkhart, IN: Mission Focus, 1989), 68.

[32] W. A. Shedd, *Islam and the Oriental Churches* (Philadelphia, PA: Presbyterian Board of Publication and Sabbath-School Work, 1904), 216-17, quoted by J. F. Coakley, *The Church of the East and the Church of England: A History of the*

This approach gave rise to controversy at the World Missionary Conference in Edinburgh. Catholic and Orthodox countries were initially to be treated as 'unreached'; after intense debate, 'Edinburgh 1910 implicitly declared Protestant proselytism of Roman Catholics, and rather less clearly of Orthodox and Oriental Christians, to be no valid part of Christian mission.'[33] Yet this confrontational outlook has persisted, sometimes in the activity of converts from Orthodoxy who seek to reach their former co-religionists and to demonstrate the errors of that tradition. (On the Orthodox side, there are ex-Evangelicals who seek to do something similar.) It was repeated at the 2010 Lausanne congress in Cape Town. One speaker asserted that the Orthodox counted as unreached peoples, and this led to some frank conversations between the few invited Orthodox observers and Evangelical leaders. The result, however, was the formation of the Lausanne-Orthodox Initiative (LOI)!

Dialogue and Co-operation

Sixteenth-century Protestants had sought dialogue with Orthodox in order to join forces against Rome and/or the Ottoman Empire, but this ended when Patriarch Jeremias II of Constantinople put an end to theological exchange, asking that future contact focus on practical assistance instead. In the West, therefore, serious and open Evangelical dialogue with ancient Eastern Christianity is largely restricted to the last three decades.[34] Apart from Evangelical involvement in bilateral theological dialogues between world communions, as between Anglicans and Orthodox or Baptists and Orthodox, several dialogues have taken place between Evangelicals and Orthodox (for books and articles about this, see the resources section of the LOI website). However, not all Evangelicals and not all Orthodox have been happy to participate in such dialogues. Much dialogue has taken place in the West rather than the Orthodox world, but the issues vary according to where the dialogue is happening. When it takes place in a majority Muslim setting, the issues change again. In practice, Evangelicals and Orthodox in the Middle East and North Africa tend more to practical co-operation (which is often quite significant) than theological dialogue.

Archbishop of Canterbury's Assyrian Mission (Oxford: Oxford University Press, 1992), 64.

[33] Brian Stanley, *The World Missionary Conference, Edinburgh 1910* (Grand Rapids, MI / Cambridge: Eerdmans, 2009), 72.

[34] Bradley Nassif, 'Eastern Orthodoxy and Evangelicalism: The Status of an Emerging Global Dialogue', in Daniel Clendenin (ed), *Eastern Orthodox Theology: A Contemporary Reader*, 2nd ed. (Grand Rapids, MI: Baker, 2003), 211-48; 'Orthodox Dialogues with Evangelical Communities', in *Orthodoxy and Ecumenism: A Handbook of Theological Education* (Geneva: World Council of Churches, 2014), 536-41; Tim Grass, 'Evangelical-Orthodox Dialogue: Past, Present and Future', *Transformation* 27 (2010), 186-98.

Dialogue objectives have shifted. Attempts to seek *theological convergence* proved frustrating, yet the experience of fellowship remained compelling. So a more pragmatic approach, of which the work of LOI is an example, has sought *closer collaboration in mission*. This has been strengthened by a broadening Evangelical understanding of what mission involves.

A persistent problem, however, has been the difficulty of moving from conversation to co-operation. Following Edinburgh 1910 there was some co-operation between Evangelicals and Eastern Christians, but relationships withered as Evangelicals distanced themselves from organized ecumenism following the Fundamentalist controversies of the 1920s. Such co-operation as there was owed much to Evangelical pragmatism. But continuing conversation has helped to create a climate in which co-operation has again become thinkable in such fields as translation and publishing, and welfare projects. However, I suspect that the more distant the link between a project and the worshipping life of local congregations, the easier it is for Evangelicals and Orthodox to co-operate in it.

Conclusion

What factors have determined which of these approaches have been adopted? *Doctrinally*, different views about the end times have shaped Evangelical engagement with Eastern Christianity. The doctrine of the Church, however, has also played a defining role. Evangelical ecclesiology has sometimes adopted an approach to history which sees the true Church as cast out and persecuted. Such an approach has predisposed many to write off the Eastern churches – until those too are persecuted and so come to share the marks of the true Church, as with the Nestorians in 1870s Turkey.

Turning to specific Evangelical ecclesiologies, it is clear that Anglicans tended to feel they had a head start in building relationships with the Eastern churches because of their episcopal order. It was hoped this would provide a model for reformed Orthodox jurisdictions. Nowadays, Orthodox apprehension at developments in parts of the Anglican communion has meant that relationships are not as warm as they were. Engagement with Anglican provinces of the Global South, which tend to be more Evangelical, might well prove more productive in terms of practical collaboration in mission.

Many Evangelicals, however, have a congregational approach to ecclesiology, in which the local congregation is the primary ecclesiological unit, rather than a diocese or jurisdiction. This makes the formation of new congregations more likely, because it can be done more easily than setting up a whole denominational structure. Such Evangelicals often have trouble seeing Orthodox parishes around them as true Christian congregations. Congregations which practise believer's baptism have found it especially difficult to engage positively with Eastern Christianity, not least because they have not accepted infant baptism as valid and have therefore (re)baptized converts. Divergent baptismal practice adds another dimension to the differences between the traditions.

Differing understandings of salvation have provided a major obstacle to better relations. Evangelical insistence on salvation through faith in Christ alone has often been contrasted with an understanding of Orthodoxy which sees it as teaching something like 'salvation by works' (often understood in the light of pre-Vatican II Catholicism). In the same way, Orthodox reject Evangelical teaching regarding salvation by faith alone. Dialogue statements have not yet offered a convincing account of how the respective views of two traditions can be regarded as compatible. However, changing understandings of such Evangelical doctrines as justification by faith alone (as seen, for example, in the work of N. T. Wright[35]) may offer new avenues of exploration. Likewise, a broadening Evangelical understanding of what it means to share in the *missio Dei* is facilitating co-operation in some areas.

As for *external factors* affecting the development of relationships, the political climate has alternately facilitated and hindered them. Ottoman decay facilitated not only Western political intervention but also Western religious intervention in the region. By contrast, recent dialogue between Baptists and the Ecumenical Patriarchate was dealt a mortal blow by NATO bombing of Serbia in 1998; and the complications arising from Western involvement in conflicts in Iraq and Syria cannot yet be adequately evaluated.

Political power could be used in various ways: to facilitate Evangelical mission, as in early nineteenth-century India, or to secure a greater measure of freedom for Eastern Christian communities, as in Turkey; on the Orthodox side, it has not infrequently been used to repress Evangelical activity. Evangelical political powerlessness, when Orthodoxy was the religion of the rulers, strongly reinforced a negative attitude towards it; this was partly the result of experience of antagonism, and partly derived from the strand of ecclesiology earlier mentioned, which sees the true Church as cast out and persecuted. At other points, Evangelicals, whose outlook was marked by a readiness to innovate, failed to grasp that centuries of Orthodox political powerlessness under Muslim domination had made any form of development very difficult for churches in those lands; their priority had to be faithful maintenance of the tradition. We cannot comprehend fully how Evangelicals and Eastern Christians have related to one another in this region without taking into account the Islamic tradition. There is much to learn from one another as we compare the various ways in which each tradition has engaged with Islam.

This has in some ways been a sad story, a tale of missed opportunities. It is not only Evangelicals who are at fault, but I write as an Evangelical,

---

[35] See N. T. Wright, *Justification: God's Plan and Paul's Vision* (London: SPCK, 2009).

confessing my own tradition's sins rather than pointing the finger at the Orthodox. At the same time, there are bright spots in the story, occasions when the gospel has truly been lived out, and I believe that the future holds great potential. We must surely agree that in spite of our failures, God has been pleased to accept and honour the service of Christians in both traditions. In the grace that has been shown lies our only hope.

14. Discipleship on the Margins

Fr Luke A. Veronis

Let me begin with a story from the Kosovo war in 1999. As the United States was bombing Serbia, half a million refugees flooded into Albania, a country of only 3.5 million people. 95 per cent of the Albanian refugees were Muslim, and they were fleeing from what they perceived as a war with Serbian Orthodox. I was serving as a missionary for the Orthodox Church of Albania at the time, and we were placed in a unique position with the refugees as fellow Albanians, yet also as Orthodox Christians. Archbishop Anastasios (Yannoulatos) quickly mobilized our church to respond to the tragic needs of the refugees. We set up a refugee camp, and then the archbishop asked all the faithful, and particularly the university students and our seminarians, to volunteer and help out wherever they could. So, when he talked with our seminarians, and we planned out how we were to visit the refugee camps each day, one student asked the archbishop: 'Should we wear our crosses when we go into the camps, so that all can see?' To this he responded: 'No. Keep your crosses under your shirts. Just live the cross by serving and sacrificing for others.'

So we did. Each day, going to the camps, talking with the refugees, listening to their stories of pain and suffering, offering aid and doing whatever we could to make their lives more bearable. Day after day we went, offering a loving presence, and slowly the refugees began responding to our students. 'Who are you? Why are you coming here every day?' And friendships developed.

Our students, who were initially uncertain, and even afraid to be among these mostly Muslim refugees, connected with them through their love and concern. Every day our students came back and shared their stories of how they felt a bond with the people and no longer looked upon them as 'refugees' or as 'Muslims' but more as fellow human beings and fellow children of God.

One man my students introduced me to was Ramazan. Numerous times, I stopped in his tent to have the traditional Turkish coffee and share in conversation. Our discussions often revolved around spiritual themes because Ramazan was continually trying to understand how this tragedy had taken place. He was friends with numerous Serbs before the war. In fact, it was his Serbian friends who helped him and his family escape alive. Yet he had seen his business looted and burned, and did not know whether his house still stood. Thankfully, all his family members were still alive, as far as he knew. For two months, he stayed in the Orthodox refugee camp. Following the end of the war, he returned home.

A week after his return, I received a phone call. It was Ramazan, telling me that he was back in Tirana, trying to buy essential supplies which were hard to find in Kosovo. He asked to meet with me. He came into my office with a neighbour from Djakova. This time I offered him coffee as he told me about his situation back home. His house had been totally looted, but at least the structure was still standing and in good shape. In general, his family was well, except for two nephews whose whereabouts were unknown. He was hoping that they were in prison in Serbia, but this was unconfirmed.

His neighbour, however, shared a more gruesome tale. He found his sister and brother-in-law burned alive in their home. He saw the skeletons himself. As we talked together, Ramazan said that he still believed that Kosovo could be a multi-ethnic country with Albanians and Serbians living together. His friend vehemently disagreed. He bluntly said that he could never live with a Serb as a neighbour. An awkward moment followed, but since I had a relationship with Ramazan, I felt that I could express my hope for the future. From a human perspective, I surely understood his friend's anger and hatred. I myself cringed and deeply felt his sorrow when his friend described the skeletal bones of his sister. Yet I gently told him that such human anger and desire for revenge would only perpetuate other acts of violence in the future. What Kosovo and the entire Balkan region needed more than ever was not human anger and revenge, but divine mercy, forgiveness and love. He looked at me, not fully understanding, but he politely listened as I told him that only through the grace and power of God could hatred be transformed into mercy and even love for one's enemies.

Surprisingly, Ramazan nodded in agreement and expressed hope for the future. 'It will be extremely difficult, seemingly impossible,' he reflected, 'yet I still have hope.' As he got up to leave my office, he handed me a large oil painting. He apologized, saying that it was not the most beautiful painting, but it was all he could find in Djakova. He offered it to me as a small token of gratitude for all his new friends in the Orthodox Church who had done so much for him and all the refugees. He said that through such concrete and loving actions of the church and her people, he still had hope in humanity despite the atrocities he had witnessed. He ended by saying: 'I have seen what true Christianity is all about.'

The topic of discipleship on the margins, which I was asked to consider, made me remember this story and reflect upon it from two perspectives. One is about discipleship from the perspective of trying to mentor our students and teach them what our faith truly means by reaching out to the stranger, to the other, to the refugee, to the Muslim. At the same time, however, was this the beginning of discipleship in the life of Ramazan, when he witnessed Christ-centred love at a critical time in his life?

Archbishop Anastasios has repeated again and again:

A Christian should never have enemies. Never call someone a 'bad communist', 'a bad atheist', or a 'bad so-and-so'. Every person has the image of God in them, and they are His children! Every day we pray 'for those who hate us and those who love us'. Thus, we cannot have enemies … The message is clear. Our salvation depends upon respect for the other, respect for the otherness. This is the deep meaning of the parable of the Good Samaritan; we see not that someone is my neighbor, but how someone becomes my neighbor. It is a process.[1]

This lesson of faith, a process of transforming strangers into neighbours and friends, became a reality as our students visited and befriended Muslim refugees every day. We modelled and practised our faith as we taught them to be disciples on the margins. Simultaneously, though, we offered a witness and became friends with the Muslim refugee strangers who no longer simply had labels – 'a Muslim' or 'a refugee' – but who had names with stories, who went from stranger to friend.

Another story from this same experience which offers an example of the power of modelling love in forming disciples on the margins came after the war ended. Sevdi and Vjolca discovered their house in Kosovo was destroyed and so chose to remain in Tirana temporarily, hoping to find a way to emigrate to Canada. As they waited day after day in the sweltering summer heat of Tirana, I suggested that maybe we could take their teenage girls to our church's summer camp for a little break. I explained to the parents that although this camp was a church camp with quite a bit of worship, Bible study and religious activity, their girls would experience a lot of fun and great fellowship in other activities, and they could participate in whatever they felt comfortable with.

Since we had built a bond of trust with the parents over the past months, they allowed their fourteen- and fifteen-year-old girls to come with me. Before they came to the camp, my wife Faith and I instructed our camp staff in how to treat these Muslim refugee girls: with loving Christian hospitality, but also with the freedom to participate in whatever they felt comfortable with. Our visitors planned to stay only for two or three nights.

On the first day of their visit, a somewhat serious incident occurred. After a day of activities and fun, time came for our evening Vesper service. All the girls of the camp came to the church, including Drita and Alba, our Kosovar visitors. When the fifteen-year-old Alba saw everyone making the sign of the cross, she immediately ran out of the church. One of the counsellors went out with her and asked her if she was okay. She simply responded: 'Where I come from, the cross is associated with violence and death. They put crosses on the homes after they destroy them. I can't stay anywhere people make the sign of the cross!'

After the service I talked with Alba and offered to take her and her sister back to Tirana immediately. Or, I told her, she could stay and participate only in whatever she felt comfortable with. Alba chose to stay, but emphasized that she would not go inside the church again.

---

[1] Luke A. Veronis, *Go Forth: Stories of Mission and Resurrection in Albania* (Ben Lomond, CA: Conciliar Press, 2009), 186.

Our camp staff and girls overwhelmed Drita and Alba with incredible love. After the initial three days, Drita and Alba asked if they could stay until the end of the camp. Their parents consented. By the final days of the camp, not only were both Kosovar girls attending every activity, including the church service, they were even reading psalms in church! On the last night of camp, Alba got up in front of all the campers and said, 'I have never experienced such love in my life as I did at this camp. I will never forget this experience! It has given me an entirely new understanding of Christianity.'

Before I took them back to their parents, they asked our camp leader for the same packet which all the other campers received. The packet included a Bible, stories of the saints, icons and other religious material. Both girls even put crosses around their necks. When I saw them wearing crosses and carrying these packets of materials, I asked them to please be very careful when they returned home. I told them not to wear the crosses, but to show all the things they had received to their parents, and ask permission from their parents about whether to keep the materials or not. I did not want the parents to think we had brainwashed their children. In the end, though, I explained to them, 'You have experienced a taste of God's Kingdom at this camp. Cherish this memory in your hearts. Seek out God, try to learn more about his teachings, and cultivate his Spirit within your hearts.'

We experience the Kingdom of Heaven by teaching disciples to reach out to the margins, but also creating disciples on the margins.

In these two stories, I cannot say whether the people in the margins became faithful disciples of Jesus Christ, but I can say they were treated with love, respect and dignity, and thus experienced a tiny taste of what it was like to be a disciple of Jesus Christ. Seeds of faith were planted within these people. Maybe one day, as they reflect on their journey through life, they will remember how they felt God's presence and experienced an authentic witness of Christianity.

Discipleship on the Margins

I have other examples of how people truly on the margins became disciples of Jesus through the respect and love they experienced from people in the Church. Right now, for example, in the church family where I serve, we have several of the most faithful members who have struggled with various drug and alcohol addictions. One almost died from an overdose several years ago, yet today comes faithfully to church every Sunday and even serves in a leadership role of our church.

Another former member had struggled with alcoholism for a number of years. She fell out of the church fellowship for decades but became sober through a Twelve Step programme. When her Twelve Step group asked to use our church hall as a meeting place, she was quite hesitant. She met with me to tell me, 'I'm not sure how comfortable I will be coming back here. Some of these people don't know about my addiction, and even though I've been sober for twenty years, they will not understand.' I emphasized to her that this community had radically changed from twenty years ago, and that this church was now a place that welcomed former addicts, welcomed those who were broken and struggling, welcomed those who were sick and in need. The Church is not a place for saints, but for sinners in need of healing and recovery and renewal, a place for all people to discover life. She was sceptical but she decided to try and come to our church, not only during her Twelve Step meetings but on a Sunday.

That was five years ago. Today, she feels loved and cherished. She has become one of my most faithful and active members who brings her grandkids every Sunday to church, and encourages two of her children who themselves are struggling with addictions. She tells everyone how she finds her peace and strength from her family of faith!

Her story reminds me of the words of Metropolitan Anthony Bloom, of blessed memory. These words aptly apply to discipleship on the margins.

> Unless we look at a person and see the beauty there is in this person, we can contribute nothing to him. One does not help a person by discerning what is wrong, what is ugly, what is distorted. Christ looked at everyone he met, at the prostitute or the thief, and saw the beauty hidden there. Perhaps it was distorted, perhaps damaged, but it was beauty none the less, and what he did was to call out this beauty.[2]

We are called to see the beauty of God's image in each and every person we encounter. This is especially important when we relate to those on the margins – those who feel rejected, despised, forgotten, hated, broken, ugly, lonely – those who feel like the OTHER.

When Jesus met the Samaritan woman at Jacob's well (Jn 4), he didn't see a woman who had been married five times, a woman so despised by society that she had to seek water from a far-away well in the middle of the day. Instead, he saw a woman filled with beauty from within and called forth that beauty! This Samaritan woman found healing and love from Christ, despite her immoral past, and became known in church history as St Fotini, one of the most beloved saints in our Orthodox Church. She is honoured twice a year in the church calendar, on her feast day on 26 February as well as on the fourth Sunday after Pascha. Imagine a woman married five times, honoured in the church twice every year!

When Jesus met Zaccheus, he did not see a chief tax-collector, a thief and a traitor to his Jewish nation. Instead he saw a lost man looking for something more, and thus he called him down from the tree, entering his house and changing his life. Zaccheus's life was transformed by Christ's visit, changing his life from that of a thief to a philanthropist and disciple of Christ, giving half his goods to the poor and repaying those he cheated fourfold! And if we

---

[2] Quoted by Allan Boyd, 'Beauty will save the World: Theophany', *Pithless Thoughts*, online at: http://pithlessthoughts.blogspot.com/2010/01/beauty-will-save-world-theophany.html.

are focusing on discipleship on the margins, we need look no farther than Jesus choosing another tax-collector to enter his inner circle of friends. Matthew the tax-collector becomes Matthew the evangelist and apostle and disciple. Christ never allowed one's fallen condition, or sinful past, to blind him from the beauty that lay hidden within.

St John Cassian emphasized: 'When someone has no compassion for another's transgressions, but pronounces a severe judgement on them, it is an obvious sign of a soul not yet purified of evil passions.'

And here lies the foundation for our Orthodox Christian understanding of discipleship on the margins. We are challenged to cultivate inner eyes to see God's beauty all around us and in everyone we meet. We live in an impure world, in which it seems so much easier to focus on the negative, to point out the evil and darkness and impurity in others. In fact, our impure hearts and minds often lead us to question and doubt even that which is most pure and beautiful. Our fallen nature and fallen world tempt us to focus on the darkness and evil all around us. That is why we see so many people tear down others, and concentrate on what they see as negative and evil.

In Genesis, we remember how God created all things good. God's original beauty and goodness still lie within all people. This goodness and beauty may be covered up by our fallen nature, it may be distorted or even damaged, yet God's goodness and beauty still exist in everyone and everything. The mission according to our Orthodox faith is to bring out this beauty in others; in the words of Metropolitan Anthony Bloom, 'to bless all things and by doing so, to participate with God synergistically in the recreation of the entire universe'.

Fr Anthony Hughes reflected on those words by noting:

> We have no time to meditate on darkness or on the evil that lives in this world. That is the work of the devil. We have the heart only to see goodness and to rejoice in it. This is the meaning of the scripture that says, *'To the pure all things are pure.'* Impure hearts see darkness in everything, and even rejoice in this darkness. Let that not be so of us. Let us participate every moment of our lives in the calling out of the beauty of creation, of our neighbors, of our friends and even our enemies. Let us call out the beauty especially within ourselves![3]

Remember, each person we meet, no matter how difficult he or she may be, was created in the image and likeness of God. Nothing can take away that divine image. A person's sinful ways and evil choices may distort or damage that image of God within them, yet our role in following our Creator and seeking to disciple others is to help each person rediscover and restore their own divine image. We must strive to bring out the divine beauty that lies hidden within them.

I remember as a seminarian around 1990 visiting a prison every week. I did this for three years, developing a number of friendships with the men incarcerated there. One of my friends there ended up spending twenty-five

---

[3] Boyd, 'Beauty will save the World'.

years in prison. I met him there as a seminarian for three years. I kept a correspondence with him over the ten-year period when I left the country and served as a missionary in Albania, sending letters back and forth. And then when I returned to the United States, I visited him again several times while he was still in prison. After twenty-five years, he was finally released.

Imagine leaving prison after twenty-five years. Leaving with the stigma of being a sex offender. Feeling despised and unwelcomed by society. Realizing it is almost impossible to find work with the label of a sex offender, extremely difficult to find a place to live, and coming to the realization that society is just waiting to send you back to prison! (40 per cent of sex offenders return to prison within three years of their release.)

With this man, however, I kept in touch and saw beauty within. We talk on the phone regularly. We have lunch monthly. I have visited each of his new apartments whenever he moved from place to place, and would offer the Orthodox tradition of blessing his house. I even began going out to lunch with him and his elderly hundred-year-old mother. I try to hold him accountable, to help him stay safe from his addiction. I encourage him to stay involved in his various support group meetings. I am sure he still has temptations, but it is now seven years since he has been out of prison, and he tries to be a follower of Jesus Christ.

I remember hearing a talk by Fr Anthony Gittens, a Roman Catholic priest who works among the 'nobodies' in Chicago, befriending and discipling them. He emphasized something that I have never forgotten: 'We Christians cannot get into the Kingdom of God until we move from the VIP category, the somebody category, and reach out to the outsider category, to the nobodies of the world! Again, let me repeat, if the only person we meet daily is the person in the mirror, people like ourselves, then we'll never enter into God's Kingdom!'

When we talk about discipleship in the margins, this implies reaching out to those in the outsider category. Too often we divide the world into the 'us' and them' categories. The 'us' are people like ourselves, with whom we identify, whether religiously, ethnically, socio-economically, politically or in whatever other ways we look at our own tribe. The 'them' are the strangers, those who are different, those who we may not understand or find difficulty relating to, and thus we reject.

In the Old Testament, the 'us' was Israel (the people of God), and the 'them' were the Gentiles. Yet today, in how many ways do we divide the world into us and them: Christian/non-Christian, Americans/Immigrants; Democrats/Republicans; Rich/Poor; Insiders/Outsiders! Ultimately, we divide the world into the 'somebodies' (who are us) and the 'nobodies' (who are those different from us).

Discipleship on the margins means imitating the life of Jesus, cultivating the mind of Christ, which implies reaching out to the nobodies of the world – to sinners, to prostitutes, to thieves, to lepers, to the poor and lame, to the marginalized, to the forgotten of the world. Our Lord's entire ministry was one of reaching out to those rejected by the world. 'I came not to condemn the world, Christ taught, 'but to save the world. I came to seek the lost. I came to reach out to the sinners! I came to bring light into darkness, good news to those in despair.'

It all begins by first noticing the other, and then acting, responding, sharing God's love.

In the gospel of the rich man and the poor beggar Lazarus, we see clearly the sin of consciously ignoring, or even unconsciously not noticing, the poor and needy right in front of us. Day after day, the rich man walked past Lazarus, without ever helping him, *maybe without ever noticing him*! Jesus concludes the gospel story by saying that Lazarus went to paradise, while the rich man went to hell. The central sin of the rich man is that he *did not notice* the poor man right outside his door. Daily, he walked out of his house, and either consciously or unconsciously passed by the poor man without even noticing him. In other words, his sin was not something that he did, but something that he did not do.

How often do we fall into the same temptation? We walk out of the church, having heard the gospel lesson to notice and help the poor, and yet we still do not see the poor who are begging for our help. So often we are quick to judge the poor as lazy people who do not want to work, yet can we say we really know these people and understand their situation? Have we sincerely befriended the poor, listened to their story, and journeyed with them in life?

And the poor are not only those who have material needs. The greatest poverty in North America is the poverty of loneliness, the poverty of feeling unloved, the poverty of feeling unwanted, the poverty of feeling marginalized.

How are we noticing the 'nobodies' of the world, reaching out to them and discipling them? How are we making them feel loved, a part of the somebodies of the world? To love, we must meet the other. We must encounter the other. We must engage the other. We must disciple them.

How many of us can say we really know these people? Knowing *about* the marginalized is no better than knowing *about* God. Our faith is one of encountering God, knowing God in an intimate way. We can only know God and encounter him by coming in contact with him in a personal way. The same could be said about those who are marginalized.

There is a story of a wise rabbi who asked his students: 'When does the night end and the day begin?' One student responded: 'When we can look in the distance and distinguish between two kinds of trees.' A good answer, but not the right one. A second student said: 'When we look into the distance and can distinguish a white thread from a black one.' A good answer, but not the right one. And after a few more attempts, the students gave up. The rabbi then answered his own question: 'We know that the night has ended and the day has begun when we can look at each person we meet, no matter who they are, and see them as our brother and sister.

Let us reflect today on how we divide the world into 'us' and 'them', to the somebodies and the nobodies, and then let us follow the call of our Lord Jesus to reach out to the other, to encounter the other in a concrete manner, to come to know the other in a personal and intimate way! For we will only enter into the Kingdom of God when we learn to notice the other, to disciple the other, to treat the other – the nobodies of the world – as precious children of God!

15. Discipleship Shifts Learned from the Margins[*]

Karen Wilk

What If …

What if … every Christian in every neighbourhood in North America (and around the world?!) actually loved their neighbours, those with whom they live in proximity – *as Jesus loves?*

What if … every Christian in every neighbourhood in North America (and around the world) sought Kingdom Shalom in word and deed for the community in which they lived?

What if … every Christian in every neighbourhood in North America (and around the world) joined together with every other Christian in their neighbourhood, and together manifested the tangible presence of God in that place as the real flesh and blood body of Jesus?

What if … as they were formed and transformed into the people of God in that place, others also participated and, together, they discovered more of who God is and what the Spirit is up to?

And *What if* … that formation became the determining factor for who they were and what they did?

And *What if* … as God did his work in, through and with them,

> they became more like Jesus *and less like consumers;*
>
> more like friends and less like service providers;
>
> more like disciples *and less like patrons;*
>
> more like radical followers *and less like fans;* more like salt, light and a city on a hill
>
> *and less like an institution, a programme and an event;*
>
> more like a community with a mission
>
> and *less like an organization* with a strategic plan;

And *WHAT IF…*

> God has moved into the neighbourhood, making his home with men and women! They're his people, he's their God. (Revelation 21.3, *The Message*)

We have many questions … How do we effectively live and share the gospel in a culture that is suspicious of institutions, and pre-packaged programs? How do we keep each other accountable and faithful to Scripture, to the leadership of the Spirit, and the history of our tradition? How do we respond to movements

---

[*] Scripture quotations in this chapter are from *The Message*. Copyright © 1993, 2002, 2018 by Eugene H. Peterson.

of the Spirit that call us back to renewed faithfulness in aspects of the life of faith that we may have neglected or need renewed attention such as evangelism and love for the neighbour in our own context?[1]

A Neighbour's Story

Sarah (name changed) grew up the daughter of a pastor, entrenched in a conservative, charismatic community where she was both nurtured and sheltered. She married young and when the marriage started to fall apart, her whole world did too. Her family told her to pray more and that she had to stay in the relationship: she had made a vow before God … but the situation got worse, even abusive, and she had to get out. Doing so however, not only black-marked her in the community and shamed her family, but left her feeling alone and abandoned, disillusioned about God, and confused about what she believed. Consequently, for a time she disassociated herself from everything to do with 'church'.

But God brought a wonderful man with a Roman Catholic background into her life and that of her young son. Together they began participating in a small church plant where they felt safe and welcome. They got involved in its ministry but it was exhausting – there were only a handful of people trying to maintain all the traditional programs and ministries; and get more people to 'come to church!' Despite the warmth of the fellowship, 'church' became a burden, draining them and others.

Sarah and her new man, however, were doing great and eventually they married and moved into our neighbourhood. Meanwhile, sadly, the church plant disbanded and this new young family wondered again about the value of the 'institutional church'. *Was that really what it was all about?* At the same time, Sarah and her new husband were beginning to discover that God was at work 'outside' the 'church', in their neighbourhood. As she would later describe it, they were being invited by the Spirit to join in with what God was already doing out ahead of them right where they lived; it was a whole new paradigm! Sarah became a block connector and found God using her as she was simply present and available to her neighbours. And when she was diagnosed with cancer, her neighbours were there for her and her family – and continue to be. This experience and their eventual commitment to our neighbourhood Sunday morning house gathering has led to huge shifts in their theology; in their understanding of what it means to be a disciple. These shifts are happening amongst the people of God in communities across North America as more and more followers of Jesus begin to recognize how the world has changed and how their modern Christendom understanding of the Church, God's mission and the nature of discipleship no longer make sense. As Alan Roxburgh puts it, 'The crisis is the ending of the Christian narrative

---

[1] Martin Contant, 'Ministry Review of Neighbourhood Life Ministry for Classis Alberta North and Christian Reformed Home Missions', 15-16 October 2014 (Edmonton, AB), 7.

as the operative, controlling map of North America culture. The emergence of postmodern maps is putting the churches into a radically different situation.'[2]

Stanley Grenz affirms: 'The shift from the familiar territory of modernity to the uncharted terrain of postmodernity has grave implications for those who seek to live as Christ's disciples in the new context.'[3] What are those shifts? What are we learning about God's mission and our call to be and make disciples as we venture out into this uncharted territory? Those are the questions I hope to address here. In order to do so, I will frame my observations with the 'posts' of David Fitch and Geoff Holsclaw: post-attractional, post-positional and post-universal, to which I will add post-commuter.[4] As I explore these shifts and their implications, I invite you to ponder: what is the Spirit up to and how is the Church to disciple *for such a time as this*?

Post-attractional

The first shift, post-attractional, might simply be articulated by saying that the dominant culture is no longer *attracted* to the Church. In the Christendom world (particularly the North American Evangelical context), the Church was able to *attract* people to its programmes and services, and discipleship happened (we presumed) when people came.

(1) Today, however, 'they' no longer seem interested in coming, no matter how 'attractive' we make 'church'.

Furthermore, we are realizing that the attractional approach was better at forming religious consumers than making disciples. Attenders simply chose the service that best suited them, went home and got on with their week, satisfied that they had done their Christian 'thing'.[5] Consequently, the call to love their neighbours, to bear witness '24-7', to disciple and be discipled was perceived as optional or peripheral, if it was considered at all. Carlson and Lueken came face to face with this reality in their megachurch and concluded that 'consumer driven church' and

---

[2] Alan Roxburgh, *Missional Map-Making: Skills for Leading in Times of Transition* (San Francisco, CA: Jossey-Bass, 2010), xx.

[3] Stanley Grenz, *A Primer on Postmodernism* (Grand Rapids, MI: Eerdmans, 1996), 162.

[4] David Fitch and Geoff Holsclaw, *Prodigal Christianity: Ten Signposts into the Missional Frontier* (San Francisco, CA: Jossey-Bass, 2013), 6-12.

[5] This is not intended to diminish the value and importance of a weekly communal gathering for the purpose of worship, fellowship and discipleship. Indeed, such a time together at the table, shaped by the Word, mutually encouraged in sharing, discernment and prayer, is essential not only for our formation, accountability and discipline (connecting us in the one, holy, catholic, apostolic Church) but for our embodiment of God's kingdom reign here and now in our neighbourhoods.

'spiritual formation are 'conflicting influences' that 'cannot coexist peacefully, for they are built on completely different foundational understandings of the life God has invited us to live'.[6] As those now participating in our Neighbourhood Life communities (NL) have articulated, 'Something was amiss, we were longing for a more integrated life.' This 'simplifying has been life-giving but we still have lots of work to do to consolidate our lives in the neighbourhood'. Others describe how they had been so involved in the 'church bubble' but were now realizing that moving beyond 'attractional church' is a call to 'a total life change', not just 'an extra thing you have to do'.

(2) A second related assumption of the attractional mode of being 'church' is its understanding of church 'success'.

Success is about numbers, more and bigger. But, more people in the pews and programmes does not necessarily mean more fully formed disciples. The latter, we are learning, requires that we ask different questions, such as: Are we being faithful? Are we loving our neighbours? Are we seeking the shalom of our community? What practices are we engaging in that bear witness to the Kingdom of God right where we live *that others might know*?

(3) A third shortcoming of the attractional paradigm concerns the individualistic approach to life and faith that it engenders.

Church is about *me*: *my* needs, *my* relationship with Jesus, *my* comfort and so forth. Catholic missionary Vincent Donovan concludes that this focus *on me* has 'consume[d] the vast majority of the church's resources, time, energy, and talent … individual responsibility, individual morality, individual vocation to the priesthood, self-fulfilment, individual holiness and salvation … with little room for community in between'.[7] Charles Taylor calls this 'the unprecedented primacy of the individual'.[8] But does catering to the individual produce disciples or have anything to with what it means to be *communitas*, the community of God's people formed by, witnessing to, and participating in God's mission?[9] Alan Roxburgh and Fred Romanuk challenge us in this way:

---

[6] Kent Carlson and Michael Lueken, *Renovation of the Church: What Happens when a Seeker Church Discovers Spiritual Formation* (Downers Grove, CA: IVP, 2011), 33.

[7] Vincent Donovan, *Christianity Rediscovered* (Maryknoll, NY: Orbis, 1978), 68.

[8] Charles Taylor, *Modern Social Imaginaries* (Durham, NC: Duke University Press 2004), 50.

[9] Alan Hirsch, quoted by Michael Frost in *Exiles: Living Missionally in a Post-Christian Culture* (Peabody, MA: Hendrickson, 2006), 123. *Communitas* is 'a community infused with a grand sense of purpose; a purpose that lies outside of its current internal reality and constitution. It's the kind of community that "happens" to people in actual pursuit of a common vision of what could be. It involves

Missional leadership is not effectiveness in meeting the inner, spiritual needs of self-actualizing and self-differentiating individuals or creating numerical growth. It is different from building healthy, non-anxious relationships among members of a congregation so that they appear attractive to people outside the church. Missional leadership is cultivating an environment that releases the missional imagination of the people of God.[10]

Not only has NL been incited to realize that church is not about meeting their needs but also that participation in God's mission is about *we. We* are called as a city on the hill, the salt and light of the world *in the world* (Mt. 5.13-16). In following, one participant was motivated to think about 'bringing the church to the people since the people were not coming to the church'. Another expressed how she was struck by 'the vision of embodying Christ together, *here* – as my kids play with the neighbour kids … organically, naturally; I'm not thinking or worrying about getting them to church'. As Henri Nouwen articulates, the togetherness of the gospel reminds us:

> It is Jesus who heals, not I; it is Jesus who speaks words of truth, not I; Jesus who is Lord, not I … we proclaim the redeeming power of God together. Indeed whenever we minister together, it is easier for people to recognize that we do not come in our own name, but in the name of the Lord Jesus who sent us. … Ministry is not only a communal experience, it is also a mutual experience.[11]

We are in this together!

Post-positional

A second 'post' which we experience as we engage on the margins is the recognition that the Church (and other similar institutions) no longer holds authority, power and position in our society. 'Our culture is increasingly less influenced by the gospel; the church has lost its place of privilege and is pushed to the margins.'[12] As a now marginalized entity, a number of the Church's long-held suppositions are called into question, including the ideas that:

   a) right thinking/believing is the main, and in many cases, the only thing that matters;

------

movement and it describes the experience of togetherness that only really happens among a group of people actually engaging in a mission outside itself.'

[10] Alan J. Roxburgh and Fred Romanuk, *The Missional Leader* (San Francisco, CA: Jossey Bass, 2006), 122.

[11] Henri Nouwen, *In the Name of Jesus: Reflections on Christian Leadership* (New York, NY: Crossroad, 1992), 58-59.

[12] Michael W. Goheen, 'A Critical Examination of David Bosch's Missional Reading of Luke', in Craig G. Bartholomew, Joel B. Green and Anthony C. Thiselton (eds), *Reading Luke: Interpretation, Reflection Formation* (Grand Rapids, MI: Zondervan, 2005), 232.

    b) church professionals are the experts and authority, and therefore carry the responsibility for discipleship;

    c) hand-in-hand with that, ordinary, lay people (on their own) do not have what is needed to disciple and be discipled.

(a) All we need is right thinking (and believing)

This modern appeal to reason led Western Christendom Christianity to assert that being a Christian meant believing the right things and ensuring (via logical argument and rational persuasion) that others did too. We are now aware that discipleship is not merely about endorsing a set of propositions' that 'simply catalog a collection of statements about God, Jesus, the Spirit, sin, redemption and so on'.[13] As one person on the margins put it, 'Either there is more to this, or it's hogwash; you've got to show me God.'

This is important for several reasons. Our neighbours are not going to believe just because we provide logical evidence that the Bible is true or can win an argument about the reality of Jesus's death and resurrection. Instead, the truth of the gospel is discovered, experienced and expressed through the whole of life and through *others'* lives. The gospel truth after all has always been a person: '*I am* the way, the truth and the life' (Jn 14.6). Furthermore, when we begin to embrace a more wholistic approach to discipleship, we discover the 'gospelling' that the Spirit is already doing out ahead of us, alerting others to the Kingdom of God come near. How meaningful it is when a neighbour remarks: 'You're not like any other religious people that I know. I like you.'

(b) We need experts

The modern belief in reason and knowledge as the only real sources of truth also led to our need for and dependence upon the experts and professionals as (often the only) disciplers. Those with the most know-how, training and skill, were listened to, trusted and given power and authority (for better and for worse), period. This is no longer the case.[14]

Many in the Church are threatened by and fearful of this loss. Nonetheless, it may be that through this 'post', the Spirit is opening up a way for the church to discover (or recover) a more Christ-like posture, in the midst of a changing, seeking world (Phil. 2). Experts presenting information or imposing rules does not make disciples. 'Finally the postmodern church', Smith proposes, must 'recognize that its primary responsibility is to live the

---

[13] James K. A. Smith, *Who's Afraid of Postmodernism? Taking Derrida, Lyotard and Foucault to Church* (Grand Rapids, MI: Baker, 2006), 74.
[14] George Hunsberger and Craig Van Gelder (eds), *The Church between Gospel and Culture: The Emerging Mission in North America* (Grand Rapids, MI: Eerdmans, 1996), 41.

story for the world and therefore Christians have a responsibility to "act well".'[15] NL participants have been aiming to 'act well' as 'they live the story' amongst their neighbours not as judges, authorities, therapists or care-givers but as friends and fellow-journeyers,[16] seeking to be 'channel[s] of grace through which God can mend a broken world',[17] but it is not easy.

(c) Not just 'laity'

It is not easy because the underlying modern positional framework of Christendom has told us that 'the average Christian' cannot disciple; we do not have the expertise (despite doctrines that in theory suggest otherwise). The subtle, perhaps unintentional, message has been: Your job (as a person in the pew), is to get your friends and neighbours into the building and then, we, 'the church' (meaning the staff / the professionals), will take care of them, disciple them, etc.[18] Already in 1967, however, Hans Küng was asserting that 'if the Church is the true people of God, it is impossible to differentiate between "church" and "laity"', observing that the latter term 'simply does not occur in the New Testament. All members of the people of God have been called by the message of Jesus Christ to faith, obedience and complete devotion in love; in this too; all members of the Church are equal.'[19] Put definitively, 'In the Church of Jesus Christ, who is the only high priest and mediator, all the faithful are priests and clergy.'[20] I wonder how different the Church and the world would be if we had heeded Küng's admonition decades ago. Could initiatives like NL be a way for the Church to commission all members to live as 'priests and clergy', humbly serving and bearing witness to the Kingdom by their faithful presence in their neighbourhoods? Since we are all priests and clergy, 'we as believers are [all] called to disciple everyone who comes into our orbit of influence – it's that simple'.[21] Thus, as NL has sought to leave *positional* behind and take up this new (ancient) *posture*, we have become more aware that it is not our 'story telling' that should be supported by our 'story living' but rather our 'story living' that, via Christ in us, is supported by our 'story telling'.[22]

---

[15] Smith, *Who's Afraid of Postmodernism*, 79.

[16] David Fitch, *The Great Giveaway*: *Reclaiming the Mission of the Church from Big Business, Parachurch Organizations, Psychotherapy, Consumer Capitalism and other Modern Maladies* (Grand Rapids, MI: Baker, 2005), ch. 7.

[17] Rick Rouse and Craig Van Gelder, *A Field Guide to the Missional Congregation: Embarking on a Journey of Transformation* (Minneapolis, MN: Augsburg 2008), 65.

[18] I confess that I perpetuated this myth in this way as a 'professional' in my Christendom church contexts. Please forgive me, holy, Spirit-filled and gifted ones in those pews!

[19] Hans Küng, *The Church* (Colorado Springs, CO: Image, 1976), 169.

[20] Küng, *The Church*, 559.

[21] Alan and Debra Hirsch, *Untamed: Reactivating a Missional Form of Discipleship* (Grand Rapids, MI: Baker, 2010), 146-47.

[22] Smith, *Who's Afraid of Postmodernism*, 79.

Post-universal Language

A third shift in today's culture that we have learned on the margins is that we are now post-universal language. There was a day (which some still assume persists in some places in North America) when everyone spoke the same language, or so we believed. Within this modern construct, the church could approach discipleship uniformly and assume that everyone understood what was being communicated, could take the same Discipleship 101, 102, etc. track, and grow from the experience. One need only walk down a busy street in any city to realize that there is no longer one common language or common understanding in our neighbourhoods. Since we all have different backgrounds, 'a phrase can mean one thing in one context and something different in another'.[23] For many in Christendom systems, however, the implications of such an observation are only beginning to be realized. The Church continues to speak 'Christianese' and expects others to understand and respond to it (as we would) even though the majority of our neighbours no longer attend church.[24]

Conversely, in our multicultural, diverse communities, showing and telling *the Story* must be far less formulaic and far more organic, contextual and relational. As Boren and Roxburgh contend, 'it's not about being trendy or catering to the culture but about being missionaries in [our] neighbourhoods, shaping the gospel in the forms and language of the local people'.[25] After all, Jesus himself did not come with one text but rather expressed and displayed *the Kingdom of God come near* in person and differently for different people. Accordingly, as one NL Community member observed, 'We're exploring faith together; I can hear my Buddhist neighbour and even learn from him; believing the Holy Spirit is at work in him.' As

---

[23] Smith, *Who's Afraid of Postmodernism*, 52.

[24] In 2005, 33% of Canadians never attended a worship service and the number who attend weekly has also declined from 30% to 21%, according to Colin Lindsay, who states that 'Canadians attend weekly religious services less than 20 years ago': Statistics Canada, 2008. Catalogue no. 89-630-X. 'Weekly attendance at religious services in Canada [was] just 13 percent, according to a December 2013 poll by the Evangelical Fellowship of Canada (EFC) and the Angus Reid Forum, a national polling firm. That 13 percent includes all faiths, not just Christians': https://www.intrust.org/Magazine/Issues/New-Year-2016/Religious-affiliation-and-attendance-in-Canada. I suspect that those percentages would be even lower now. The greatest drop has been in the boomer generation (those born between 1944 and 1964) (from 39% attending weekly to 22%) which parallels an informal survey of the Christian Reformed Church showing the greatest dropout rate in this age group. Furthermore, the percentage of Canadian teenagers (age 15-19) who identify as affiliated with a Protestant tradition dropped from over 35% to 13% between 1984 and 2008: Reginald W. Bibby and others, *The Emerging Millennials: How Canada's Newest Generation is Responding to Change & Choice* (Lethbridge, AB: Project Teen Canada Books, 2009), 176. More information about religious trends can be found at: www.pewresearchcenter.org.

[25] Alan Roxburgh and M. Scott Boren, *Introducing the Missional Church: What it is, Why it Matters, How to become one* (Grand Rapids, MI: Baker, 2009), 131.

Earl Creps has pointed out, 'listening to the voices of others is an essential part of being the church'.[26]

We need the community. A second aspect of the post-universal language shift is the acknowledgement that 'we can't interpret a text, thing or event without the conventions and rules of an interpretative community; indeed language itself is inherently communal and intersubjective'.[27] In other words, contrary to our primarily individualistic approaches to evangelism and discipleship, we are (re)learning that, our sharing and interpretations invite us to discover a God and a story (not a model or a doctrine) that embrace many voices. On the margins, we hear from our younger brothers and sisters ('out of the mouths of babes'); we are attentive to those of different ethnic, socio-economic, national and denominational backgrounds; we make space for 'nones and dones'[28] and, we are the better for it! On the margins, we are realizing that 'we don't have to prove anything or argue for God's existence', rather, being a disciple and discipling is about 'trying to live the gospel with friendship and love'. 'Since its God's mission, we're more relaxed about getting involved with our neighbours in our typical daily lives and waiting for the Holy Spirit to make apparent an opportunity for us to act, pray, proclaim or console. God generates connections.' 'Spiritual conversations just flow naturally, they're part of our life together.'[29]

Post-commuter

We are witnessing a resurgence of interest in questions of place – it comes in multiple forms such as rediscovering the local or understanding what the Christian life has to do with presence. This is quite a significant shift in which many of us are trying to sort out what it means to be located, to have our lives shaped by the notion of neighborhood.[30]

---

[26] Earl Creps, *Off Road Disciplines: Spiritual Adventures of Missional Leaders* (San Francisco, CA: Jossey-Bass, 2006), 69.

[27] Smith, *Who's Afraid of Postmodernism*, 56.

[28] A common reference in North American church culture: 'In today's lingo "Nones" are those identified as having little or no experience with the church or the Bible. When surveyed, these respondents record "no religion." The "Dones" are those who report having had involvement, membership or leadership in the church. However, now they indicate in effect: "Been there, done that, doesn't work for me anymore."': Jim Farrer, 'Six Insights about "Nones" and "Dones"', Biblical Leadership, 7 August 2017, online at: https://www.biblicalleadership.com/blogs/six-insights-about-nones-and-dones, last accessed: 3 January 2021.

[29] Quotations from interviews which I conducted with Edmonton Neighbourhood Life participants in the autumn of 2014.

[30] Alan Roxburgh, 'Editorial: Questions of Place', *Journal of Missional Practice*, Winter 2018, available online at: http://journalofmissionalpractice.com/questions-of-place/, last accessed: 3 January 2021.

A fourth and final postmodern shift affecting our discipleship today is what I have labelled 'post-commuter'. North American culture has once again begun to realize the significance of the local, of place, of being rooted. In fact, there is increasing evidence in our communities of a 'late-modern cultural nostalgia for the local, a concept lost amid the big box stores and MacDonaldized franchises now homogenizing every square inch of the United States'.[31] Indeed, it is much more than nostalgia. As one NL couple reflected, 'We're learning the importance of proximity' and how this post-commuter shift impacts the Church, her identity, discipleship and witness.

Neighbourhood matters. For example, in my hometown, Edmonton, many city officials, civil servants, community leaders and neighbourhood boards are convinced of the power and significance of the local community for the social and personal well-being of citizens and the metropolis as a whole.[32] Edmonton has a 'Great Neighbourhoods' programme and numerous 'Go Local' emphases, including a walkability index as well as the Abundant Community Initiative (ACI), a foundational principle of which is 'human scale'. The culture is realizing that 'living above place' has allowed us to develop structures that keep cause-and-effect relationships far apart in space and time where we cannot have first-hand experience of them and therefore 'we have lost touch with social, economic, environmental and global impact'.[33]

This trend towards the local is also evident in our personal choices. For instance, a young family new to our neighbourhood explained that they were planning to stay for twenty-plus years. (In contrast, when we moved to Edmonton twenty-plus years ago, we said, 'two years max' as did most of our peers.) A NL Community member acknowledged that their move from another city after seventeen years was precipitated not by a job but by a search 'for a place to call home; a community of people who cared about each other, that we could contribute to and feel a part of'. Another couple shared how, as a young family moving into a new community, they had experienced the significance of 'next door' relationships: 'there is so much more to our life together, it is multidimensional'. Andy Crouch has concluded that while 'the twentieth-century American dream was to move

---

[31] Alden Bass, 'Closer to Home than we Realize: A Review of *No Home like Place: A Christian Theology of Place* by Leonard Hjalmarson', *Englewood Review of Books*, 22 August 2014, online at: http://erb.kingdomnow.org/leonard-hjalmarson-no-place-like-home-review/, accessed 4 March 2015.

[32] For example, John McKnight and Peter Block, *The Abundant Community: Awakening the Power of Families and Neighborhoods* (Oakland, CA: APA and Berrett Koehler, 2010); Will Miller and Glenn Sparks, *Refrigerator Rights: Creating Connections and Restoring Relationships* (Amherst, MA: White River Press, 2007; Later editions published as *Our Crucial Need for Close Connection*).

[33] Paul Sparks, Tim Soerens and Dwight J. Friesen, *The New Parish: How Neighborhood Churches are Transforming Mission, Discipleship and Community* (Downers Grove, IL: Intervarsity Press, 2014), 24.

out and move up; the twenty-first century dream seems to be to put down deeper roots'.[34] Wendell Berry believes that 'being rooted is perhaps the least recognized and most important need of humans'.[35]

There are also good theological reasons to renew our understanding of the significance of, and to recover a sense of, place and particularity. As one NL Community participant bluntly asserted, 'Commuter church might actually be contrary to who God is.' As Alden Bass observes, 'localism is the reigning philosophy of the day, and theologians have not been exempt from its pull'.[36] Nonetheless, while the 'pull' is being explored by numerous present-day theologians and practitioners, most of today's North American church attenders continue to commute often a significant distance to 'go to church'.[37]

As associations of commuters, North American churches have functioned and sought to achieve their purposes in 'spaces'. Commuter congregations occupy a generic space once or twice a week under the assumption that what we do *there* will attract and bear witness, disciple and grow those who attend and those whom we want to attend. As a result, the church is not a stakeholder in the neighbourhood and while perhaps able to be a service provider and 'do outreach' *there*, she is not an incarnational presence. Consequently, for church members who volunteer in this space, there is no sense of personal ownership or commitment. As outside Christian volunteers, we can choose when to engage, and can opt in and out of caring at all because we feel no particular responsibility for the people or the place. In contrast, as one NL member noted, 'being a neighbour makes it more real and integrated, like church is supposed to be – an extension into all of life – and neighbours can reveal how God works, how the world works and [thus] the context in which we live'.

Commuter church participation in a neighbourhood also fosters a certain response in the neighbourhood receiving the volunteers and services. The neighbours recognize that the church has its own agenda, and that it may, or may not, understand or have the best interests of the neighbourhood in mind. Indeed, a commuter congregation can engender negative responses from the residents who perceive them as outsiders using their resources and their place.

---

[34] Andy Crouch, 'Ten most significant Cultural Trends of the last Decade', quoted in Leonard Hjalmarson, *No Home like Place: A Christian Theology of Place* (Portland, OR: Urban Loft, 2014), 126.

[35] Leonard Hjalmarson, 'Becoming Doctors of the Church' (DM7015 Lecture, Northern Seminary, Chicago, IL, 23-27 January 2012).

[36] Bass, 'Closer to Home'.

[37] See, for example, Michael Frost, *Incarnate: The Body of Christ in an Age of Disengagement* (Downers Grove, IL: Intervarsity Press, 2014); Hjalmarson, *No Home like Place*; Sparks, Soerens and Friesen, *The New Parish*; C. Christopher Smith and John Pattison, *Slow Church: Cultivating Community in the Patient Way of Jesus* (Downers Grove, IL: Intervarsity Press, 2014).

The occupation of *space* as opposed to *place* forces us to wrestle again with what it means to be the church. Can we fulfil our mandate as God's people simply by doing good deeds somewhere / anywhere and going home? Might a church that operates in a space, a building which is not the 'habitus' of its people, be missing something critical, not only to its witness but also to its identity and formation as the people of God? What did Jesus mean when he prayed for the Church to be one? As the culture is rediscovering the importance of place, perhaps the Spirit is also nudging the Church to re-examine what it means for her to be 'the *personal presence* of Jesus by the Spirit *in* the world'.[38] 'A disembodied church', it has been quipped, 'doesn't have a leg to stand on!'

By contrast, the good news in the Scriptures portrays *a God who goes on mission in person and in place*. The wonder of the Incarnation is the presence of the loving God *in* our ordinary, everyday lives. To this the Church is now made, empowered and called to bear witness *in her very being*, as an incarnational presence. If this be so, the post-commuter shift in our culture is an invitation from the Spirit for the Church to think again about the implications of her formation in detached spaces around a myriad of affinities, from doctrine to musical preference. Meanwhile, fresh expressions of church, such as NL, are seeking to do experiments as the body of Christ in person and in place. In this new (ancient) paradigm, church is less about a space, a service and an organization and more about being a community of Jesus-followers doing life together in a neighbourhood such that they alert others to God's Kingdom come *near*. Perhaps Michael W. Smith's struggle to find his 'place in this world' is actually the struggle of an ethereal church now stirred by the wind of the Spirit to reimagine what it means to be the people of God by finding her place in this world.[39]

In Summary: Spies of a New Cultural Paradigms

As we have been experiencing the cultural shifts of our postmodern, post-Christendom context, the Spirit it seems, has been inviting us to trust and follow the Triune One into ancient-new places, postures, practices and paradigms.

This journey reminds me of the account in Numbers 13 of Moses sending the twelve spies to scout out the promised land in order to assure the people that this was a good way, a God-way, forward. Moses sought to provide his people with the assurances, which many in our churches may also need, as we face our own journey out of the wilderness. How will the body of Christ continue to proceed; trusting that *though foreign*, the land flows with milk and honey; *though remote*, God is present; *though not tilled in our ways*, the

---

[38] Craig Van Gelder, 'Incarnating the Gospel in Culture' (DM 7613 Lectures, Northern Seminary, Chicago, IL, 18-22 June 2012). Emphasis mine.
[39] Michael W. Smith, *Go West Young Man*, Album, (US, Reunion Records, 1990), Track 1.

fruit is good and plentiful; and *though inhabited*, we need not fear: this *place* is God's place, plan and gift!

Two spies (Joshua and Caleb) come back and, like many NL participants on the margins, are wide-eyed with anticipation. They have seen the potential of the promised land, the joy and wonder of following God to the place which he has already prepared for them and to which he is sending them with his power and authority. As one NL member declared, 'We've experienced the faithfulness of God; he'll be there, he is there when you're on his mission, you don't have to worry! It's so freeing! God has gone ahead and will be there long after we're gone. God is pursuing people; we just look for the ways the Spirit is doing that in our neighbours – and in us too!'

Others see only the giants in the land. Nonetheless, for those out ahead, kingdom discipleship is taking on new forms consonant with the promised land that they are settling in.[40] They are praying that as the Church is willing to enter into and inhabit her changing context(s), the Spirit will continue to reveal new entry points and develop new or renewed beliefs and practices to shape her into *more and more* of what she is *already* called and made to be: the sign, instrument and foretaste of the triune God who reigns both now and for evermore.

From 'Posts' to Signposts: What's on the Other Side?

In our NL Communities, the 'posts' have become not merely descriptions of what we know is being left behind, but sign*posts* as to where we are going. Posts demand an answer to the question, what's next: if not *that*, then what? The journeys of NL participants are a response to that question, not prescriptively but descriptively. They point to a way of being and doing by which the Church can disciple and bear witness *today*. This entry point might be summed up as *communitas*: authentic, Spirit-led relational community that participates in the mission of God as she lives in, with and amongst her neighbours. *Communitas*, an expression of faithful presence, is what comes out 'on the other side' of the four posts, namely incarnational engagement (versus attractional), humble posture (versus positional), life as witness or story living (versus universal language) and place and proximity (versus commuter). It is not simply theoretical work but an anticipation of, and a link to, the 'daily practices and lifelong pursuits' that, as Lau Branson affirms, embody the gospel.[41] Thus, NL participants feel called and empowered to engage in postures and practices that envision and cultivate new forms of an ancient discipleship DNA of church as

---

[40] Schreiter's approach as described by Stanley Grenz and John Franke, *Beyond Foundationalism: Shaping Theology in a Postmodern Context* (Louisville, KY: Westminster John Knox, 2001), 155.

[41] Mark Lau Branson, *Memories, Hopes and Conversations: Appreciative Inquiry and Congregational Change* (Herndon, VA: Alban Institute, 2004), 62.

'God's *personal presence* in the world [in our neighbourhoods] through the Spirit'.[42]

Postures and Practices

Prompted by their stories and experiences, NL participants have been developing postures and practices that are shaping them to 'participate [more] fully in God's mission in [their] particular context[s]'.[43] Nancy Ammerman asserts that 'practices are the pathways that shape our lives. Practices take us from the memories of the past and steer us through the uncertainties of the present.'[44] NL practices are framed by three postures that we believe bear witness to the incarnational, missional God. These postures have been helping us to discover how to disciple and be *communitas* in our neighbourhoods, tangibly revealing the reign of God, the oneness of the body that Jesus prayed for, and the keeping of the great commandment (Jn 17.11). The three postures that NL has found significant are 'Among', 'In' and 'With'. Although we have yet to live into them fully, we are nonetheless aware that the articulation of them, the stories told around them, and our ongoing experimentation are shaping and guiding us anew as 'his family of disciples' in our neighbourhoods.[45]

(a) The Posture and Practices of AMONG

Our first posture is that of 'Living Among' our neighbours as neighbours.[46] Jesus identified himself as embodying the Kingdom of God *among* the people (Lk. 17.21). 'Among' practices include sharing our lives and practising hospitality, celebration and God's 'one another' plan.[47]

(b) The Posture and Practices of IN

Our second set of practices focuses on how disciples are to abide *in* Christ. Jesus's example and instructions are reiterated in John's first letter.[48] The

---

[42] Craig Van Gelder, *The Essence of the Church: A Community Created by the Spirit* (Grand Rapids, MI: Baker, 2000), 25. Emphasis mine.

[43] Craig Van Gelder, *The Ministry of the Missional Church* (Grand Rapids, MI: Baker, 2007), 182.

[44] Nancy T. Ammerman et al., *Studying Congregations: A New Handbook* (Nashville, TN: Abingdon, 1998), 34.

[45] Brad Harper and Paul Louis Metzger, *Exploring Ecclesiology: An Evangelical and Ecumenical Introduction* (Ada, MI: Brazos Press, 2009), 27.

[46] 'Living among' is articulated in verses such as Mt. 4.23; 18.20; Mk 6.6b; 9.19a; Lk. 7.16; 17.20-21; 22.27, 37; 24.36; Jn 1.14, 26-27; 20.19; Ac. 2.22; 4.12; 1 Jn 4.9; Rev. 21.3.

[47] 'God's One Another Plan' refers to over thirty Bible verses that employ the 'one another' phrase, e.g. Rom. 12.10; Col. 3.13, 16; 1 Thess. 5.11, 15; Jas 4.11.

[48] 1 Jn 2.5b-6, 24, 28; 3.17-18, 24; 4.13-19.

cultivation of 'in' practices are instrumental as we seek to be *communitas,* as described above, in our neighbourhoods. For us to embody and bear witness to the Kingdom of God near and to be shaped by it and, by love for our neighbours, we must continue to nurture our personal and communal relationship with the Triune God. 'In' practices thus include what have been traditionally called spiritual disciplines, such as prayer, dwelling in the text, sabbath-keeping and sharing in the sacraments. In all of these, God's ordinary people embrace a missional attentiveness aimed at discovering what God is up to in the neighbourhood and joining the Spirit at work there.

(c) The Posture and Practices of WITH

In our third cluster of practices, we assume the posture of 'with', serving *with* the people of peace (Lk. 10), *with* our neighbours and neighbourhoods that we all might increasingly experience God's yet-to-be-grasped Shalom Kingdom and recognize our parts in God's story. This is the 'discipline of nurturing [a] good place means inhabiting [it], believing in [it], investing in [it] and doing everything we can to make [it] fully human … investing both resources and energy in order to create a community of shalom; a community of completeness and wholeness in which people individually and collectively experience health, prosperity, security and spiritual renewal'.[49]

Thus, by practising 'with-ness', we are seeking to collaborate, engage and be present in the midst of neighbourhood life. Again, there are practices that we believe guide us into humble engagement *with* our neighbours as Christ-followers. They include compassion in action; seeking peace and justice; stewarding well the earth and all its assets; giving generously and cheerfully; and sharing and affirming every neighbour's gifts, wisdom and resources.

Conclusion: The 'Sent to Follow' Adventure

As these postures and practices are being tried out, enacted and 'made flesh' by participants on this journey, they are meeting the Triune One and discovering more of what they are called and made to be as Christ's disciples, right where God has placed them.

As I ponder the wonder and joy of these experiences – this 'experiment on the margins' – I speculate as to why the Church has so often settled for so much less. Such pondering reminds me of the typical answer I get to the question: What does it mean to be a Christian (a disciple of Christ)? 'Well, it means I believe in Jesus as my Lord and Saviour; and I go to church, pray, read my Bible and try to be a good person.'

And that's it. How motivating is *that*?

---

[49] Simon Carey Holt, *God Next Door: Spirituality and Mission in the Neighbourhood* (Brunswick East, Vic.: Acorn Press, 2007), 132.

I wonder, in contrast, how Jesus's first followers might answer the question. I imagine them saying, with passion, conviction and intensity something like this:

> Well, it's been the craziest, most exciting, wild, life-changing experience you could ever imagine, *more than we could have ever imagined!* We have never before experienced such love and acceptance. It's so empowering and freeing! Yet Jesus is always pushing us – sending, challenging, confusing and inspiring us. Our heads are spinning and our hearts are pounding almost all the time. He's got us being friends with people we would have never even glanced at before; and going places and hanging out where we never would have dreamed of finding ourselves. We're learning to listen, to follow, to trust and to love *everyone.* Life will never be the same again – *we'll* never be the same again. Although it scares us half to death most of the time and we've had to let a lot of things go, we wouldn't trade it for anything. Of course, there have been sacrifices, not least of which are our agendas and self-righteousness. We've even had to leave some people behind … yet there's no life like it; in fact, there's no life! Wherever Jesus leads, wherever he sends, *that's* where *the* Kingdom is and that's where we want to be. Shalom, joy, grace, mystery, sacrifice, adventure – that's how we would describe being a disciple of Jesus: *the way, the truth, the life.*

I wonder what being a disciple of Jesus will look like for you and me, and the church in the next decade, the next century. As we step out into this new promised land, where we have been sent to follow, may we see, not giants but giant grapes, the fruit of the Triune One at work in, amongst, with and through us for the sake of his kingdom and in his name. Amen.

16. The Future of African *Christian* Theology: Convergences between Ancient Ethiopian Orthodoxy and Contemporary Evangelicalism

Tekletsadik Belachew

This chapter explores the links between ancient African Orthodoxy (i.e. Coptic and particularly Ethiopian Orthodoxy), and contemporary Evangelicalism. Major similarities between Ethiopian Orthodox theology and contemporary African Christian theology are evident when considering cosmological views and the prevalence of the supernatural; the deployment of alternative theological methods, different from those of scholasticism or the Enlightenment; the prevalence of a sense of mystery (mystical or apophatic theology) in relation to spirituality and prayer; and features such as ethical conservatism, symbolism (in textuality, orality and iconography), and the use of liturgies and rituals. It will argue that the concept of tradition or memory can serve as an embryonic tie uniting newer African Christian theologies – including those of Catholicism, Evangelicalism and the African Independent Churches – with the enduring legacy of their spiritual ancestors, that of ancient African Orthodoxy. This argument alters the assumed and habitual periodization of the history of African Christian theology, and relieves African Christian theology of over-dependence on post-Enlightenment, scholastic 'Western' theology and on purely secular sources, without denying the value of inter-connectedness in theologizing, especially in an era of world Christianity.

Orthodox and Evangelical theological traditions can cross-fertilize one another in an African setting. For Evangelicals, dialogue with the Orthodox can provide a sense of appreciation for the living and ancient tradition, *Sankofa*, a return to the sources. Orthodox can learn lessons from African Evangelical innovation on different theological issues. Tradition and innovation are not mutually exclusive.

Common Roots of Africa's Ancient Christian Past

As Joachim Persoon observed, 'The relationship between Ethiopian and wider African Christianity is a neglected area of research.'[1] An African dimension of Ethiopian Christianity is yet to be explored. Christian faith in Africa is as old as

---

[1] Joachim Persoon, 'New Perspectives on Ethiopian and African Christianity: Communalities and Contrasts in the Twentieth Century Experience', *Exchange* 34 (2005), 306. A number of scholars have been preoccupied with the Judaic element in Ethiopian Christianity at the expense of the African element.

Christianity itself. Unfortunately, most of the ancient Church Fathers are often mistakenly portrayed as Europeans. For so long, theological texts depicted African Church Fathers and Mothers as if they were Europeans. But against such disremembering, a number of growing ecclesiastical and scholarly voices in and out of Africa are paying a deserved tribute to the continent's ancient gifts to world Christianity.

Pope Paul VI, on 29 October 1967, greeted Africans by recalling Africa's glorious memories of the Christian past, starting from Mark the Evangelist and going on to numerous saints, martyrs, monks and nuns (Desert Fathers and Mothers), theologians, teachers and leaders.

> In conveying our greetings to Africa, we cannot but recall the glories of her Christian past.
>
> We think of the Christian churches of Africa whose origins go back to the time of the Apostles and are traditionally associated with the name and teaching of Mark the Evangelist. We think of their countless saints, martyrs, confessors and virgins, and recall the fact that from the second to the fourth century Christian life in north Africa was vigorous and had a leading place in theological study and literary production.
>
> The names of the great doctors and writers come at once to mind, men like Origen, St. Athanasius, and St. Cyril, leaders of Alexandrian school, and at the other end of the north African coastline, Tertullian, St. Cyprian and above all St. Augustine, one of the most brilliant lights of the Christian world. We shall mention the great saints of the desert. Paul, Anthony, and Pachomius, the first founders of monastic life, which later spread through their example in both the East and the West. And among many others we want to mention St. Frumentius, known by the name of Abba Salama, who was consecrated bishop by St. Athanasius and became the Apostle of Ethiopia.
>
> The noble examples, as also the saintly African Popes, Victor I, Melchiades and Gelasius I, belong to the common heritage of the Church, and the Christian writers of Africa remain today a basic source for deepening our knowledge of the history of salvation in the light of the Word of God.[2]

An American Evangelical, Thomas C. Oden (1931-2016), founded and directed the Center for Early African Christianity (CEAC), in consultation with African scholars and church leaders.[3] The twenty-nine volumes of the *Ancient Christian Commentary on Scripture* (ACCS) and the realization of

---

[2] Pope Paul VI, *Africae Terrarum* ('On Africa'), 29 October 1967 (Washington DC: United States Catholic Conference, 1967), 3.

[3] See Thomas C. Oden's works: *How Africa Shaped the Christian Mind: Rediscovering the African Seedbed of Western Christianity* (Downers Grove, IL: IVP, 2007); *The African Memory of Mark: Reassessing Early Church Tradition* (Downers Grove, IL: IVP Academic, 2011); *Early Libyan Christianity: Uncovering a North African Tradition* (Downers Grove, IL: IVP Academic, 2011); *The Rebirth of African Orthodoxy: Return to Foundations* (Nashville, TN: Abingdon, 2016); *Africa's Gift: A Christian Legacy* (New Haven, CT: ICCS Press, [2015]); Thomas C. Oden with Curt Niccum (eds), *The Songs of Africa: The Ethiopian Canticles* (New Haven, CT: ICCS Press, 2017).

the ancient African contribution led to the formation of CEAC.[4] Joel C. Elowsky, who served as managing director of ACCS and a research director of CEAC, reported:

> When the Center for Early African Christianity formed during the last decade, it was decided that a consultation should be held on the continent of Africa. The question was where such a meeting should be held. It was decided that the logical place was to be Addis Ababa in Ethiopia because Ethiopia had not only one of the earliest Christian communities in sub-Saharan Africa, but also one of the most enduring.[5]

An African Evangelical theologian (of the diaspora), Tite Tiénou, points to the lack of continuity in contemporary African Christianity:

> Alexandria, in Egypt, and Carthage, in Tunisia, were important centers for Christian theology. For many centuries Christianity flourished in Nubia. The Christian faith has had continuous existence in Egypt and Ethiopia. There is, however, little continuity between these earlier forms and expressions of African Christianity and Christianity as it exists in most of Africa today.[6]

At times, Evangelicalism confuses the Reformation's *sola scriptura* (Scripture alone) with a total rejection of tradition. But that was never the intended meaning of *sola scriptura*. Most of the reformers were indebted to the Church Fathers. It does not negate tradition, for Scripture is never alone.[7] No serious Evangelical scholar can subscribe to an attitude which discounts tradition by appealing to *sola Scriptura* or *nuda Scriptura*.[8] On the other hand, we should distinguish between tradition (the living faith of the dead) and traditionalism (the dead faith of the living).[9] For the Orthodox, tradition does not mean custom or something remote to the Bible.[10] Thus the living

---

[4] See all patristic publications published by IVP; the Ancient Christian Commentary Series has been seminal in this respect. Subsequently, there were the five-volume on Ancient Christian Doctrine series, as well as Ancient Christian Texts.

[5] Joel Elowsky, 'Ethiopian Christianity: Review of *Abyssinian Christianity* by Abba Abraham Buruk Woldegaber and Mario Alexis Portella (Pismo Beach, CA: BP Editing, 2012)', 2014, online at the CEAC blog: https://www.earlyafricanchristianity.com/blog/.

[6] Tite Tiénou, 'Methodology in African Christian Theologies … Revisited', unpublished paper given to a symposium at Trinity Evangelical Divinity School, Deerfield, IL, 30 April 2015 (used with the author's kind permission).

[7] See Irenaeus of Lyons, *Against Heresies, Book III*, ed. Robert M. Grant, Early Church Fathers (London and New York, Routledge, 1997), 123-42; Kevin J. Vanhoozer, *The Drama of Doctrine: A Canonical-Linguistic Approach to Christian Theology* (Louisville, KY: Westminster John Knox, 2005), 154.

[8] See Martin Chemnitz (1522-86), 'Concerning Traditions: From the First Decree of the Fourth Session of the Council of Trent', in *Examination of the Council of Trent, Part I*, trans. Fred Kramer (St Louis, MO: Concordia, 1971).

[9] For further elaboration, see Joel C. Elowsky, 'Scripture and Tradition in an Evangelical Context', *Concordia Journal* 42 (2016), 54. This formulation of the distinction is credited to Jaroslav Pelikan.

[10] St Irenaeus of Lyons provided a foundational theology of Tradition in *Against Heresies*. He regarded holy Tradition as a standard for arriving at the truth. Whereas

nature of tradition and the necessary distinction between tradition and traditions may pave the way for dialogue.[11]

African Christian theology ought to wrestle with both Scripture and the history of exegesis. In this regard, as Tiénou recommended, '[f]or active theology to exist in Africa, theologians must *understand the Church*, diachronically and synchronically; they must *understand African cultures in the multiplicity of their dimensions*; they must *understand Scripture*.'[12] The Botswana theologian Musa W. Dube underlined the long history of reading the Bible in diverse African contexts.

> Historically, Christianity in North Africa is as old as the early church. The latter gave us the prevailing Egyptian Coptic Church and the Ethiopian Orthodox church and a whole line of celebrated church fathers such as Origen of Alexandria, Tertullian, and Augustine of Hippo. While North African Christianity was the earliest, sub-Saharan Christianity is now the most thriving. The history of the latter covers five centuries. The Bible has been read within pre-colonial, colonial, struggle-for-independence, post-independence, neocolonial and globalization contexts.[13]

The Bible has a long history, a formative role and an enduring legacy in Africa. Let us turn to examine how the memory of ancient African Christianity survived, starting from Mark the Evangelist and gospel writer.

African Orthodoxy as a Church with a Memory

Christianity in Africa has a two-thousand-year-old story. Ghanaian theologian Kwame Bediako (1945-2008), after delivering the Frumentius lectures (established to honour the first bishop of the Ethiopian Orthodox Church) in Addis Ababa in February 2001, reflected on the Ethiopian Orthodox Church. In two articles, he articulated the thesis that 'The Ethiopian Orthodox Church is a church with a memory.'[14] Furthermore, he stated, the Ethiopian memory of the Bible goes back three thousand years, to the Old Testament story of the Ethiopian

---

Gnostics respect neither Scripture nor Tradition, the succession of clergy in the churches is traceable to the apostles. However, a distinction must be made between traditions and Tradition.

[11] John Meyendorff, *Living Tradition: Orthodox Witness in the Contemporary World* (Crestwood, NY: SVS Press, 1978), 21.

[12] Tiénou, 'Methodology'.

[13] Musa W. Dube, 'Introduction: The Scramble for Africa as the Biblical Scramble for Africa: Postcolonial Perspectives', in Musa W. Dube, Andrew Mbuvi and Dora Mbuwayesango, (eds), *Postcolonial Perspectives in African Biblical Interpretations* (Atlanta, GA: Society of Biblical Literature, 2012), 1-2.

[14] Kwame Bediako, '"Ethiopia shall soon stretch out her hands to God" (Ps. 68:31). African Christians Living the Gospel: A Turning Point in Christian History?', in Kwame Bediako et al. (eds), *A New Day Dawning: African Christians living the Gospel. Essays in Honor of Dr. J. J. (Hans) Visser* (Zoetermeer: Uitgeverij Boekencentrum, 2004), 33; Kwame Bediako, 'Africa and Christian Identity: Recovering an Ancient Story', *Princeton Seminary Bulletin* 21 (2004), 153-61.

Queen of Sheba and King Solomon of Israel.[15] This story is archived in the *Kebrà Nagast* ('The Glory of the Kings').[16] He also listed a number of examples of what the Ethiopian Church remembers in connection with the Coptic Church of Egypt. In particular, there was the great leader, St Athanasius, patriarch of Alexandria, who consecrated St Frumentius as the first bishop of Ethiopia in the fourth century. But Ethiopian Orthodoxy's memory goes back further, to St Mark.[17] Mark, the gospel writer and narrator, was an African born in Cyrene (Libya), who collaborated closely with Peter the apostle and travelled across three continents. He founded the church in Alexandria and ordained leaders for Cyrene before being martyred in Alexandria on 26 April 68. To this day, the Coptic Church of Egypt and the Ethiopian Orthodox Church venerate Mark the Evangelist as an African apostle and gospel compiler. In addition, Alexandria is regarded as the See of St Mark.[18]

Giyorgis of Sägla, a fifteenth-century Ethiopian monk and theologian, remarked: 'He who is likened to a lion is Mark. He destroyed the idolatrous altars throughout the provinces of Egypt roaring like a lion, teaching the Gospel.'[19] Similarly, Lisane-Worq Gebre-Giyorgis, a present-day Ethiopian Orthodox scholar, displays an Ethiopian memory of Mark as the apostle of Africa:

> … twenty-seven years passed after the ascension of the Lord, but due to the remoteness of the nation(s) they were not able to reach all by the Gospel. They cast lots and dispersed according to their portion (nations), then Mark the Evangelist took the whole of Africa as his lot to share the Gospel, then he taught the Gospel to the people and baptized them. When the number of the assembly grew, through his preaching and the unity of the congregation, the Church was established in Alexandria in the name of the Paraclete. On *Sene* [June] 5, Year of Mercy 61 [Ethiopian calendar], the liturgy was conducted for the first time.[20]

Thus the evangelization and discipleship of Africa is tied to Mark the gospel writer, an African apostle and the earliest martyr. Let us now explore the development of African martyrdom literature and its lingering effect.

---

[15] Bediako, 'African Christians', 32-33.

[16] See *Kebra Nagast: The Queen of Sheba and her only Son Menyelik I*, trans. E. A. Wallis Budge (London: Oxford University Press, 1932).

[17] For instance, there are theological corpuses available including the *Haymanota Abaw* (a compilation of theological work) and the *Qerlos* (a corpus attributed mainly to St Cyril of Alexandria but including other patristic sources). See Alessandro Bausi and Alberto Camplani, 'New Ethiopic Documents for the History of Christian Egypt', *Zeitschrift für Antikes Christentum / Journal of Ancient Christianity* 17 (2013), 215-47.

[18] Oden, *African Memory*.

[19] Giyorgis of Sägla, *Mäshafä Säatat*, *'The Book of Hours'*, *'The Book of the Glory of Day and Night' or Horologium* (Addis Ababa: Tinsae Zegubae, 1986), 58 (my translation from Ge'ez-Amharic).

[20] Lisane-Work Gebre-Giyorgis, *Tintawi Serate Mahlet ZeAbune Yared Liqe. The Ancient Order of Singing of our Father Yared, the Master / the Melodious* (Addis Ababa: Maison des Études Ethiopiennes, 1997), 80 (my translation from Amharic).

From Ancient Martyrdom to the Synaxarium

For ancient Christians in Africa and elsewhere, martyrdom was a public liturgy.[21] The public confession, procession and sacrifice contrasted with the pagan experience of Roman emperor-worship. For Christians, the parallel was the sacrifice of Christ and the Eucharist. So the martyrdom texts were used to train the catechumens for 'their own quasi-eucharistic sacrifice of martyrdom'.[22] Christian martyrs combated the violence of pagan religio-political persecution, not as victims but as victim-victors.[23]

Martyrdom as public liturgical procession was a testimony in community with others. They were imitating the death of Christ, from the perspective of an eschatological hope of the Kingdom of God above worldly powers.[24] It was a 'gift of love' (a eucharistic term), the martyrs appealing to the suffering of Christ and the Old Testament prophets. As Young explains, there was a distinction between the eucharistic sacrifice and that of martyrdom: 'when the eucharist was still private, not open to non-Christian view, the martyrs' sacrifice was public and dramatic'.[25] The martyrs viewed their lives in terms of the parable of the sower: they died to yield fruit, to win the lives (even at the spectacles) of potential catechumens, for their object was the conversion of the world.[26]

Origen wrote two books on martyrdom: *Contra Celsum*, a response to a pagan accuser of Christian martyrdom, and an *Exhortation to Martyrdom*, intended to equip the faithful to memorize Scripture quotations. His writings on martyrdom drew attention to three aspects, as athletic contest, as fulfilment of mystical spirituality and as eucharistic sacrifice. Origen asserted that 'those who [are] confessing Christ participate in a heavenly liturgy'. Being a confessor makes one a true martyr, but not every confessor ends up being a martyr; and 'martyrs are sacrificial priests'. Finally, in *Exhortation to Martyrdom*, Origen noted that martyrs are to go 'in procession before the world'.[27]

Martyrdom literature continued to be developed in Egypt and Ethiopia, especially in the Synaxarium. The Ethiopic Synaxarium expanded the Arabic version and continued its use in the liturgy. There is also the continuing tradition expressed in the genre of hagiographic literature known as *Gädl*, commemorating the lives of saints and martyrs. For instance, *The Life of Takla Haimanot* (*c.*1215-1313) is a celebrated testimony to its subject's faith,

---

[21] Robin Darling Young, *In Procession before the World: Martyrdom as Public Liturgy in Early Christianity* (Milwaukee, WI: Marquette University Press, 2001).

[22] Young, *In Procession*, 2.

[23] Inspiration for the martyrdom texts came from different textual sources, including Jewish, New Testament (including Revelation, Hebrews and 1 Peter) and post-apostolic texts (1 Clement).

[24] Young, *In Procession*, 10, 13.

[25] Young, *In Procession*, 12.

[26] Young, *In Procession*, 37.

[27] Young, *In Procession*, 14, 56, 59.

both in the Ethiopian Orthodox and the Coptic churches. Its missiological implications are yet to be explored. It is a witness that has transformed the lives of multitudes. Andrew F. Walls remarked that Takla Haymanot trained others in the life of prayer, in copying biblical manuscripts, and in an ascetic lifestyle, so that disciples were ready to evangelize and not to shy away from spiritual or worldly powers.[28] Walls added: 'There are not many places in the world where a church has a continuous history of nearly 1700 years. East Africa is one of them, and the witness of Takla Haymanot and his like is part of the reason.'[29]

We have already discussed the common roots of ancient African Christianity exemplified in the memory of the Ethiopian Orthodox Church. We turn now to explore the commonalities between ancient African Orthodoxy and newer African Evangelicalism.

Commonalities in Theological Outlook

African Christianity matters not only because of its ancient legacy but also because of its phenomenal contemporary demographic growth.[30] As Walls put it: 'The theology that matters will be theology where the people are.'[31] Without denying the academic and public dimensions of theologizing, the church is the primary locus for this. Thus African Christianity matters for world Christianity and Christian theological scholarship. What, then, are the main features of contemporary African Christianity and what are the areas of possible convergence?

Prayer and the Sense of Mystery in African Cosmologies

In doing theology, African Evangelicals can learn from the Orthodox in the domains of spiritual exegesis and the centrality of worship.[32] In Alexandrian and Axumite (Ethiopian) Christianity, theology and worship (especially anaphoras as eucharistic prayers in the liturgy) are intertwined.

Commonalities in African theologies are best discovered through an African cosmology or shared through religio-cultural worldviews that manifest themselves in and through embodied spirituality and prayer.[33] An

---

[28] Andrew F. Walls, 'The Cost of Discipleship: The Witness of the African Church', *Word and World* 25.4 (Fall 2005), 439.

[29] Walls, 'The Cost of Discipleship', 440.

[30] John L. Allen Jr, *The Future Church: How Ten Trends are Revolutionizing the Catholic Church* (New York & London: Doubleday, 2009), especially ch. 4.

[31] Quoted by Kwame Bediako. 'African Theology as a Challenge for Western Theology', in Martien E. Brinkman and Dirk van Keulen (eds), *Christian Identity in Cross-Cultural Perspective* (Amsterdam: Meinema, Zoetermeer, 2003), 54.

[32] See Brian E. Daley, 'Some Reflections on Orthodoxy as a Theological Resource', *Pro Ecclesia* 6 (1997), 400-5.

[33] Persoon, 'New Perspectives'. 309.

African cosmology embraces both the material and spiritual worlds and is significantly different from that of Western Christianity, which has been decisively shaped by scholasticism and the Enlightenment.[34] The Enlightenment's narrow view of the universe affected how people experienced the Bible, prayer, liturgy and theology. The Enlightenment universe is a purely human realm, unlike the enchanted world that includes transcendental realities and the spirit realm. In Hiebert's words, such unbelief in the 'excluded middle' involves the transcendental celestial powers of angels and demons.[35] It is a secular dualism that compartmentalizes religion and science.[36]

An African holistic cosmology is close to the biblical worldview and is mediated through symbolism, ritual, spirituality, prayer and healing. In it, belief in the supernatural may lead to a holistic theology of the cosmos, which in turn shapes one's sense of mystery, prayer, miracle and healing. As Persoon explains:

> Biblical and African ideas are combined in the grassroots indigenisation processes of cosmological beliefs that have occurred in Ethiopia and among AICs [African Independent Churches]. True to widespread African concepts the faithful view themselves as 'surrounded by an active, dangerous spirit world that requires constant and vigilant intervention to be safe and whole … Christianity has not evaded the issues of a crowded dynamic universe of persons, souls, spirits and evil. Hence, there was a strong emphasis on exorcism and spiritual healing.[37]

This sense of holistic spirituality expressed in prayer, healing, exorcism and a concern for health demonstrates how African cosmology defies the divide between the sacred and the secular.[38]

From a Christian point of view, as Tiénou noted, 'Worship precedes theology. We all learn to pray before we learn to reflect on the contents and meanings of our prayers.'[39] He adds: 'right theology begins, continues and ends with right prayer'.[40] Unfortunately, African Evangelicals have not reflected adequately on theology, spirituality and prayer in the light of their lived experience and religious background.[41] Yet pre-Christian African

---

[34] See Kallistos Ware, 'Scholasticism and Orthodoxy: Theological Method as a Factor in the Schism', *Eastern Churches Review* 5 (1973), 16-27.

[35] Paul G. Hiebert, 'The Flaw of the Excluded Middle', in Ralph Winter (ed), *Perspective on the World Christian Movement*, 3rd ed. (Pasadena, CA: William Carey Library, 1999), 417.

[36] Hiebert, 'Flaw', 418.

[37] Persoon, 'New Perspectives', 319.

[38] See Laurenti Magesa, *What is Not Sacred: African Spirituality* (Maryknoll, NY: Orbis, 2013).

[39] Tite Tiénou, 'Lessons from the Prayer Habits of the Church in Africa', in D. A. Carson (ed), *Teach Us to Pray* (Grand Rapids, MI: Baker / Exeter: Paternoster, 1990), 268.

[40] Tiénou, 'Lessons', 268.

[41] Tiénou, 'Lessons', 268.

religiosity, structured around the triangle of God, man and the adversary, shaped the basic structure of African Christian prayer. According to Tiénou, the lessons that can be learned from the prayer habits of the Church in Africa are, first and foremost, that 'our theological stories are useless if they are not rooted in prayer', and second, 'the importance of community prayer'.[42] Thus an African narrative theology is closely tied to prayer and stories of the lived experiences of Christians past and present. African narrative theology ought to take seriously the history of exegesis and the living faith of the dead. It is vital to keep prayer and theology together.[43] 'If prayer is the mother of theology, then anyone interested in developing an authentic African Christian theology should seek a greater understanding of prayer in African Christian communities.'[44]

In the Ethiopian Orthodox tradition, theology is best expressed through the liturgy. What one finds in the liturgy is reflected in the *Ammestu a'amada mestir* (አምስቱ አዕማደ ምሥጢር), the five fundamental mysteries of the faith. The *mestir* (Ge'ez and Amharic ምሥጢር) or mysteries are the doctrines of the Trinity, the Incarnation, baptism, the Eucharist and the resurrection of the dead. Summarizing the ancient desert spirituality of Egypt, Syrian, and Palestine, Bradley Nassif noted that 'a disembodied faith can be anemic because spiritual life is physically rooted in the incarnation'.[45] Similarly, the holy icons are liturgical and dogmatic affirmations of the incarnate Christ who becomes truly human for us and for our salvation. The doctrine of the incarnation as well as the holy icons thus exclude docetic tendencies which deny the true humanity of Christ, the goodness of creation, the materiality of salvation and the embodied nature of spirituality.

The reading of Scriptures, inner spirituality and contemplation, and intellectual acumen – each of which impacts the larger society – are never compartmentalized. Evagrius Ponticus famously put it like this: 'If you are a theologian, you truly pray. If you truly pray, you are [will be] a theologian.'[46] Such prayer is always communal and liturgical, as he shows in *Ad Monachos*.[47] A further quotation from Evagrius solidifies this argument for the interconnection of theology and liturgy as a way of life in antiquity:

> Flesh of Christ: virtues of *praktike*
> He who eats it, passionless shall he be.
> Blood of Christ: contemplation of created things;

---

[42] Tiénou, 'Lessons', 270.

[43] Tiénou, 'Lessons', 271.

[44] Tiénou, 'Lessons', 268.

[45] Bradley Nassif, *Bringing Jesus to the Desert* (Grand Rapids, MI: Zondervan, 2011), 19

[46] Evagrius Ponticus, *The Praktikos and Chapters on Prayer*, trans. John Eudes Bamerger (Kalamazoo, MI: Cistercian Publications, 1972), 65 ('The 153 Chapters on Prayer', no. 60).

[47] Robin Darling Young, '*Theologia* in the Early Church', *Communion* 24 (1997), 690.

he who drinks it, by it becomes wise.
Breast of the Lord: knowledge of God;
he who rests against it, a theologian shall he be.[48]

In the early church, the pursuit of spirituality, including prayer and other ascetic practices, were part and parcel of the intellectual's endeavour. Four early African theologians, Tertullian, Cyprian, Origen and Augustine, wrote *On the Lord's Prayer*.[49] These treatises emerged from their practice in the Christian family of North Africa and explicate the content and posture of prayer, giving attention to both mind and body. Early African and Alexandrian theology, in the words of Joel C. Elowsky 'mirror what African theology today strives to be: theologically and intellectually rooted while also practically engaged'.[50]

African Theology in/through Symbolism and Sacraments

Numerous African Evangelical theologians have suggested that African theology is not restricted to the textual.[51] African theologies are expressed in oral forms such as discourses, rites and rituals, and liturgical performances. Clifton R. Clarke has contended for the epistemological value of orality and symbolism in African theology.[52] Symbolism exists in orality, iconography and metaphorical or poetic theology. Spiritual discourses of power find expression in the religious use of symbolism, as in the veneration of icons, crosses, the *Tabot* or ark and other artifacts.

Both the Ethiopian Orthodox and the African Independent Churches 'have a great veneration of the cross, the ultimate metonym of sacred power'.[53] Ogbu Kalu (1943-2009), a noted Nigerian Evangelical, speaks of the multifaceted faith expressions of Ethiopian Christianity in this way:

> Ethiopian contributions to Christian art, architecture, music, literacy and liturgy have remained enduring. The Ethiopian church, with its large number of aesthetic crosses, remained in splendid isolation and served as an ingredient of the national culture, until Europe rediscovered it in the fifteenth century in the quest for the mythical kingdom of Prester John. This contact saved it from

---

[48] Young, '*Theologia*', 690.

[49] Tertullian, Cyprian and Origen, *On the Lord's Prayer*, trans. Alistair Stewart-Sykes (Crestwood, NY: SVS Press, 2004).

[50] Joel C. Elowsky, 'Early Alexandrian Theology as a Way of Life', in David T. Ngong (ed), *A New History of African Christian Thought: From Cape to Cairo* (Abingdon: Routledge, 2016), 40.

[51] Kwame Bediako, 'Five Theses on Modern African Christianity: A Manifesto', in Robert L. Gallagher and Paul Hertig (eds), *Landmark Essays in Mission and World Christianity* (Maryknoll, NY: Orbis, 2009), 95-115.

[52] Clifton R. Clarke, 'African Epistemology and Christian Faith: Towards the Epistemic Use of Orality and Symbolism in African Christian Scholarship', *Journal of African Christian Thought* 9 (2006), 56-64.

[53] Persoon, 'New Perspectives', 319.

the jihadist attack of the imam, Ahmed Gran (the left-handed), but it exposed it to disruptive foreign influences, especially efforts to annex it to Rome.[54]

Similarly, ancient Egyptian Christianity produced a rich theological and spiritual literature. Today, the Coptic Church passes on its legacy mainly, and vividly, through the holy icons. In McGuckin's words:

> As Alexandria's role as university city, and cauldron of theological change, ended for the Christians, the Icon stepped forward, as it were, to continue to resist both the old religion, and the new (Islam). Mutely the Egyptian church continued to show its deep devotion to Christ, the *Theotokos,* and its martyred saintly *fellahin,* in the quiet majesty of the holy icons.[55]

Symbolism is vital for contemporary African theology. In this regard, Jean-Marc Éla, a Catholic theologian from Cameroon, observed that 'in Africa, the invisible is as real as the visible; the two are inseparable, and communicate with each other through appropriate symbols'.[56] Such an epistemological outlook is different from the post-Enlightenment and scholastic outlook that is dominant in the West. The pervasiveness of symbolism in Africa demonstrates that 'African civilization is a civilization of symbols … Africans live then in a "forest of symbols," a unique way of maintaining their relationship to the universe.'[57] In many places in Africa, oral symbolism and religions have great affinity. 'In Africa, religion is a system of signs and symbols that attributes primacy to the spoken word. Africa's symbolic system, which can lead to an understanding of the African "language," includes forms of oral expression, gestures, rituals, actions, and so on, embracing institutions, objects and beings.'[58] Symbolism in different forms such as folklore and poetry is thus indispensable in African theology, including Ethiopian Orthodoxy. African theology contributes to the rediscovery of symbolic language that scholasticism eliminated. The value of storytelling in Africa has diverse functions: simply telling the story, passing on knowledge and theologizing.[59] In such theologizing, the infinite God is approached with human humility. Mabiala Justin-Robert Kenzo, an Evangelical theologian born and raised in the Democratic Republic of Congo, noted that theological poetry represents a 'multifaceted form of

---

[54] Ogbu Kalu (ed), *African Christianity: An African Story* (Trenton, NJ: Africa World Press, 2005), 29.

[55] J. A. McGuckin, 'Early Christian Egypt and the Origins of the Icon', in Richard Temple (ed), *Masterpieces of Early Christian Art* (London: Temple Gallery, 2005), 14.

[56] Jean-Marc Éla, *My Faith as an African,* trans. Johan Pairman Brown and Susan Perry (Eugene, OR: Wipf & Stock, 1988), 21.

[57] Éla, *My Faith as an African,* 35.

[58] Éla, *My Faith as an African,* 35.

[59] Daniel Assefa and Tekletsadik Belachew, 'Values Expressed through African Symbols: An Ethiopian Theological Reflection', *International Bulletin of Mission Research* 41 (2017), 312-24.

symbolic innovation, metaphorical innovation and narrative innovation'.[60] Theological poetry and iconography are both liturgical and apophatic. A contemporary philosopher and Greek Orthodox theologian, Christos Yannaras, has argued for this apophatic dimension of poetry and icons: 'The apophatic attitude leads Christian theology to use the language of poetry and images for the interpretation of dogmas much more than the language of conventional logic and schematic concepts.'[61] The sense of mystery is expressed in various art forms, particularly iconography and poetry. For generations, the traditional Ethiopian Orthodox Church school has offered a rigorous study of *Qene*, a type of poetic improvisation with rhyme, rhythm, and metre. The inspiration for *Qene* comes from metaphors borrowed from Scripture, nature, and tradition. Symbolism and paradox are important elements, used to express theological mysteries that allow important tensions to stand. *Qene* improvisation is used primarily in the liturgy to praise God in new poems which are turned into songs and accompanied with liturgical dance. *Qene* poetry as exegesis and theology yields to the sense of wonder, praise, and prayer.[62] McGuckin, in his introduction to the translation from the Latin version of the *Harp of Glory: Enzra Sebhat*, a theological poem originally written in Ge'ez (Ethiopic) around the fifteenth century, described the unknown riches of the Ethiopian church as an 'ecumenical sadness'.[63] Even the most enlightened pan-Africanists and African nationalists, who dig deep in every well in their quest to reclaim the stories of Africa and restore her dignity, often neglect the textual and other intellectual contributions of pre-colonial early Africa. What hinders the exploration of such theological riches of Africa by Africans and non-Africans?

A negative view of African theology results from the presumed divorce between textual, oral and iconographic discourses. Oral traditions are mistakenly perceived as inferior, an error with powerful Afro-pessimistic implications since Africa is habitually regarded as the oral continent *par excellence*. This false dichotomy neglects the fact that the gospel progressed from oral forms to a textual medium. It also undermines the textual contributions of Africa, particularly those of early African Christianity.

In the next section, we shall examine two African metaphors that may help us find ways of being rooted in the Christian tradition and relevant

---

[60] Mabiala Justin-Robert Kenzo, *Dialectic of Sedimentation and Innovation: Paul Ricoeur on Creativity* (New York & Oxford, Peter Lang, 2009), 256.

[61] Christos Yannaras, *Elements of Faith: An Introduction to Orthodox Theology* (Edinburgh: T. & T. Clark, 1991), 71.

[62] See Alaka Imbakom Kalewold, *Traditional Ethiopian Church Education* (New York: Teacher's College Press, 1970); Daniel Assefa and Tekletsadik Belachew, 'Ethiopian traditional and living Oral Poetry (*Qene*) as Biblical Hermeneutics', *International Bulletin of Missionary Research*, forthcoming.

[63] John A. McGuckin, *Harp of Glory: Enzra Sebhat (An Alphabetical Hymn of Praise for the Ever-Blessed Virgin Mary from the Ethiopian Orthodox Church*, Popular Patristic Series 39 (Crestwood, NY: SVS Press, 2010).

theological innovation. They are an Akan symbol, *Sankofa*, and an African philosophy *Ubuntu*. Such concepts may enrich the future of African theology as it learns from the wisdom of the past and from one another.

Sankofa: *The Audacity to Remember*

The myth of 'Africa without history' fails to acknowledge the early Christian intellectual movement from South to North, from Africa to elsewhere, including Europe and America.[64] Africa's gift has been utilized without proper acknowledgment. Due to many factors, particularly the internalization of negative stereotypes, contemporary African Christianity is in danger of forgetting the legacy of Africa's Christian past. Yet the ancient faith has much to offer, including a wealth of spiritual resources, to present-day Christians living in Africa and the Diaspora. The spirituality and intellectual vitality of these 'living stones'—be they laypeople, clergy, teachers, theologians, martyrs or Desert Fathers and Mothers—is a vast gold mine awaiting African theological *Sankofa*. That is, they beckon a return to our roots, a reclaiming of our ancestors and the telling of their stories. Our excavation of their memories may both root us in history and empower our vision.

The metaphor of *Sankofa* is relevant to the contemporary problem of forgetting the ancient African Christian legacy. *Sankofa* is an Akan cultural icon and metaphor borrowed from Ghana. It is a bird that stands and looks backwards in order to go forward, symbolizing 'a look back into the future'. By going back to the past, we can move toward the future in a way that affects our present reality positively. *Sankofa* thus evokes memory, as a call to the memory of 'ancient-future' that signifies 'returning to your roots, recapturing what you've lost and moving forward'. Memory of the living tradition is an important aspect of being Christian, and truthful remembrance is not a mere attempt to dwell in the past (nostalgia) or a wishful dream. For Africans, the audacity to remember the past stands against the tides of historical amnesia or repeated erasures of memory. This is true to African Christian memory. But theological institutes, their curriculum, textbooks, educators and in turn their students, have been largely miseducated about the legacy of ancient African Christianity. By contrast, in Scripture, the story of the Passover (Ex. 12) underscores the significance of memory. Later, Joshua ordered the representatives of Israel to gather stones to comprise a memorial. He commanded the Israelites to tell their children, when asking about the meaning of the stones, how God had dried up the Jordan so the Israelites could cross it (Josh. 4.21-2). In the New Testament, the sacrament of the Lord's supper (the Eucharist) also carries a powerful dimension of remembrance and re-enactment of Christian life.

The African memory has double dimensions, namely Africa in the Bible and the Bible in Africa. Africa in the Bible remembers how different parts of

---

[64] CEAC video, 2010, online at: https://www.youtube.com/watch?v=2_H0wRvfL8g.

Africa such as Egypt, Ethiopia or Cyrene (Libya) participate in the stories of the biblical narrative of both Old and New Testament, although the five hundred years of vibrant early Libyan Christianity have been almost forgotten.[65] The Bible in Africa is all about the formative role of ancient Christian African teachers, theologians, spiritual believers and exegetes.

We read the Bible as a historical document, and the history of biblical interpretation has been shaped by early African Christianity (which, in turn, shapes world history). Alexandria was the home for the translation of the Hebrew Old Testament into Greek, the Septuagint (LXX). In Ethiopia, the Bible was translated into the vernacular Ge'ez (classic Ethiopic) in the fifth century, making it one of the first seven ancient languages into which the Bible was translated.[66] Early African teachers contributed to the translation and interpretation of Scripture. Outstanding exegetes and theologians include Didymus the Blind, Cyril of Alexandria and Augustine of Hippo. Origen the Egyptian (*c.*185-254) deserves to be acknowledged as the father of biblical criticism, as one of the earliest Church Fathers to develop a theory of biblical interpretation.[67] A prolific writer, he produced a massive body of commentaries, as well as systematic and philosophical texts. A wealthy friend provided the facility and manpower to record Origen's texts in writing while Origen himself dictated them. Later, Origen transferred his library and taught at Caesarea. Other early African teachers were also sought after and invited to teach the Bible outside Africa. A further contribution of early African Christianity is the teaching centres, particularly in Alexandria, upon which European universities were patterned.

Christianity is not a Western religion. And Christianity in Africa is not a recent colonial and missionary experiment. Despite naïve ideas to the contrary, early African Christianity contributed enormously to the formation of Christian doctrines and practices. Amongst noteworthy early African theologians, teachers, philosophers, and exegetes are Clement of Alexandria, Cyprian of Carthage, Didymus the Blind, Fulgentius, Lactantius, Marius Victorinus and Minucius Felix. No one doubts the great doctrinal contributions of these figures. But their identity as Africans has been contested or forgotten. One of the many reasons for negating their African identity centres on the fact that their original writings were in Latin or Greek. However, language is not an exclusive identity marker. The fact that the New Testament was written in Greek does not alter the Jewish identity of the authors, and it is not typically suggested that Paul and Peter were Greek

---

[65] Oden, *Early Libyan Christianity*.

[66] Ephraim Isaac, 'The Bible in Ethiopic', in Richard Marsden and E. Ann Matter (eds), *The New Cambridge History of the Bible*, 2: *From 600 to 1450* (Cambridge: CUP, 2012), 110-22; Ephraim Isaac, *The Ethiopian Orthodox Tawahido Church* (Trenton, NJ: Red Sea Press, 2012).

[67] See Nancy R. Heisey, *Origen the Egyptian: A Literary and Historical Consideration of the Egyptian Background in Origen's Writings on Martyrdom* (Nairobi: Pauline Publications Africa, 2000).

rather than Jewish! Similarly, the African identity of a number of early intellectuals has been questioned, for example, that of Tertullian, who wrote in Latin.[68]

Tertullian, one of the great African theologians, is known for coining the Latin term for the doctrine of the Trinity, and Athanasius of Alexandria is best known as a pragmatic theologian and church leader who refuted the heretical teaching of Arius. Athanasius also influenced the decisions of the ecumenical council of Nicaea and the creed setting out the doctrines of Christ and the Trinity. These controversies were debated and settled in Africa before they achieved an ecumenical consensus elsewhere.

The influence of early African Christianity also extends to Christian practices such as monasticism, prayer, and ecumenism, which were shaped significantly in Africa. Early African church thinkers (both clergy and laypeople), whose ascetic lifestyle was demonstrated through different Christian practices such as prayer and endurance in the face of severe persecution and even martyrdom, were known mostly for their deep spirituality. Mark in Alexandria and Cyprian in the Maghreb gave their lives as a living offering. Vibia Perpetua also became a martyr in resisting the Roman cult and died in Carthage's amphitheatre. Many other early African Christians faced persecution and ultimately honoured God in martyrdom.

We echo the writer of Hebrews, who declares that he has run out of time to recount the heroic faith of godly men and women (11.32). How much more can *we* say? It would also take us too long to retell the stories of African Christian saints such as Mark the evangelist, Cyprian the bishop, and Perpetua the mother who fearlessly and resiliently faced martyrdom in front of everybody. These saints celebrated the Lord of life without the fear of suffering and death. As Tertullian is said to have argued, 'The blood of the martyrs is the seed of the church.'

Let us consider another feature of African Christianity. Monasticism flourished under the leadership of monks such as Anthony, Pachomius and Macarius of Egypt. St Athanasius's classic *Life of St Anthony* helped to propagate monastic movements outside Africa, in Europe. The Desert Fathers and Mothers provided counselling for those who were spiritually and emotionally distressed. Evagrius Ponticus was inspired by Origen and shaped Egyptian spirituality. Evagrius founded the disciplines of Christian psychology and counselling, along with St Augustine of Hippo (in present-day Algeria). Exploration of their wisdom may still bring comfort and consolation to contemporary Africa.

---

[68] See David E. Wilhite, *Tertullian the African: An Anthropological Reading of Tertullian's Context and Identities* (Berlin: Walter de Gruyter, 2007).

Ubuntu as a Hermeneutics of Gift and Hospitality

Here we explore briefly the meaning of *ubuntu* and its implications for African Christian scholarship. *Ubuntu* is an understanding of human personhood and relations that can be found in different African terminologies and languages. Arguably, *ubuntu* has ecclesiological and ecumenical implications, and consequences for the rethinking of African theology. *Ubuntu* represents a commonly held worldview grounded in an African cosmology. It also shapes African anthropology or personhood: a human person is not an isolated individual entity but connected and constituted in the community of others, humans, non-human creations (visible and invisible) and the Creator. The South African expression, *Ubuntu ungamuntu ngabanye abantu,* 'people are people through other people' or 'a human being is a human being because of other human beings' is fundamental.[69] The concept of *Ubuntu* was propagated by Archbishop Desmond Tutu.[70] Kenyan Anglican theologian John S. Mbiti expressed *ubuntu* in this way: 'I am, because we are; and since we are, therefore I am.' This is a cardinal point for African anthropology.[71] *Ubuntu* captures what is an African philosophy of personhood held commonly across the continent.

According to Francis B. Nyamnjoh, *ubuntu* is a philosophy of life that 'espouses a fundamental respect [for] the rights of others, as well as a deep allegiance to the collective identity ... through compassion, interconnectedness, interdependence, and deep-rootedness in community'. A person is known through another person. Human personhood is constituted by the community of others. Ubuntu is constituted from family, extended family, relatives, friends, strangers and others, as well as non-human creatures. Human existence is interconnected, whether for flourishing or diminishing.

> Ubuntu is sharing what one has, and acknowledging and providing for the fact that one's 'humanity is caught up, is inextricably bound up' with the humanity of others – hence the affirmation 'a person is a person through other people', 'I am human because I belong', and I am 'diminished when others are humiliated or diminished.'

On one hand, *ubuntu* exists in striking contrast with Descartes' axiom: 'I think, therefore I am.' Such a notion focuses on the autonomy of the individual and the supremacy of reason that downplays faith, tradition and

---

[69] Francis B. Nyamnjoh, 'Ubuntuism and Africa: Actualised, Misappropriated, Endangered and Reappraised', Africa Day Memorial Lecture, University of the Free State, Bloemfontein, 22 May 2019, 1 (used by kind permission of the author). Colloquially, it can be said 'I am because you are' or 'We are together.' See also Francis B. Nyamnjoh, *'C'est l'homme qui fait l'homme'. Cul-de-sac Ubuntu-ism in Côte D'Ivoire* (Bamenda: Langaa Research & Publishing, 2015).

[70] Desmond Tutu, *No Future Without Forgiveness* (Johannesburg & London: Random House, 1999).

[71] John S. Mbiti, *African Religions and Philosophy* (Nairobi & London: Heinemann, 1989; first published 1969), 108-9. It is not only the identity but also the existence of an individual described in corporate life.

ultimately God. On the other hand, the ideal of *Ubuntuism* values human interconnectedness in a way that cannot be reduced to a parochial African value. It is a human value which can be shared universally and is applicable for Christian theological discourse. In this regard, Nyamnjoh insisted: 'The notion of *ubuntu* and its ethics of caring, sharing and considerateness are not uniquely African, even if African civilizations are widely understood to be governed by its philosophy.'[72]

> Ubuntu is not something to be relegated to small-scale village communities. Ubuntu is capable of serving as a moral theory of human rights in any context, however modern, identifying and exhibiting solidarity with others, such that the violation of human rights and dignity are egregious degradations of that capacity for community.[73]

The ideals of *ubuntu* such as trust, conviviality and support are not without contradictions, tensions and violations. *Ubuntuism* as an ideal when either being fulfilled imperfectly or betrayed can be a lens for evaluating a moral crisis, involving the human person both as an individual and communal. *Ubuntu* is a communitarian ethic that adopts a non-instrumental reciprocity as a means of exchanging of gifts beyond the material, fundamentally as donation of the self to the beloved other.

If we depend on God, then our interdependence with one another will be theologically right and morally appropriate. For a Christian, true *Ubuntuism* includes kinship in Christ and in one another as a Christian family. In the words of Mbiti, 'I am because Christ is.'[74] He also insists on the solidarity with Christ transposed into the solidarity with one another, and the multiple existence of an individual anchored in such confession as 'Because Christ is, therefore I am both individually and corporately.'[75]

These philosophical outlooks, *Sankofa* and *Ubuntu*, are practically lived experiences. In Ethiopia, tradition as memory is preserved. *Ubuntu* as African hospitality and convivial scholarship is also exhibited in the traditional education system.

---

[72] Nyamnjoh, 'Ubuntuism', 2.

[73] Nyamnjoh, *'C'est l'homme qui fait l'homme'*, 18.

[74] John Mbiti, 'African Concept of Human Relations', *Ministry* 9 (1969), 162. This also compels us to acknowledge humans are reciprocally and mutually receiving-givers. Humans are recipients from the source, the Triune God in Christ, the giver and the gift in love and who himself is love. This evokes what Luther is credited with saying: 'In the court of God, we are all beggars'. See Robert Benne, *Reasonable Ethics: A Christian Approach to Social, Economic, and Political Concerns* (St Louis, MO: Concordia, 2005); and the reflection on Paul and Luther by Miroslav Volf, *Free of Charge: Giving and Forgiving in a Culture Stripped of Grace* (Grand Rapids, MI: Zondervan, 2006).

[75] Mbiti, 'African Concept of Human Relations', 162.

Conclusion

Tradition and innovation are not mutually exclusive. The classical misrepresentation of the Orthodox as archaic must be rejected if one wants to take African Christianity and its ancient pillars of the faith seriously. Also, Evangelicalism's reference to the Reformation's *Sola Scriptura* must not be confused with a rejection of tradition. The Orthodox Church is 'at once "ever ancient and ever new"'.[76] The oldest living African churches today are the Coptic and Ethiopic Orthodox Churches, preserving the legacy of ancient Christianity in Africa. Evangelicals, Charismatic-Pentecostals, Independent and other denominational churches of Africa and the African Diaspora are also entitled to share in this early Christian heritage.[77] They must give due respect to the ancient African churches who archived the living tradition through texts, liturgy, the commemoration of the saints, oral tradition, poetry and iconography.

Losing a sense of tradition by not exhibiting such respect hinders churches from delving into the wealth of early African Christian memory and the associated rich resources. We stand on the shoulders of our African spiritual ancestors (martyrs, teachers, clergy and intellectuals), who have already run the race of faith and are watching us as a 'huge crowd of witnesses' (Heb. 12.1). We should not neglect them – they are our roots – nor should we abandon such rich treasures.[78] Remembrance of the past should lead us to envision the future by going back to the ancient resources in search of spiritual wisdom. As Bediako put it: 'If the historian is the "wise man" conserving what has been achieved, that a people may know who they are, the theologian is the "prophet", driving the present generation to look beyond immediate horizons and urging that the true achievement is the construction of the future.'[79]

Thus, the African theologian of the future is a historian who cherishes the glorious memory of ancient African fathers and mothers as well as a prophet who can read the signs of the current times and propose a comforting message. The future of African theology is as a model that incorporates both

---

[76] John A. McGuckin. *The Orthodox Church: An Introduction to its History, Doctrine, and Spiritual Culture* (Oxford: Blackwell, 2010), xi.

[77] Paisius Altschul (ed), *An Unbroken Circle: Linking Ancient African Christianity to the African-American Experience* (St Louis, MO: Brotherhood of St Moses the Black, 1997).

[78] See Daniel Assefa, 'Treasures from the Ethiopian Orthodox Täwahədo Church', in Agbonkhianmeghe E. Orobator (ed), *The Church We Want: Foundations, Theology and Mission of the Church in Africa* (Nairobi: Pauline Publications Africa, 2015), 310-21.

[79] Kwame Bediako, 'Christ in Africa: Some Reflections on the Contribution of Christianity to the Africa Becoming', in Christopher Fyfe (ed), *African Futures: Proceedings of a Conference held at the Centre of African Studies, University of Edinburgh, December 9-11, 1987* (Edinburgh: Edinburgh UP, 1988), 449.

tradition and innovation. This model involves both sedimentation (in the living Christian tradition) and innovation relevant to the changing context.[80]

Ethiopian Orthodox Christianity is typically associated with diverse artistic expressions appealing to the senses and the soul. The rich theological vocabulary and textual tradition are not complete without the visual traditions (such as icons and architecture) and oral traditions (such as poetry, songs, and liturgy). Such treasures offer rich sources to the vibrant and growing contemporary African Evangelicalism. May the future of African theology be with a long memory, a sense of mystery and wonder that also innovates using symbols and metaphors. Indeed, theology that matters addresses where the Church is, but also treasures the long memory of the living tradition in and beyond Africa.

Theology that matters is where the Church is and where the Church remembers the treasures of the living tradition. The recovery of the gifts of Africa revitalizes the phenomenal growth of various forms of African Christianity, including Orthodoxy and Evangelicalism. Respecting the Christian ancestors of the faith requires acknowledgement of the contribution of the Church Fathers and Mothers in reading and interpreting the Bible.

A dialogue should be marked with mutual recognition of gifts (past and present) with which Africa has been endowed. *Sankofa* serves as a symbol of return, an excavation of the common roots, a remembering of the past, in order to reshape and revitalize the future. Epistemic humility is the key to learning from the riches of the living tradition. The memory of ancient African Christianity has survived in ruins, texts, oral stories, and the liturgy. Africa in the Bible and the Bible in Africa has a long history. Again, Bediako put it clearly: 'The Ethiopian Orthodox Church is a church with a memory.'

The future of African theology combines shared roots in the memory of the past and commonalities in theological outlook, in the prayer life of the African churches, and in the sense of mystery expressed. Orality and iconic symbolism, as well as sacraments and liturgical rites, are dominant manifestations of mystical theology. The two metaphorical expressions *sankofa* and *ubuntu* provide helpful insights into the future of African theology. They can dispel ecumenical sadness and enrich the sense of being a Christian family. *Sankofa* evokes the memory of the Christian traditional past, while *ubuntu* as a philosophy of personhood, gift, and hospitality recognizes the loved human and ecclesial other as oneself.

---

[80] Kenzo, *Dialectic*, xiv.

17. Mission and Martyrdom:
A Reappraisal of Mark in African Context[*]

Revd Canon Mark Oxbrow

Introduction

The Christian concept of witness, in Greek μάρτυς or 'martyr', derives from the twofold promise contained in the very last words of the Lord before ascending: 'But you will receive power when the Holy Spirit comes on you; and you will be my witnesses in Jerusalem, and in all Judea and Samaria, and to the ends of the earth' (Acts 1.8) The first, pneumatological element of this promise is of course a reaffirmation of Jesus's words before and after his death and resurrection (Jn 14.26; Lk. 24.49; Acts 1.4-5), but the second element is a much clearer statement of what we, through sanctification or *theosis*, will become. This 'being a witness' is never presented as an option, a choice, a response to a command, but rather the inevitable consequence of the reception, through grace, of the Holy Spirit. Here we shall explore what it meant for a young African migrant of the first century to find himself living the life of a witness, a martyr, as he is drawn ever deeper into the life of God through the indwelling of the Holy Spirit. We may never know, but it is logistically and socially possible that as an inquisitive teenager Mark was actually present when the resurrected Christ promised him, 'you [Mark] will receive power when the Holy Spirit comes on you; and you will be my witness[es] in Jerusalem, and in all Judea and Samaria, and to the ends of the earth'. The story we are about to explore, in a somewhat speculative manner, is not just an intriguing historical investigation; it is a missional challenge for every young African today.

A Young Man in a Linen Garment

We begin our recollection of Mark with one of the most intriguing vignettes in his gospel. I refer to Mark 14.51-2, which reports that as Jesus was arrested, 'A young man, wearing nothing but a linen garment, was following Jesus. When they seized him, he fled naked, leaving his garment behind.' Why is this small, seemingly inconsequential, story included here when it appears to have so little impact on the world transforming events that are unfolding through the arrest, death and resurrection of the Son of God? Many scholars have concluded that this can only have been included because the young man in question was in fact

---

[*] Scripture quotations in this chapter are from the Holy Bible, New International Version®, NIV® Copyright ©1973, 1978, 1984, 2011 by Biblica, Inc.® Used by permission. All rights reserved worldwide.

the young Mark. If so, then this passage is not only an interesting aside but it represents, at least in the story of Mark that we follow here, highly important theological perspectives. I name just three.

Firstly, the young man is described as 'following Jesus'. Mark, assuming it is him, self-identifies as a follower of Jesus. His motives for following are not revealed. Perhaps he was just an inquisitive teenager, or he sniffed a night-time adventure, or he was deeply interested in this man whom he was later to describe boldly as 'Jesus, the Messiah, the Son of God' (Mk 1.1). Nineteen times in his gospel Mark speaks of those who follow Jesus, but their motives differ. Some followed out of total commitment, having given up everything to be with Jesus; others followed because they were hungry; and a number of women, we are told, followed so that they could care for Jesus. As a young man, a teenager, Mark is here, in the garden of arrest, learning to follow, to be a disciple.

Secondly, by implication, we learn that Mark was a witness, a μάρτυς. He was an eye-witness to the arrest of Jesus and spoke of what he saw and knew. At that young age, Mark knew nothing of the witness he was to bear across the Mediterranean world in later years, nor of the martyrdom which would fulfil and complete this witness; but he knew what he had seen, he knew he had witnessed something very important that would later shape his life. Finally, in the darkness of that garden, surrounded by sword-wielding soldiers, the young Mark experienced vulnerability. He was young, unarmed, dressed only in a linen cloth (probably his sleeping garment) and even that was stripped from him so that he had to run home naked. This vulnerability was important: it was to shape his understanding of discipleship and it would later help him as he ministered to a community which knew, and knows even today, extreme vulnerability as people of a minority faith in a hostile world. This strange vignette hidden in the final chapters of his gospel introduces us to the saint who was a follower, a witness and a martyr living in vulnerability for the sake of the uniquely vulnerable Son of God.

The African Roots of Orthodox Faith
and the Orthodox Roots of African Faith

This chapter has a strong African flavour for two reasons. Firstly, the historical evidence gives St Mark a strong African identity; secondly, today we face a growing desire by African Christians to recover the African roots and identity of Christian faith. Let me begin by addressing the second of these.

The unfortunate combined hegemony of the English language, Western theological writing and Global North leadership within the global Christian and missionary movements over several centuries has blinded many of us to the highly significant African influence on the shaping of Christian theology, witness and service. With the contemporary growth of the African church (Orthodox, Catholic, Protestant, Pentecostal, and African Instituted Churches), we see an increasing desire to recover African roots. Thomas

Oden opens his recent work on Orthodoxy and Africa with these words: 'Classic African Christian teaching in the patristic period (100-750 AD) preceded modern colonialism by over a thousand years. Many young African women and men are now re-examining these lost roots. They are hungry for accurate information on their brilliant Christian ancestors.'[1] Serving for thirty years in leadership of mission agencies, I often despaired at the theological library shelves in Nairobi, Lusaka and Addis Ababa that groaned under the weight of Luther, Bultmann and Rick Warren but with no trace to be found of Tertullian, Augustine of Hippo, Frumentius of Ethiopia, John Mbiti of Kenya, Kwame Bediako of Ghana or any of the other highly significant African theologians. A deliberate programme of recovering our African roots (and I say 'our' because these roots are just as important to Europeans and Asians as to Africans) is long overdue.

One of the challenges we face is that the New Testament canon focuses almost entirely on one strand of the expansion of the early church and this bias has been reinforced by English-speaking church historians whose focus has almost always been on Rome, Mount Athos, Geneva and Azua Street rather than Edessa, the great theological melting pot of the Eastern churches; Baghdad, the seat of Patriarch Timothy I, the premier theologian of the Church of the East and, after him, of many Oriental Orthodox church leaders; Alexandria, the home of some of the greatest early biblical scholars; and Carthage, the home of Tertullian, our first major Christian apologist. Amongst Orthodox historians, there has at least been a little more acknowledgement of the significance of the Syrian and other oriental church traditions of the East, but still far too little honouring of the African heritage of the undivided church, a heritage I intend to honour here.

This is not the place to explore in full the African heritage we have ignored for so many centuries, but we need at least to place Mark, the first bishop of Alexandria, in context by naming some of the best-known African fathers of the faith, many of whom are often treated in the literature as if they were Greeks or Romans! We begin with one of Mark's successors, Clement of Alexandria (*c*.150-*c*.215), the catechist and tutor of Origen; closely followed by Tertullian of Carthage (*c*.160-*c*.225), one of the first great apologists. Also from Carthage, we honour one of the martyrs of the Church, Cyprian (*c*.200-*c*.250), who provides such a good example of pastoral ministry and the witness of a sacrificial life. Further east, we find Marcus Minucius Felix (d.250), of Berber extraction, another great apologist of the early church. Then comes Origen himself (*c*.185-*c*.254), born in Alexandria in Egypt and the first theologian to expound Christian doctrine in a systematic way. Another significant Berber from North Africa was Lucius Lactantius (*c*.250-*c*.325), who became an advisor to the first Christian emperor, Constantine, guiding his religious policy as it developed. The giant amongst North African

---

[1] Thomas Oden, *The Rebirth of African Orthodoxy: Return to Foundations* (Nashville, TN: Abingdon, 2016), 3.

Christians is probably Augustine of Hippo (*c*.354-*c*.430), born in present-day Algeria. His work of catechesis, *De doctrina christiana*,[2] remains a benchmark for anyone working on Christian formation even today. One of his pupils, Optatus of Milevis, also a Berber, was a key apologist for orthodoxy against the Donatists. Having started with Clement of Alexandria, we cannot end this list without mentioning Cyril, also of Alexandria (*c*.376-444), a central figure in the Council of Ephesus (431) and the surrounding Christological disputes. These are but a small sample of the African Fathers of the Church. The undivided church, Orthodoxy and Evangelicalism alike, has firm roots in the soil of Africa. But what of St Mark?

Mark the African

Mark certainly ended his life in Egypt, but where was he born? In his interesting, if somewhat speculative, work, *The African Memory of Mark: Reassessing Early Church Tradition*,[3] Thomas Oden advances the theory that Mark always had a heart for Africa because he was in fact born in Africa, in Cyrene (in contemporary Libya), to be precise. How did this come about?

The evidence begins with the pre-Nicene *Martyrium Marci*,[4] which records the ancient tradition, maintained to this day within the Coptic and other Orthodox communities, that 'This Saint [Mark] was born in Cyrene (one of the five Western cities, Pentapolis – in North Africa.'[5] To find a native of Cyrene in Jerusalem at the time of Jesus is in no way unexpected, firstly because of the biblical references to Simon of Cyrene (Mk 15.21), the man whom the Roman soldiers forced to carry Christ's cross, and the presence of residents from 'the parts of Libya near Cyrene' (Acts 2.10) on the day of Pentecost, but also because of what we know about the social and political upheavals in Cyrene at this time. It is also worth noting that although Matthew and Luke repeat the tradition, probably drawing on Mark, that Simon of Cyrene carried the cross of Christ, only Mark speaks of him as 'the father of Alexander and Rufus' (Mk 15.21), implying that the Cyrenian community was one with which Mark was familiar and with which he felt a personal connection. Secondly, turning to the situation in the Pentapolis itself, we find a region of North Africa which had known considerable prosperity and had attracted a significant Jewish diaspora, some of whom

---

[2] See St Augustine, *Teaching Christianity (De Doctrina Christiana)*, trans. and notes by E. Hill, ed. J. E. Rotelle (Hyde Park, NY: New City Press, 1996).

[3] T.C. Oden, *The African Memory of Mark: Reassessing Early Church Tradition* (Downers Grove, IL: IVP Academic, 2011).

[4] An English translation of the *Martyrium Marci*, an early Egyptian document which has not been accurately dated but which comes from some time between the second and fourth centuries, can be found in E. A. Wallis Budge (ed), 'The Martyrdom of St Mark the Evangelist', in *The Contendings of the Apostles*, 1: *The English Translation* (Oxford: Oxford University Press, 1901), 309-18.

[5] *Martyrium Marci* 1.

had accumulated personal wealth through trading and other business enterprises.[6] Both Suetonius[7] and Josephus[8] report tribal conflicts and rising civil unrest in the Pentapolis between 5-15 CE and the migration of more wealthy Jewish families to the safer context of Israel. The suggestion of Oden and others is that the young Mark,[9] with his mother Mary, was a part of this migration to Jerusalem, where the family, using the wealth gained in the diaspora, established a substantial household and exhibited the capacity to act as 'patrons' to a new Jewish prophet and his associates.

So far, we are on fairly solid ground in connecting the John Mark of Acts, the valued companion of Peter, Paul and Barnabas, with the migrant Jewish community from North Africa who found themselves in Jerusalem about the time of the public ministry of Jesus. Where the argument, advanced by Oden, becomes a little more speculative is when he links this early evangelist and author of the second canonical gospel with the events of the last week of Jesus's life in Jerusalem. Much depends on the story with which we began, the assumption that the houses mentioned in Mark 14.14 and Acts 12.12 are identical, and a number of later church traditions. If Mark was the young boy who followed Jesus and his disciples into the garden and witnessed his arrest, then he almost certainly belonged to the household where the Last Supper was held. How would any other teenager have known what was going on that night, as the meal had been arranged in secrecy? It also makes sense that Jesus would arrange that meal in the home of one of his more wealthy patrons, Mary the mother of John Mark, and that later, when Peter is released by an angel from prison (Acts 12.7-12), he should flee to the house he knows best as the Jerusalem 'sanctuary' of his new community, the house of the Last Supper, the home clearly identified by Luke in Acts 12 as that of John Mark and his mother.[10] The fact that Mary hosted the Passover meal and

---

[6] For an analysis of the economic situation of the Jewish community in the region of Cyrene in the first century CE, see Shim'on Applebaum, *Jews and Greeks in Ancient Cyrene* (Leiden: E. J. Brill, 1979), 130-200.

[7] Shim'on Applebaum, 'The Social and Economic Status of the Jews in the Diaspora', in S. Safrai and M. Stern (eds), *The Jewish People in the First Century: Historical Geography, Political History, Social, Cultural and Religious Life and Institutions*, Vol. 2 (Maastricht: Van Gorcum, 1987), drawing on Suetonius, *Vespasian* 16.

[8] Flavius Josephus, 'Wars of the Jews', in *The Works of Flavius Josephus* (trans. William Whiston; London, T. Nelson, 1886), 783.

[9] It is also worth noting that Luke, in Acts, tells us that Mark's full name was 'John Mark', an interesting name which brings together both Hebrew (John) and Latin (Mark) cultural roots, again indicative of the multi-cultural experience of diaspora communities. A young boy born in the Jerusalem of the early first century, under despised Roman occupation, would be unlikely to have been given a Roman, Latin name.

[10] Oden goes further to suggest that the home of John Mark and his mother was also the home where the disciples gathered after the crucifixion and where resurrection appearances took place and eventually the Holy Spirit descended upon the disciples

provided sanctuary for Peter implies further that she was one of the close followers of Jesus and part of the earliest Christian community, or church, in Jerusalem. Mark's father is never mentioned,[11] which might imply that Mary was a single mother (possibly as a result of some tragedy in Cyrene). This would have placed Mark, as a son over the age of twelve, in a position of responsibility within the home used by Jesus and his followers as a meeting place and quite likely also a follower of, or believer in, the new prophet Jesus from his early teens onwards. Most of this cannot be substantiated from Scripture but is authenticated by church tradition, some of which is very ancient.

Another strong indication of the African roots of Mark is the way in which, during his extensive missionary journeys over several decades, he appears to be drawn back constantly to Africa, where he was eventually to lead the church of Alexandria and die as a martyr, giving his blood to the soil of this great continent.

Mark the Migrant

We find ourselves on much firmer ground when we move on to the record in the Acts. Mark's first appearance in this story is a little puzzling, but it supports a strong tradition. After Peter is released from prison and flees to the home of Mary and John Mark, he departs (it seems very rapidly and probably for his own safety) to 'another place' (Acts 12.17), which tradition suggests was Egypt, mirroring the earlier flight of the Holy Family to Egypt. But then in Acts 12.25 we are told that, following the death of Herod, 'when Barnabas and Saul (Paul) had finished their mission, they returned to Jerusalem, taking with them John, also called Mark'. This implies two important things. Firstly, Paul did not waste his time in his place of sanctuary but was in mission there, and secondly that he had not gone there alone but with Barnabas and Mark. We can understand why he might have chosen Barnabas as a travelling companion when he had to flee Jerusalem but why also take Mark. Other than being the cousin of Barnabas (Col. 4.10), there are three reasons why this young man could have been chosen by Peter, or perhaps nominated by his mother, to join the two older men on this dangerous journey. If our suppositions about Mark so far are correct, then Mark was an experienced migrant. He knew how to survive on the road, how to navigate his

---

empowering them for mission: Oden, *African Memory*, ch. 6. If we accept this hypothesis, and the evidence that Oden advances is substantial, then this also places the young Mark in very close proximity to the resurrected Christ and the outpouring of God's Spirit, experiences which may well have empowered him for the amazing ministry of the rest of his life.

[11] There is however an ancient tradition that Aristobulus, whose 'household' Paul greets in his epistle from Rome (Rom. 16.10) was from Cyrene and was the father of Mark. The greeting of Aristobulus' household but not him personally may well imply that Aristobulus has died, perhaps even in Cyrene before John Mark and his mother migrated to Jerusalem.

way through aggressive officialdom, how to settle in a new culture and learn a new language. If Egypt was Peter's place of refuge, then Mark had likely already travelled through that country on his way from Cyrene to Jerusalem some years before. Secondly, Mark could have been chosen because of his status within a wealthy family. Peter was a fisherman, no doubt of limited means, but Mark could command the resources, and perhaps the personal connections, needed for a successful migration and resettlement. Finally, we have already seen that Mark was likely one of the inner circle of early disciples of Jesus, present (but probably behind a curtain) at the Last Supper, the arrest, and maybe the resurrection appearances and Pentecost itself: so he would have been the ideal witness and spiritual companion for an older believer prone to doubts.

In Acts 13.5, we hear of John (Mark) accompanying Barnabas and Paul on their missionary journey to Cyprus and Perga as their 'helper'. So began, for Mark, many years of travel and mission. Paul seems to have been upset when Mark left Perga to return to Jerusalem (Acts 13.13), and consequently refused to take him on a later journey; Barnabas therefore took his young cousin with him to Cyprus (Acts 15.37-40). That rift with Paul was obviously healed at a later date because Paul writes to Timothy from Rome: 'Only Luke is with me, get Mark and bring him with you, because he is helpful to me in my ministry' (2 Tim. 4.11). This is not the place to map out all of Mark's likely criss-crossing of the Mediterranean Sea in support of the mission work of Peter, Paul and Barnabas but we do know that he later found himself back in Egypt, a migrant returning to his roots on African soil.

My purpose here is to highlight the strength and insights which Mark brought to mission and ministry from his identity as a migrant and, in so doing, to alert us to the gift that contemporary African migrants can be to the universal Church. Migrants, whether forced into migration or moving out of choice, are resilient, and know how to survive and to rely on divine providence. They often have many cross-cultural skills and experience of dealing with the authorities, knowing how to find shelter, to build community, to preserve a faith tradition, and so much more. In our xenophobic world, many African migrants drown in the Mediterranean but many others cross successfully to bring the gospel of God's love and reviving Spirit to Europe and beyond.[12]

---

[12] There is, of course, much more to be said about the similar and very different experiences of first-century and contemporary migrants across and around the Mediterranean Sea, for which there is not space here, but a number of people, including me, are undertaking further studies in this area, especially as migration becomes such a significant twenty-first-century phenomenon. See, for example, Martha Frederiks, 'Religion, Migration and Identity: A Conceptual and Theological Exploration', *Mission Studies* 32 (2015), 181-202; Afe Adogame and Cordule Weisskoppel (eds), *Religion in the Context of African Migration* (Bayreuth: Breitinger, 2005); Paul Woods, *Theologising Migration: Otherness and Liminality in East Asia* (Oxford, Regnum, 2015).

Mark the Youth

We turn now to Mark the young man. We do not know exactly how old Mark was when he first met Jesus, or when he set out with Peter and Barnabas to find a place of refuge, but we can be almost certain that he was the youngest of those early disciples to respond to the call to cross-cultural mission. We do know that he died on 26 April 68 as a bishop and martyr,[13] probably still in his early fifties or younger. The fact that such a young man should have an important role in the establishment of the Church, not only in Africa but also in southern Europe and at the gateway to Asia (in Antioch), is counter-cultural for first-century Middle Eastern society, which tended to value the wisdom and leadership of elders, but also highly symbolic of the call that Jesus gave to place the child in the midst (Mt. 18.2) of our consideration of eternal matters.

Africa is currently a young continent with 41 per cent of its population under fifteen years of age.[14] Most churches, whether Orthodox, Catholic or Evangelical, struggle to bring children and youth into the local and global mission of the Church. In recent years, the Child Theology Movement has focused on 'Doing theology with a child in the midst'. One of the founders of the movement, Keith White, writes:

> Our contention is that the little child [of Mt. 18.2] (about whom we know nothing) was called and placed by Jesus into the midst of an existing form of theology in order to challenge and change it. Jesus interrupted and challenged the beliefs and lives of any who sought to follow him. The call is not to change the disciples' attitudes to the child (although such attitudes most certainly will change if they get the point). Rather the child is invited into the unfolding story of Jesus as he proclaims, signs and seeks the Kingdom of God. In our view, there is no way the child can be abstracted (decontextualised) from the narrative of Matthew, the person of Jesus, the theological arguing of the disciples, the culture of the time or the nature of the Kingdom of God. The sign of the child in the midst is not self-evident in any time or culture, but rather chosen by God in Christ to challenge our theology and lives.[15]

---

[13] The date of 26 April 68 is given by the *Coptic Synaxarion* (Chicago, IL: St George Coptic Orthodox Church, 1987), vol. 1, 30. Other sources such as Jerome, in *Lives of Illustrious Men*, trans. E. C. Richardson (London: Aeterna Press, 2016), 14; the Coptic-Arabic history of Sawīrus ibn al-Muqaffaʻ, *History of the Patriarchs of the Egyptian Church: Known as the History of the Holy Church*, ed. Yasa ʻAbad al-Masih et al., vol. 1 (Cairo: Sociéte d'archéologie copte, 1943); and Eutychius of Alexandria (in his *Nazm al-Jauhar*) all offer or imply earlier dates.

[14] http://worldpopulationreview.com/continents/africa-population/, accessed 21 October 2019.

[15] Keith White, in the foreword to *Anvil* 35.1 (March 2019), 14. This edition of *Anvil* is themed around Child Theology and also includes a useful article by Frances Young: 'Child Theology: A Theological Response'. This topic was also the subject of a theological consultation sponsored by the 4/14 Movement in Seoul, Korea, in 2013, the papers from which have been published as Dan Brewer and John Baxter-Brown (eds), *Children & Youth as Partners in Mission* (Penang: Compassion International, 2013).

Perhaps the young Mark is the 'child' who is being placed in our midst today to challenge our theology, our mission praxis and our lived discipleship. Even more significantly, Mark challenges us to open up our theological discourse to the children and youth of Africa and to listen to the voices of young people globally.

Mark the Witness

We have already noted that Mark was, in all probability, amongst those who followed Jesus during his ministry, and, in his gospel writing he gives prominence to those who for different reasons chose to become followers of Jesus. Discipleship is at the heart of his witness. The important consideration before us now, however, is the character of that discipleship: what did following Jesus look like for Mark? If we take the oldest Greek manuscripts of Mark's Gospel as authoritative and the ending therefore to be at 16.8,[16] then Mark's final words are:

> Don't be alarmed, [the angel] said [to the women]. 'You are looking for Jesus the Nazarene, who was crucified. He has risen! He is not here. See the place where they laid him. But go, tell his disciples and Peter, "He is going ahead of you into Galilee. There you will see him, just as he told you."' Trembling and bewildered, the women went out and fled from the tomb. They said nothing to anyone, because they were afraid. (Mk 16.6-8)

The words here, 'they said nothing to anyone', and their motive, 'because they were afraid', as we will see, stand as a powerful motif for the character of African discipleship in the first three centuries. In fact, it seems that this ending was so shocking to later custodians of the text that their additions (both the longer and shorter versions) set out to correct this denial of verbal witness. The longer version adds 'they went forth and preached everywhere' (Mk 16.20) and the shorter version adds, 'Jesus himself sent out, by means of them, from east to west, the sacred and imperishable proclamation of eternal salvation.'

As Alan Kreider has recently pointed out,[17] the witness of the early Fathers of the African church, the successors to Mark, the first bishop of Alexandria, is that proclamation, evangelism, verbal witness, was hardly on their agenda. For at least three centuries, the church of Africa grew through the witness of

---

[16] Some manuscripts add a further twelve verses (Mk 16.9-20), whilst others add just a lengthened version of v.8. These longer versions of the ending of Mark's Gospel are also missing from the oldest form of the Syriac and three of the oldest Armenian manuscripts of the gospel. Eusebius and Jerome both note that this ending is missing from the best Greek manuscripts available to them. Rawlinson asserts that the evidence points to the longer endings 'having formed no part of the oldest texts current in Africa, Alexandria, Caesarea, Antioch': A. E. J. Rawlinson, *St Mark* (London: Methuen, 1925).

[17] Alan Kreider, *The Patient Ferment of the Early Church* (Grand Rapids, IL: Baker, 2016).

holy lives. Clement of Alexandria uses the models of Daniel and Jonah to suggest that in a hostile environment the Christian's witness should be one of 'language, life and behaviour'.[18] In his catechesis, he focuses on the training of new believers in distinctive Christian values and the adoption of a new lifestyle. In the second century (but in the Middle East), Justin Martyr points in a similar manner to the witness of life. As Kreider records, 'Justin contended that christocentric patience was potent. It didn't merely change people's attitudes, and it didn't take people out of the world. It formed people who made a difference in the world, including the business world, and they attracted people to the faith because their patience made them different enough to be intriguing and because they held out hope.'[19] Origen, the great theologian, in his catechetical homilies, focuses not so much on theology as on behaviour, reminding his readers that their behaviour was the basis on which outsiders – Greeks, philosophers and 'common folk' – would make decisions for or against Jesus.[20] For a more theologically nuanced rationale of this focus on the witness of Christian living, we turn to Tertullian, who links Christian living in an unbelieving world with the Incarnation. He asserts that the Christians' patient approach to life, accepting suffering and even martyrdom, and looking always to the needs of others, 'attracts the heathen',[21] in the same way that the life of God incarnate in Jesus attracted the first disciples. Finally, this theme is taken even further by Cyprian who, commenting on Matthew 5.43-48, suggests that, through baptism and a heavenly birth, his readers can 'become like God' (*simile Deo*). As God perfects them, 'the patience of God the Father' abides in them and enables them 'to possess among our virtues what can be put on a par with the divine merits!'[22] It is this sanctification, deification or *theosis*, which, Cyprian suggests, creates lives that witness to the power of salvation to be found in the gospel of Christ.

The thesis of Kreider's work is that the African church of the first three centuries grew because of the 'habitus', the 'Christ-like behaviour' and life-style of the Christian community which was both intriguing and attractive to those outside the faith. He maintains that the African church of those early years had no strategy for evangelism and little verbal proclamation of the gospel, and yet it grew at a rate rarely seen in subsequent centuries. To what

---

[18] Clement, *Stromateis* 2.104.1, trans. John Ferguson, Fathers of the Church 85 (Washington DC, Catholic University of America Press, 1991), 226.

[19] Kreider, *Patient Ferment*, 293.

[20] Origen, *Homilies on Jeremiah* 14.8, trans. Roy J. Deferrari et al., Fathers of the Church 97 (Washington DC, Catholic University of America Press, 1998), 143.

[21] Tertullian, *Patience* 15.3, in *Tertullian: Disciplinary, Moral and Ascetical Works*, trans. Roy J. Deferrari et al., Fathers of the Church 40 (Washington, DC, Catholic University of America Press, 1959), 220.

[22] Cyprian, *The Good of Patience* 5, in *St Cyprian: Treatises*, trans. Roy J. Deferrari et al., Fathers of the Church 36 (Washington DC, Catholic University of America Press, 1958), 267.

degree Mark was instrumental in setting this tone in first-century Alexandria we shall probably never know, but this African approach does pose an important question for contemporary mission. In his concluding chapter, Kreider argues that Constantine and Augustine of Hippo (Roman emperor and African bishop) and the Council of Nicaea set in motion the demise of church growth through the African witness of Christ-like lives and replaced it with the coercive, violent growth of a powerful church, the Christendom project. The question for us, in a post-Christendom era, is whether our witness, and the church growth which it can engender, might be better shaped by the early African model than by a desire to recover the powers of Christendom. In work currently being undertaken within the Anglican Communion, we are discovering that discipleship that focuses on character formation and living 'lives worthy of the Gospel of Christ' (Phil. 1.27) in every sector of contemporary society may well be the way forward in Christian witness and the growth of the Church. In this, the wider Church has a lot to learn from the Orthodox understanding of the transformation of human character through the indwelling of the Spirit of Christ and from our African Church Fathers.

Mark the Evangelist of the Spirit

The first bishop of Alexandria, John Mark, companion of Peter, Paul and Barnabas, is of course best known to us through his gospel, as one of the four evangelists. There is a strong tradition that the gospel was written in Rome and relies heavily on the testimony of Peter at the end of his ministry. The gospel is, however, much more that simply the dictated work of Peter with Mark acting as interpreter. As we read the gospel, again and again we see in it the hand of an African leader, a man who already has experience of, and is looking forward to, planting more churches on African soil. Firstly, there is an earthiness to the Gospel of Mark, a connection to the blood, sweat, tears and laughter of ordinary human lives. We see here none of the high philosophy of John, the refined language of the educated doctor Luke, or the deeply Jewish traditions of the stable faith community into which Matthew spoke, but rather the practical application of a costly discipleship. Secondly, we see clearly here in Mark an aliveness to the spirit world. If we allow ourselves to be immersed in the ethos of Mark's Gospel, we find ourselves in a liminal space between the world of the supernatural powers – God, Satan and the spirits – and the human world of injustice, brutality and compassion, the two worlds inexorably entwined. Mark opens his gospel with Isaiah's great cry of hope: into the wilderness of our daily experience enters the voice, the Word of God, demanding the straightening of our ways, a highway in this world for the divine (Mk 1.2-3, quoting Isa. 40.3). Then the prophet John announces the arrival not of a political leader, a messianic king or a social reformer but the divine Spirit of God (Mk 1.8). The liminality of our experience allows for the arrival of Godself in the wilderness of our lives. No sooner has the arrival of the Spirit been announced than the same Spirit descends in the form of a dove upon a man who is declared to be the beloved divine Son of God (Mk 1.11). For a few verses, the divine Spirit of God seems to be running the show but we get no further than verse 23 before the 'unclean spirit' rises to contest the intrusion of the Spirit, 'the Holy One of God' (Mk 1.24), into the traditionally acknowledged territory of the spirits of this world. Let battle commence! As we read on, we are immediately transported into a world of spiritual contest, evocative of the spirit-enlivened world of any African village.

Mark's Gospel stands as a challenge to the duality of much of contemporary Western theology which does not take seriously the 'super-reality' of the spiritual realm. As Orthodox theologians often remind us, it is the physical realm that is temporal, temporary and passing and the spiritual realm which is eternally sustained in the life of the Trinity, but in the incarnate Lord the two cannot be wrenched apart.

Before leaving this reflection on Mark as the evangelist of the Spirit, it is helpful to note two further points. Firstly, although it is highly likely that Mark was a witness to the outpouring of the Spirit at Pentecost,[23] and his mentor, Peter, was a key participant on that life-changing day (Acts 2.14-15), his gospel makes no mention of this event nor of the earlier promise of Jesus to send the Spirit (Jn 14.26; 15.26; 16.7). This is surprising. I conjecture that the reason for this may be that for Mark, following the resurrection and the testimony of the centurion, 'Truly this man was the Son of God' (Mk 15.39), the Spirit of God is to be seen in all its fullness in the Son and in the manifestation of the Spirit it is the Son we encounter. Not only has the divine invaded the world of humanity but the way has been opened up for humanity to find its true being in divinity. Secondly, we should note that Mark's acute awareness of the world of the spirits does not lead to a 'spiritualization' of the gospel but rather to a very earthy political agenda for justice, peace and human dignity in the here and now,[24] to living a life worthy of the gospel of Christ in this complex 'wilderness' of a world in which we find ourselves today.

Mark the Church Planter

The record of Mark's ministry which Luke provides in his Acts of the Apostles suggests that he travelled widely in Asia Minor, Greece and on to Rome as a mentee or apprentice of Peter, Paul and Barnabas, learning from his elders and so being prepared as the 'apostle to Africa', his native land. According to Sawīrus

---

[23] Thomas Oden has argued quite convincingly that the upper room where the disciples received the Holy Spirit was very likely the same room as that used for the Last Supper in the home of John Mark and his mother: Oden, *African Memory*, 94-8.

[24] For a much fuller treatment of this aspect of Mark's Gospel, see Ched Myers, *Binding the Strong Man: A Political Reading of Mark's Story of Jesus* (Maryknoll, NJ: Orbis, 1988); and on the 'political agenda' of the gospel, Alan Richardson, *The Political Christ* (London: SCM Press, 1973).

ibn al-Muqaffaʻ,[25] Bishop of al-Ašmūnīn in the tenth century, on leaving Rome Mark first travelled to Alexandria and then on to his home region of Cyrene in Upper Libya to plant churches amongst the Jewish community there.[26] It is clear from the tradition that Mark's ministry spread far beyond the Jewish diaspora community, as he spent some years in an area of Libya known as the Pentapolis (five towns), planting churches and training church leaders amongst the native populations. The exact details of his ministry in north Africa are not clear but Thomas Oden quotes one standard Coptic chronology which suggests that in Alexandria Mark

> … ordained a bishop (Anianos), three priests and several deacons to look after the congregation if anything befell him. He left Alexandria to Berce [in the Pentapolis], then to Rome, where he met St. Peter and St. Paul and remained there until their martyrdom in 64AD. Upon returning to Alexandria in 65AD, St. Mark found his people firm in faith and thus decided to visit the Pentapolis. There he spent two years preaching and performing miracles, ordaining bishops and priests and winning more converts. Finally he returned to Alexandria and was overjoyed to find that Christians had multiplied so much that they were able to build a considerable church in the suburban district of Baucalis.[27]

This traditional record of Mark's ministry paints the picture of someone who was an evangelist and church planter at heart. Having witnessed the martyrdom of his mentors and elders in Rome, he returns to Alexandria which is rapidly becoming the centre of church life in first-century Africa, but he is restless there and immediately moves out to the Pentapolis to continue his mission work. The fact that we are told that in those two years he ordained several bishops, as well as priests, suggests that the church was growing and new congregations were being established right across the region. Sawīrus talks of Mark's church planting work in 'the province of Egypt, of Africa and Pentapolis, and *all those regions*',[28] and the earlier *Martyrium Marci* speaks of his ordaining 'church leaders for the whole Pentapolis region'.[29] Finally, according to the tradition, it took not one but two angelic visions to persuade Mark to leave his church planting work in Libya and return to the leadership of the church in Alexandria.[30] Planting ecclesial communities of witnessing Christians was the core of Mark's discipleship and ministry and in a sense a precursor of, if not a contributing factor to, his eventual martyrdom.

---

[25] Sawīrus ibn al-Muqaffaʻ, *History*, vol. 1, 141-42.

[26] Sawīrus here is recording earlier traditions, particularly those from the *Martyrium Marci*.

[27] Oden, *African Memory*, 139, quoting http://www.suscopts.org/coptic-orthodox/church/saint-mark/.

[28] Sawīrus ibn al-Muqaffaʻ, *History*, vol. 1, 141 (emphasis added).

[29] *Martyrium Marci* 6-10.

[30] Oden, *African Memory*, 140.

Mark the Witness and Martyr

This chapter began by emphasizing the etymological connection between the English words 'witness' and 'martyr', but so far we have focused primarily on the witness of Mark rather than his martyrdom. This has been a deliberate argument, not just for a continuity between the two but for a deep dependence of the one on the other. The indication is that martyrdom was no surprise for Mark and may even have been received as the most appropriate summation of his life of witness.

Recent research by the Center for the Study of Global Christianity indicates that, in the five decades from 1960 to 2010, there have been at least 11 million Christian martyrs.[31] During the 1970s and 1980s, these martyrs were predominantly eastern Europeans and those from the former Soviet Union but today they are more likely to be Africans, citizens of South Sudan, Eritrea, Egypt, Nigeria, Cameroon or the Central African Republic. Despite these figures, most contemporary Christians, even those of us working in the mission or development sectors, will not have met a Christian who was later martyred, let alone witnessed the death of a martyr. This was not the case for Mark. His teenage discipleship began with the crucifixion, the martyrdom, of Jesus; he would have almost certainly known Stephen, the first Christian martyr; he witnessed the martyrdom of his mentors Peter and Paul in Rome; and it is likely that he saw opposition to the gospel and death as the church grew in north Africa and challenged many vested cultic interests.

Stronger evidence of Mark's expectation of a violent response to the witness of Christians comes from his gospel itself. In recording Jesus's words about the 'end times', Mark's text runs parallel with that of Matthew and Luke (who, many scholars believe, are using Mark's text as their source at this point: Mk 13.1-37; cf. Mt. 24.1-44; Lk. 21.5-24) but has its own distinct emphasis. Whilst Matthew, with his Jewish hearers in mind, emphasizes Jesus's call to careful reading of the signs of the times and faithful patience as they wait for the Lord's return, and Luke has a similar emphasis on resolute forbearance in the face of suffering, Mark has a much clearer focus on witness. He is more specific about the opportunities for witness that will be provided in the hostile councils and synagogues. Jesus is recorded as saying: 'They will deliver you up to councils; and you will be beaten in synagogues; and you will stand before governors and kings *for my sake*, to bear testimony before them' (Mk 13.9).[32] In Mark this is immediately followed by: 'And the gospel must first be preached to all nations' (Mk 13.10, which is there in Mt. 24.14 but separated from the 'tribulation' and 'put you to death' of Mt. 24.9). There is no doubt here in Mark that the

---

[31] T. M. Johnson and others, 'Christianity 2018: More African Christians and Counting Martyrs', *International Bulletin of Missionary Research* 42.1 (January 2018), 25.

[32] Note the almost exact parallel in Lk. 21.12-13 but not in Mt. 24.9.

suffering and death which will ultimately come are an integral part of the witness to all nations.

In the following verses of Mark's Gospel, we see not only an underlining of this link between martyrdom and witness but also of the theme addressed earlier in this chapter, the role of the Spirit in Christian discipleship. Jesus says: 'Whenever you are arrested and brought to trial, do not worry beforehand about what to say [your witness]. Just say whatever is given you at the time, for it is not you speaking, but the Holy Spirit' (Mk 13.11-12).[33] Again, Spirit-inspired witness is central to occasions of suffering and martyrdom. On this passage, Martin Hengel writes:

> I do not believe that we can understand Mark 13:10, bracketed as it is by Mark 13:9 and Mark 13:11-12, which are texts about persecution, without looking at the effect of the Gospel. Mark 13:9-11 cannot be understood without reference to the paradigmatic significance of the death of Jesus (Mark 15:39). Like the suffering of Jesus, so too that of his community has the character of witness. Campenhausen[34] therefore rightly cites Mark 15:39 in connection with the missionary effect of martyrdom, which is expressed most clearly in Tertullian, *Apologeticum* 50:21f.: *semen est sanguis Christianorum.*[35]

Here and elsewhere Hengel holds up the confession of the Roman centurion on the death of Jesus, 'Truly this man was the Son of God' (Mk 15.39), as the 'climax of the whole Gospel', effectively completing what Mark has begun with the first words of his book, 'The beginning of the gospel of Jesus Christ, the Son of God'. Here, as Hengel says, 'the commander of the execution squad becomes the first 'confessor':[36] death, martyrdom, witness and confession are held together as one.

The centrality of witness to the gospel in Mark's thinking, and its connection with martyrdom, draw us to one final verse, which stands not at the beginning or end of his book but rather at the very heart of it, when Jesus first begins to speak about his own death. This passage, 'whoever loses their life for me and for the gospel will save it' (Mk 8.35), has parallels in Matthew 16.25 and Luke 9.24, but it is only Mark who includes 'the gospel'. Again, we see Mark's overriding concern for mission, for the preaching of the gospel, for witness. One can almost imagine that while Mark was being dragged by the throat around the streets of Alexandra, as his life-blood drained out into the dust, he may have played those words over and over in his mind: 'whoever loses their life for me and for the gospel will save it.'

The facts of Mark's martyrdom are wrapped in tradition and somewhat confused, with at least three sites claimed for his death and more for his burial, but it is clear that the growth of the church in Alexandria, and the

---

[33] Matthew does not record this saying but Luke has it at an earlier point, at 12.11-12.

[34] Hans von Campenhausen, *Die Idee des Martyriums in der alten Kirche* (Göttingen: Vandenhoeck & Ruprecht, 1936).

[35] Martin Hengel, *Studies in the Gospel of Mark* (London: SCM, 1985) 134 n.143.

[36] Hengel, *Studies*, 24.

consequent influence of Christians, inflamed public opinion and the anger of a mob, who reputedly dragged Mark through the streets and the cattle market with a rope around his neck until his life was ended. What is important for us today is not how or where Mark died but how he lived and why he died a martyr's death. Just over two centuries later, in the era of Constantine when another African leader, Augustine of Hippo, was embracing the emperors' use of power to suppress heretics and preserve the true faith, Lactantius, a Berber African and quite possibly a descendant of one of Mark's early converts in Libya, stuck firmly to the African tradition of patient witness, writing: 'Religion must be defended not by killing but by dying, not by violence but by patience'.[37] Two millennia later, the world watched, half in horror and half in faith, as, in the sands of the desert outside Sirte in Libya, twenty-one Coptic Christians patiently knelt in silent witness to await their martyrdom at the hands of terrorist executioners. The cord that binds together St Mark the evangelist, the Berber teacher Lactantius and the Coptic workmen from Sirte is the single strand of witness and martyrdom – μαρτύρια.

Conclusion

This chapter has attempted to pick up some of the major themes of Mark's life which are relevant to the mission of the Church in Africa today. Migration, youth, witness, the Spirit, church planting and martyrdom are all live issues for the fastest growing Christian continent today – the Christian family which is most likely to shape the future of global Christianity in this twenty-first century. I have argued that African Christians will be better served in their leadership of Christian futures by the recovery of early African spirituality, patterns of discipleship, theology and history than by any post-colonial acceptance, rejection or critique of Western Christianity. Mark, the evangelist, witness and martyr, is as good a place to start as any.

To conclude, we return to Thomas Oden and one of his earlier books, *How Africa Shaped the Christian Mind: Rediscovering the African Seedbed of Western Christianity*, because it so effectively turns the tables and challenges Western Christians to take seriously the African Christian heritage. He writes:

> The rapid spread of early African Christianity was due in part to the heartbreaking African history of martyrdom. This is a history of African blood on African soil. For African believers the martyrs pointed to the continuity of the communion of saints. They bore their cross in Africa. They evoked a luminous awareness of their relation with esteemed ancestors. … The readiness to die for the sake of the truth is intrinsic to baptismal faith. In fact, it is the core meaning of baptism as a participation in the death and resurrection of the

---

[37] Lactantius, *Divine Institutes* 5.19.22 (A. Bowen and P. Garnsey, *Lactantius: Divine Institutes* [Translated Texts for Historians 40; Liverpool: Liverpool University Press, 2003], 324).

Lord of glory. There is a kind of temporary vindication that comes from winning a short-term historical battle [even two centuries of colonisation]. But that does not account for the faith of multiple generations of witnesses following Jesus and Mark. … The meaning of the struggle of the early African martyrs begs to be understood in modern Africa. It was a countercultural, risk-laden, sacrificial, pre-Constantinian struggle for integrity in the face of overwhelming political power. … It was amid that period of martyrdom that the teachings of African orthodoxy were decisively refined. It was in that context that Africa gave birth to the enduring ecumenical doctrines of creation, providence, sin, atonement, resurrection and the church – its liturgy, eucharistic life, teaching and discipleship, refined by the fires of African experience. Living towards eternal life through death became the experiential basis for translating the Christian gospel into African terms.[38]

---

[38] T. C. Oden, *How Africa shaped the Christian Mind: Recovering the African Seedbed of Western Christianity* (Downers Grove, IL: IVP, 2007), 115-20.

18. St Mark, from Mission to Martyrdom: A Coptic Perspective*

Dr Irini Thabet

Behold, I send my messenger before your face,
who will prepare your way before you.
The voice of one crying in the wilderness:
'Prepare the way of the Lord;
make his paths straight.' (Mk 1.2-3)

This is how St Mark begins his gospel. And this is how we received the good news that he brought to us about our Lord and Saviour Jesus Christ. By 'we', I mean Christians not only in Egypt, but in all of Africa as well. Like John the Baptist's voice, St Mark's voice cried in the wilderness of the hearts of our ancestors, telling them, and also telling us: 'Prepare the way of the Lord; make his paths straight' (Mk 1.3).

A Developing Personality

It is absolutely challenging to approach the personality of St Mark, a great saint, apostle, missionary, evangelist and martyr; a personality that is so rich and full of accomplishments even though he was martyred in his early sixties.

Who was St Mark before his evangelical mission began? Was he that 'certain young man [who] followed Him [Jesus], having a linen cloth thrown around his naked body. And [when] the young men laid hold of him, he left the linen cloth and fled from them naked' (Mk 14.51-52)? Was he the one who left Paul and Barnabas in Perga to go to Jerusalem, causing a conflict between his uncle Barnabas and Paul? Or was he the one about whom Paul wrote to Timothy, saying: 'Get Mark and bring him with you, for he is useful to me for ministry' (2 Tim. 4.11)? Or the one whom Peter has called 'My son Mark' (1 Pet. 5.13)?

---

* I am very grateful to His Holiness Pope Tawadros for giving me this opportunity to survey the life, mission and martyrdom of his predecessor St Mark, and to enjoy getting closer to our great evangelist. These two are, as we say in Arabic, خير خلف لخير سلف, 'The best ancestor to the best predecessor.' I also wish to thank Dr Ishak Agban, Professor of History and dean of the Institute of Coptic Studies, and Dr Saeed Hakeem, Professor of Theology in the Theological Seminary of Anba Rueiss, for their great help with ideas and sources to consult.

Mark was all the aforementioned; a young man who grew up in a well-off family and had good education, who therefore was not to be arrested but ran away almost naked. He also was the one who left Paul and Barnabas. Yet he was willing to learn and to develop; a missionary who would grow in the knowledge of his Saviour and work more in his vineyard. That is how Mark became useful, not only to Paul but to all the countries where he preached and to the churches he built: ours is one of them. And that is how he was no more the one who runs away, but rather the apostle who faces all kinds of danger to complete his evangelism.

This great development is stamped by the symbol of St Mark: the lion. Yes, the lion in Revelation 4 and the lion with wings that Venice adopts as its city symbol refer to St Mark, the first patriarch in the Coptic Church. For two thousand years, all the popes of Alexandria, successors to the see of St Mark, have had statues of lions surrounding their chair, even inside the church, to show the love and pride that we have towards our great saint.

A Fisherman

Mark had a developing personality and also a fisherman's talent. Although he was not a fisherman as his older relative Peter was, he was one of the seventy apostles called by Jesus. Therefore, his mission was to be a fisherman: he followed Jesus to become a fisher of men as mentioned in Matthew 4.19.

In Fr Mennassa Youhanna's book, *The History of the Church*, you can read how Mark worked as a fisher of people when he met Inianus in Alexandria.[1] Fr Mennassa wrote that St Mark was walking for a long time in the city, watching the streets and observing people, until his shoe was torn. He went to a shoemaker, Inianus, and when he attempted to fix the shoe, he cut his hand badly. This made Inianus cry, saying *o énas theós*, which means 'O, the one god'. Immediately, Mark used the words to begin a conversation about who the one god was, after healing the hand of Inianus, of course. Like Paul, who talked to the Athenians in the Areopagus about the unknown god to fish for souls, St Mark began from the cry of 'the one god' and won his first Egyptian family, that of the shoemaker, who became a pious Christian and the first to be ordained by St Mark.

In his famous book about St Mark, *The African Memory of Mark*, Thomas C. Oden verified the account of the meeting of Mark and Inianus; but more importantly, Oden described the evangelism of Mark, saying: 'Geographically he covered more of the earth than Paul, witnessing on all three known continents.'[2]

---

[1] Mennassa Youhanna, *The History of the Church* (Cairo, 1924), 11-16, online at: https://www.goodreads.com/book/show/13633472 (in Arabic).
[2] T.C. Oden, *The African Memory of Mark: Reassessing Early Church Tradition* (Downers Grove, IL: IVP, 2011), 44.

A Man with a Vision

Mark was a self-developing person, a fisherman in his evangelical mission, and also a man of vision. His mission had a very ambitious vision. This is not merely history but a present reality that the church in Egypt lives daily, thanks to the vision of St Mark. Let us see how this vision worked out.

The School of Alexandria

He had the vision of a teacher. St Mark was the only apostle who established a Christian university, the first in the world, the school of Alexandria. Seeing that Alexandria was a city of philosophy and science, and that both were turning people away from God, he foresaw that ideas must be beaten by ideas, and that a Christian school was the way of a wise fisherman to draw the attention of learned Alexandrians. It worked successfully, and he was very much envied for that success.

The school of Alexandria, though it ceased for centuries, came back powerfully to enlighten the Coptic congregation through theological studies. It has always been, and is still, a spiritual university of which many popes of Alexandria were deans, and from which many more have graduated. As Oden says,

> Mark's life would end in the most populous city of Africa: Alexandria on the coast of the Nile delta. Out of this city, the most influential intellectual center of the whole Mediterranean world, came the first Christian school. It was a catechetical school, designed to communicate the gospel to the world. Its distinctive learning process, from apostolic texts and in dialogue with culture, was born in Africa.[3]

The Gospel of St Mark

He had the vision of a writer. St Mark did not only establish the first theological university, but also wrote the first gospel. Most historians believe that he wrote his gospel before St Luke wrote his. These were then followed by St Matthew, then St John. Mark was a missionary writer who looked forward to generations and generations of believers and well-educated Christians, who would prefer to read the word of God and read the good news than to read anything else.

When he wrote his gospel in Egypt (according to St John Chrysostom), St Mark thought of world Christianity rather than Coptic Christianity. A vision with heavenly wings led the evangelist to cry in the wilderness with the written word, short but deep, and full of miracles that tell the world about the Messiah. As a writer, Mark produced a narrative with detailed description but was able to keep it concise. His frequently repeated word 'immediately' says it all. And his message, as is well known, was: 'For even the Son of Man

---

[3] Oden, *African Memory*, 22-23.

did not come to be served, but to serve, and to give His life a ransom for many' (Mk 10.45).

Liturgy and Establishing a Church

St Mark had the vision of a worshipper. He foresaw that prayers needed to be composed so that the church community could worship God together. He also ordained priests and deacons with Inianus the patriarch, so that they could pass on the liturgy – and they did – to future generations. Consequently, the very first liturgical prayers that St Mark composed constitute the core of the holy mass we as Copts pray still. Although he did not write it, St Mark's holy mass was written by St Athanasius the Apostolic, twentieth pope of Alexandria, and was rewritten with added litanies by St Cyril the Great, the twenty-fourth pope of Alexandria.

In the prayer for the consecration of the elements which is at the heart of the liturgy ascribed to St Mark, he described Jesus's first Eucharist, saying: 'He took bread into His holy hands, which are without spot or blemish, blessed, and life-giving. He looked up toward heaven to You, O God, who are His Father and Master of everyone. And when He had given thanks, He blessed it, and sanctified it.'[4] Seeing Jesus looking up toward heaven in the upper room of his mother's and his house, Mark was the one who described the scene in detail. None of the other evangelists mentioned that Jesus 'looked up'. It is noteworthy to mention that the holy communion has been taken in Egypt, as was the very first Passover which was also held in Egypt before the Exodus. I can imagine St Mark powerfully praying: 'The worship of idols, utterly uproot from the world. Satan and all his evil powers, trample and humiliate under our feet speedily.' And 'Arise, O Lord God, let all Your enemies be scattered, and let all who hate Your holy name flee before Your face.' Those prayers we still pray in the twenty-first century with faith and understanding.

Monasticism

St Mark had the vision of an ascetic apostle. He led an early monastic life. Like St Paul, he did not have a wife or family. Nor is it mentioned that he had brothers or sisters. His life was completely devoted to his sacred mission. Abandoning comfort and riches, seeking to engage in evangelism everywhere possible, and teaching by example what a true Christian ascetic life is like, Mark was the early inspiration of monasticism.

Monasticism began in Egypt through St Anthony the Great and others during the fourth century. The words of the Gospel of St Mark were read in the church when Anthony was attentively listening. 'Then Jesus, looking at

---

[4] Liturgy of St Basil the Great. On the liturgies used by the Coptic Church, see *Catholic Encyclopedia*, *s.v.* 'The Alexandrine Liturgy', online at: https://www.catholicity.com/encyclopedia/a/alexandrine_liturgy.html.

him, loved him, and said to him: 'One thing you lack: Go your way, sell whatever you have and give to the poor, and you will have treasure in heaven; and come, take up the cross, and follow Me' (Mk 10.21). Anthony received the words as a personal message to him, sold all he had and followed Jesus. St Mark's life and words about Jesus outlived him to flourish throughout the history of the Coptic monasteries and their influence even crossed the seas to Europe. We owe St Mark a great deal.

Martyrdom

St Mark had the vision of a martyr. The key word 'immediately' describes the vision he had of what he should quickly complete before being martyred. St Mark worked hard and speedily: he established the church in Egypt, ordained Inianus, three priests and seven deacons, established the school of Alexandria, wrote his gospel, and taught the church to pray his liturgy in a few years. He also went to establish the churches of the Pentapolis, which are still part of the see of St Mark now, although our Libya churches have recently been closed because of the troubles there. All this work was completed in a short space of time, before he was martyred in Alexandria during the Resurrection celebrations.

Oden says: 'Out of Mark's life and death came an enduring gift to all early Christians: the emergence of African Christianity.'[5] The consecration of the streets of Alexandria with his holy blood has been manifested in our Coptic Orthodox Church through ages of martyrs. Even down to very recent years, the legacy of martyrdom that St Mark established in the Church has been, and remains, alive. In St Mark's homeland, Libya, twenty-one were slaughtered in the name of Christ, following the example of all our ancestors and our beloved evangelist St Mark, and proving to the whole world that it was not history, nor memory, but a faith lived daily in this holy land that Christ himself visited.

How do we see St Mark and all those who gave their bodies to testify to their faith? We can view them through the lens of the biblical text:

> [Those] who through faith subdued kingdoms, worked righteousness, obtained promises, stopped the mouths of lions, quenched the violence of fire, escaped the edge of the sword, out of weakness were made strong, became valiant in battle, turned to flight the armies of the aliens. ...

> Others were tortured, not accepting deliverance, that they might obtain a better resurrection. Still others had trial of mockings and scourgings, yes, and of chains and imprisonment. They were stoned, they were sawn in two, were tempted, were slain with the sword. They wandered about in sheepskins and goatskins, being destitute, afflicted, tormented – of whom the world was not worthy. (Heb. 11.33-38)

To conclude, from mission to martyrdom, St Mark has been like his master. His name Mark, which means a heavy hammer, is considered a sign

---

[5] Oden, *African Memory*, 23.

because his preaching hammered and destroyed the idols of Egypt just as the visit of Jesus Christ to Egypt as a child was said to have destroyed the idols half a century before, in fulfilment of Isaiah 19.1. His symbol, the lion taken from the Book of Revelation, reminds us of the words spoken of our Lord Jesus Christ: 'Behold, the Lion of the tribe of Judah, the Root of David' (Rev. 5.5). St Mark introduced Jesus to all the lands he visited by means of his power, his search for souls, his teaching, praying, pious life and martyrdom.

May his prayers keep us, and may his example enlighten the way for us.

19. Understanding the Blessing of Persecution: Reflections on Philippians*

Dr Myrto Theocharous

Introduction

Fr Tadros Y. Malaty writes the following in his *Introduction to the Coptic Orthodox Church*:

> The Copts insisted on starting their calendar by the beginning of the reign of Diocletian, in 284 AD, calling it 'Anno Martyri,' for in his reign the Church gained numerous numbers of martyrs, who are now glorified in Paradise. About the eleventh of September of every year we celebrate the commencement of a new Coptic year, calling it 'Feast of El-Nayrouz,' in which we celebrate the Feast of Martyrs, as a spiritual preparation for starting a new year.
>
> By this unique understanding, the Church of Alexandria has shown the world her deep spiritual faith, her vision that leads to eternity and her concept of martyrdom. She did not consider martyrdom as death or something terrible, but rather a new birth which is an entry to paradise.[1]

One can only admire the faith and devotion of our Coptic brothers and sisters, not only to God, but to their community that transcends death. They call death 'a new birth', thus establishing an image in our minds that we, as Christians, are never really separated from our parent. We are carried in the darkness of the womb, only to be delivered into a new life, a transcendent life.

The Coptic Church remains connected to the martyrs in a very concrete way, and this is something that Protestants have lost in their rejection of relics: the connection to the tangible remains of the saints. I will not enter a theological discussion about relics here. However, one does not need to agree with the veneration of bones in order to recognize that there is a certain theological understanding about the human body behind these practices that is already present in some form or another in the writings of the apostle Paul; a theological understanding which we all, hopefully, share.

---

* Scripture quotations in this chapter are from the New Revised Standard Version Bible, copyright © 1989 National Council of the Churches of Christ in the United States of America. Used by permission. All rights reserved worldwide.

[1] Fr Tadros Y. Malaty, *Introduction to the Coptic Orthodox Church* (Alexandria: St George's Coptic Orthodox Church, 1993), 27.

The Body

The physical body is extremely important for Paul. He is no Platonist. He does not despise created matter. The body, for him, is the realm in which testimony to God is given. Within his own Jewish heritage, this was primarily done through the sign of circumcision, an issue that comes up many times in his letters.

Therefore, he is not accustomed to despising the body; he considers it to be the greatest instrument of the believer for the purpose of demonstrating to whom one belongs. This he makes clear from the first chapter of Philippians, in which he mentions his body and how he exalts Christ with it in verse 20: 'It is my eager expectation and hope that I will not be put to shame in any way, but that by my speaking with all boldness, Christ will be exalted now as always *in my body*, whether by life or by death.'

Paul moves beyond the *ethnic* bodily sign of circumcision to other ways in which his body expresses allegiance to, and glorifies, his Saviour. He sees that it is through physical suffering that the gospel is advanced (1.12). The chains that constrained his body were actually effective in dispelling all fear from his brothers and sisters. One would have expected that Paul's chains would *impart* fear to the Church, but the exact opposite had happened. His chained body infused the Church with confidence for a bold witness.

Therefore Paul concludes that it is not departing from the body, but inhabiting it, that bears fruit. It is not a useless mass of flesh and bones, but it grows the Kingdom of God demonstrably, it plants churches in the Gentile world, and it encourages believers to continue the work of the gospel (1.22). Now we must keep in mind that it was much harder for Paul to say this than it is for us today. We forget that 'modern medicine makes it much easier to celebrate bodies. Our progenitors didn't have Novocain, C-sections, or sodium pentothal. The burden of the flesh was much heavier upon them',[2] as Dale Allison reminds us. Platonism would have been the most attractive philosophy to hold, as it correlated with their lived experience. Yet Paul insists on the value of the body.

The body will exalt Jesus whether it lives or dies, according to Paul. Death is a gain, surely, because in death one is with Christ and physical miseries come to an end. That is a much better state (*pollō mallon kreisson*, 1.23). This agrees with the record of Jesus saying on the cross to the repentant criminal: 'Truly I tell you, today you will be with me in Paradise' (Lk. 23.43).

However, while it is a personal gain for Paul to move on from this life, he prefers bodily suffering precisely because it generates more fruit for the kingdom. The suffering of his body is love for the Church in action. Jesus himself did not choose to remain outside the body in the fleshless 'form' of God for his own benefit, but took on a body 'the form of human flesh' for the sake of the Church (2.5-8). So how could Paul prefer to move in the

---

[2] Dale C. Allison Jr, *Night Comes: Death, Imagination, and the Last Things* (Grand Rapids, MI: Eerdmans, 2016), 33.

opposite direction to that which Jesus took? He does not. He chooses the community, even if that means carrying a body of pain.

Paul makes it even more graphic that he is referring to the actual shape our flesh and bones take, by using expressions about the bodily *form*. He is not speaking of an abstract concept of humanness, but about an actual human shape. This is the reason he goes out of his way to stress the shape that Christ took, by using expressions such as 'form of a slave, likeness of humans, shape of a human being' (*all' heauton ekenōsen morphēn doulou labōn en homoiōmati anthrōpōn genomenos kai schēmati euretheis hōs anthrōpos*, 2.7). You do not get more tangible than that!

The word μορφή (*morphē*) ('form') is the physical appearance of a person and it is regularly used in the Bible as a synonym for the body or body parts. This applies especially to the face of a person, that may be altered as its expression changes due to fear or sadness (Theodotion, Dan. 3.19; 4.36; 5.6, 9, 10; 7.28). *Morphē* ('form') is also the tangible figure that the idea of a statue takes in the hands of a sculptor (Isa. 44.13 LXX).

Therefore, when we get to our central text, Philippians 3.10, and after Paul has used the word *morphē* twice already, he adopts a rare compound word made of the term *morphē*: *summorphizomenos* or *summorphoumenos* (lit. 'co-shaped'). He is speaking about sharing the same form as Christ, but he is not speaking of the exalted form of Christ, the pre-existent form of God of which Christ had emptied himself, but of the form of his death. And we do have an idea of what that looked like: beaten, bleeding, chained, naked, bruised, hungry, thirsty, pierced.

In other words, for Paul, identification with Christ has to include identification with Christ's degraded body that was subjected to death; the imitation of Christ is not simply a spiritual exercise, but is visible and fully felt in our physical bodies. The body is the realm of our humiliation. Not that Paul is encouraging self-inflicted suffering, neither is he congratulating his persecutors for oppressing him. He is saying that this physical humiliation is valuable since it is this same humiliation that Christ embraced by emptying himself from his divine form and taking on a body that *could* be humiliated. In a sense, Paul is not passively mourning what is done to his body, but he is actively embracing this humiliation in the manner of his Saviour's *kenosis* ('emptying').

These exact same events or circumstances of affliction can be interpreted as humiliation in the eyes of the powerful, but from the standpoint of the persecuted they amount to active resistance. It is the choice of allegiance to the incarnated God who emptied himself into a suffering body of death.

Here let us pause and remember our Coptic brothers and sisters who have held firmly to this same position, especially during the last decade, in the midst of their own persecution. We remember the Easter church bombings, the pilgrims killed by extremists, the fifteen girls (if not more) in Minya who were kidnapped in 2017 to be forced to marry Muslims and convert to Islam, and the constant discrimination in all areas of life by local authorities.[3] These are unwanted beatings, no doubt, but the active resistance of our brothers and sisters understands these sufferings as being of the same form as those of our Saviour. We, the more privileged ones who are witnessing the suffering of our brothers and sisters from afar, see the same form of Christ in them, the same beaten body of our Lord demonstrated before us from Egypt. His body of death is tangible, it is visible and it is local to Egypt (as well as in other places of persecution). We can actually go and stand before their blood-stained clothes in the cultural centre of Cairo's Coptic Cathedral. We see it and as a result we are emboldened in the gospel as well.

What will happen to this tangible *morphē* ('form') of humiliation and death that is before us? Paul says in 3.21: 'He will transform the body of our humiliation that it may be conformed [lit. 'co-shaped'; here he uses another compound adjective of *morphē*: *summorphon*] to the body of his glory, by the power that also enables him to make all things subject to himself.' Again, the emphasis is on the physical transformation of the *sōma* (body) into the *morphē* (form) of Christ's current glorious resurrected body. Our suffering body that now participates in the form of his death is also to be made into the form of his glory, thus following the same pattern that Christ's body has been through. Nowhere do we see an escape from the body, a rejection of physical suffering. Instead, we see continuity from one to the other: the same body that is in pain before death, somehow mysteriously connected to its glorious self beyond death. Death is not oblivion. It is the passage that will reveal the reality of glory that is now hidden in these fragile figures that carry us around. And the greater the affliction of these fragile bodies in the present, the more magnified will the glory of this coming transformation be! This great contrast will be a great testimony!

Joy and Resurrection

However, the physical body is used by some of Paul's Jewish contemporaries as well, in order to attain to life in the world to come. He calls them 'mutilators of the flesh' (3.2). They are those who 'put confidence in the flesh' (3.3). This is the attitude that Paul himself had before encountering Jesus: circumcision, pride in ethnic identity, zeal for persecuting the Church and for keeping the law to the letter (3.4-6). It is the body in the service of achievement.

In second-century BC Jewish accounts of martyrdom, we often see not simply strict law-keeping by devout Jews, but a full-on war between the Maccabees and pro-Hellenist Jews who wanted to assimilate elements of the

---

[3] Harriet Sherwood, 'Christians in Egypt face unprecedented persecution, report says', *The Guardian*, 10 January 2018, online at:
https://www.theguardian.com/world/2018/jan/10/christians-egypt-unprecedented-persecution-report; 'The History of Religious Persecution in Egypt', *Forb in Full*, 11 March 2019, online at: https://forbinfull.org/2019/03/11/long-read-the-history-of-religious-persecution-in-egypt/.

Greek way of life to their Jewishness, such as participation in the gymnasia and even disguising their physical mark of circumcision in order to join the games (1 Macc. 1.11-15). The Maccabees felt persecuted by the pro-Hellenists but also by the Seleucid king Antiochus Epiphanes, who wanted to impose Hellenism in Judaea. The Maccabees were zealous in their devotion to God and were willing to go into battle to die for their Jewishness, with the rallying cry: 'Let everyone who is zealous for the law and supports the covenant come out with me!' (1 Macc. 2.27)[4]

The sufferings of these martyrs were often understood, among other things, to be chastisements for personal sins, i.e. as personal atonement (2 Macc. 7.18, 32, 33), or chastisements for national sins (Dan. 9.8; 2 Macc. 6.12-16; 7.38).[5] These Jews had similar aspirations to resurrection; these were, in fact, the precursors of the belief in a bodily resurrection that Christians later inherited. The Church was inspired by them. Origen, for example, in his *Exhortation to Martyrdom* 22-27, regarded the Maccabees as great examples to the Christians of courage and perseverance under torture.[6]

Paul, however, differs from his Jewish compatriots, a certain group of them at least, in that he no longer regards such zeal, and the labour of the physical body, as the agents that *generate* their heavenly reward. Such an understanding would make the work of Jesus Christ redundant, since the labour by itself would be adequate to achieve the world to come.

Radical forms of the understanding that one's death can gain paradise perhaps characterize the violent martyrdom of Islamic extremists who are looking to win paradise through their suicide and their killing of others. Far from this, Paul grounds his understanding of suffering and resurrection on the resurrection *already* attained by Jesus himself. Jesus's resurrection is the starting-point. It is not an aspiration regarding a possible event in the distant future. For Paul, the resurrection that gives meaning to his suffering is an event that lies both in the past (Christ's resurrection) *and* in the future (the Church's resurrection). Suffering is bracketed by resurrection; thus the sufferer is animated by it.

Let us look at this bracketing as it becomes most apparent in 3.10-11: 'I want to know Christ and the power of his resurrection and the sharing of his sufferings by becoming like him in his death, if somehow I may attain the resurrection from the dead.' Resurrection is simultaneously what enables us to endure suffering and the goal to which suffering takes us. Resurrection is not something that our suffering earns. God does not want God's children to go through ordeals in order to win a prize. It is not a bargain with God because it has already been achieved. So it is both the animating power that enables the martyr to endure and the reward as well. Paul himself clarifies this, lest someone interprets his suffering as simply a substitute for the

---

[4] John S. Pobee, *Persecution and Martyrdom in the Theology of Paul* (JSNT Supplement 6; Sheffield: JSOT Press, 1985), 19-25.

[5] Pobee, *Persecution and Martyrdom*, 34-36.

[6] Rowan A. Greer, *Origen* (New York: Paulist Press, 1979), 55-59.

'works of the law' of his former life. He says in 3:12: 'I press on to make it my own, because Christ Jesus has made me his own.' He is bracketed in Jesus! 'Attaining' is not about winning a reward, but it is about knowing him, as Paul says in 3.10, and that means knowing the full journey of Jesus from his humiliation to his glorification. Recently Rowan Williams gave primary importance to the role of the body in knowing, as opposed to living solely in our heads.[7] Paul is clearly embracing the experiential knowledge of Christ that his physical suffering is offering him.

This understanding of suffering and resurrection clarifies why Paul insists on joy in this beautiful letter to the Philippians. Paul mentions 'joy' in this letter close to ten times, something which has always troubled me. I could never understand how one could rejoice in the midst of suffering without it being simply a pretence or shallow sentiment. When I am attacked by others, especially by my fellow believers, I am in pain, even anger. Joy is the last thing that I experience and the last thing I would want someone to exhort me to. I believe that his command to rejoice in the Lord makes sense in the light of this particular suffering, i.e. the suffering which is *not* a means of achieving the favour of God or earning resurrection. This kind of suffering, which is not dependent on the effectuality of one's human efforts and the uncertainty that goes with it, cannot be anything other than a source of joy.[8] Any other kind of suffering would be a source of anxiety, fear, angst, competition. It would be identical to having confidence in the flesh. Instead, we may rest in the fact that it is Christ who is the generating power, the cause, the one who controls and secures power over death, and the one who is faithful to bring about the resurrection. Paul's task is that of 'eagerly (actively) awaiting' this to be initiated from heaven: 'But our citizenship is in heaven, and it is from there that we are expecting a Savior, the Lord Jesus Christ. He will transform the body of our humiliation that it may be conformed to the body of his glory, by the power that also enables him to make all things subject to himself' (3.20-21).

Dale Allison writes:

> If there's an agent in death, it can only be God. We're reduced to hope. Our incapacity makes us like Jesus on the cross. All he could do was close his eyes and commit his spirit to Another.

> Maybe, once we become acclimatized to whatever ultimately awaits us, there'll be a place for our decisions and our efforts. But at the moment when we pass from here to there, it'll be like our first coming into this world. When born, we were ignorant and passive, and we couldn't provide for ourselves. All we could

---

[7] Rowan Williams, *Being Human: Bodies, Minds, Persons* (London: SPCK, 2018), 49-68.

[8] On the understanding that Paul is not doubting the certainty of the future resurrection, see Judith M. Gundry Volf, *Paul and Perseverance: Staying In and Falling Away* (Louisville, KY: John Knox Press, 1990), 254-60.

do was instinctively cry out for nourishment and comfort. And as it was in our beginning, so will it be at our end.[9]

This truth, this surrendering to the agent who is guaranteed to take us through the waters of death, is Paul's source of joy and ours (1.6). We are safe, even when we fall into the unsafe hands of our oppressors. We stand secure, even when we are threatened by our enemies, because our bodies have a future; they are firmly held through the grave and beyond.

At the same time, nothing that we currently do to the body is meaningless. Paul hopes to send Timothy back to the Philippians because he will show genuine concern for their welfare, he says (2.19-24). The Philippians, too, had already sent Epaphroditus to take care of Paul's needs and he even risked his life through serious illness in order to serve Paul (2.25-30). If this body has no future or hope of being transformed, if there is absolute discontinuity between our fragile bodies and our glorified ones, then why would one spend a single second caring for them?

Jesus himself cared for bodies, healing and feeding them, during his earthly ministry. He even welcomed care for his own body by people such as the Samaritan woman whom he asked for water, the women who ministered to him in his travels, or the woman with the alabaster jar who anointed his feet. And even in his death we see Joseph of Arimathea taking care of his dead body, as well as the women with burial spices looking to anoint him in the tomb. Interestingly, even in what is thought to be a post-resurrection scene in Matthew 25.31-46, the determining factor for people's fate seems to be their approach to the tangible physical needs of others, and through those to Jesus: 'I was hungry and you gave me food, I was thirsty and you gave me something to drink, I was a stranger and you welcomed me, I was naked and you gave me clothing, I was sick and you took care of me, I was in prison and you visited me' (25.35-36). How remarkable that our attitude towards physical bodies *now* has effects which are carried over beyond the grave, and that it is even determinative of our lives in the coming kingdom!

George Makeen[10] challenges us to think about the questions that our doctrines and theological language raise in young people who are disconnected from church. 'What does belief in physical resurrection would mean for my life?' a young person could ask. But, before rushing to reply, can we point them to how the Church lives and what the Church does so that they could conclude by themselves: 'yes, it is obvious that the resurrection of people's bodies is the future you people anticipate'?

---

[9] Allison, *Night Comes*, 43.
[10] 'Witness through the Media', presentation given at the Lausanne-Orthodox Initiative Consultation, Monastery of St Bishoy, Wadi el-Natrun, Egypt, 6 November 2019.

Bibliography of Helpful Works on Discipleship and Christian Formation

Prof. Nathan Hoppé and Revd Canon Mark Oxbrow

This selected bibliography brings together books and articles from Orthodox and Evangelical sources suggested by the contributors to this book. The primary focus of the bibliography is Christian formation and discipleship, living a life worthy of the gospel of Jesus Christ, but we have also included a number of texts which help to bridge the gap of understanding between Evangelical and Orthodox communities as well as those which provide background to topics covered by particular chapters in this book, such as African Christian spirituality and theological formation. The bibliography includes popular as well as academic writings but is restricted to texts in the English language.

Addison, Steve. *Pioneering Movements: Leadership that Multiplies Disciples and Churches*. Downers Grove, IL: IVP, 2015.

Anastasios, Archbishop. *Mission in Christ's Way*. Brookline, MA: Holy Cross Orthodox Press, 2010.

Anastasios, Archbishop. *In Africa*. Brookline, MA: Holy Cross Orthodox Press, 2015.

Arnold, J. Heinrich. *Discipleship: Living for Christ in the Daily Grind*. New York: Plough Publishing, 2011.

Arseniev, Nikolas. *Russian Piety*. Trans. Asheleigh Moorhouse. London: Faith Press, 1964.

Assefa, Daniel, and Tekletsadik Belachew. 'Values Expressed through African Symbols: An Ethiopian Theological Reflection'. *International Bulletin of Mission Research* 41 (2017).

St Athanasius Academy of Orthodox Theology. *The Orthodox Study Bible*. Nashville, TN: Thomas Nelson, 2008.

Bauckham, Richard. *Bible and Mission: Christian Witness in a Postmodern World*. Grand Rapids, MI: Baker, 2004.

Bediako, Kwame. *Theology and Identity*. Oxford: Regnum, 1992.

Bediako, Kwame. 'Africa and Christian Identity: Recovering an Ancient Story'. *Princeton Seminary Bulletin* 21 (2004).

Bediako, Kwame and Mathilde Jansen., eds. *A New Day Dawning. African Christians Living the Gospel: Essays in Honour of Dr J. J. (Hans) Visser*. Zoetermeer: Uitgeverij Boekencentrum, 2004.

Behr, John. *Becoming Human*. Crestwood, NY: St Vladimir's Seminary Press, 2013.

Belachew, Tekletsadik. 'Christianity's African Roots'. In *Africa Study Bible*. Carol Stream, IL: Tyndale House Publishers, 2017, 1466-1468.

Blackaby, Henry T., Richard Blackaby, and Claude V. King. *Experiencing God: Knowing and doing the Will of God*. Revised and expanded edn. Nashville, TN: Lifeway Press, 2007.

Bloom, Anthony. *Beginning to Pray*. Mahwah, NJ: Paulist Press, 1970.

Bloom, Anthony. *The Essence of Prayer*. London: Darton, Longman & Todd, 1986.

Bloom, Anthony. *Living Prayer*. London: Darton, Longman and Todd, 1998.

Bondi, Roberta. *To Love as God Loves: Conversations with the Early Church*. Minneapolis, MN: Fortress Press, 1987.

Bonhoeffer, Dietrich. *The Cost of Discipleship*. London: SCM Press, 1959.

Bonhoeffer, Dietrich. *Life Together*. New York, NY: HarperOne, 2009.

Bouteneff, Peter. *How to be a Sinner*. Yonkers, NY: St Vladimir's Seminary Press, 2018.

Bouteneff, Vera. *Father Arseny (1893-1973): Priest, Prisoner, Spiritual Father*. Crestwood, NY: St Vladimir's Seminary Press, 1998.

Braun, Jon. *Divine Energy: The Orthodox Path to Christian Victory*. Chesterton, IN: Ancient Faith Publishing, 1991.

Breen, Mike. *Building a Discipling Culture*. Greenville, SC: 3DM Publishing, 2011.

Bretherton, Luke. *Hospitality as Holiness: Christian Witness amid Moral Diversity*. Portland, OR: Routledge, 2010.

Bria, Ion. *The Liturgy after the Liturgy: Mission and Witness from an Orthodox Perspective*. Geneva: WCC Publications, 1996.

Brianchaninov, Ignatius. *The Arena*. Jordanville, NY: Holy Trinity Publications, 2012.

Brock, Sebastian P. *St. Ephrem the Syrian: Hymns on Paradise*. New York: St Vladimir's Seminary Press, 1990.

Brock, Sebastian P. *The Luminous Eye: The Spiritual World Vision of Saint Ephrem the Syrian*. Cistercian Studies 124. Kalamazoo: Cistercian Publications, 1992.

Brock, Sebastian P. *The Bride of Light*. Kottayam: St Ephrem Ecumenical Research Institute, 1994.

Brock, Sebastian. P., and George A. Kiraz. *Ephrem the Syrian: Select Poems*. Provo, UT: Brigham Young University Press, 2006.

Bunyan, John. *Pilgrim's Progress*. London: Harper Press, 2013.

Christensen, Michael J., and Jeffery A. Wittung, eds. *Partakers of the Divine Nature: The History and Development of Deification in the Christian Traditions*. Grand Rapids, MI: Baker, 2008.

Chryssavgis, John. *Soul Mending*. Brookline, MA: Holy Cross Orthodox Press, 2000.

Ciobotea, Metropolitan Daniel. *Confessing the Truth in Love: Orthodox Perceptions of Life, Mission and Unity*. Iaşi: Trintas, 2001.

Climacus, John. *The Ladder of Divine Ascent*. Mahwah, NJ: Missionary Society of St Paul, 1982.

Cochrane, Steve. *Many Monks across the Sea: Church of the East Monastic Mission in Ninth-Century Asia*. Oxford: Regnum, 2017.

Coleman, Robert E. *The Master Plan of Evangelism*. Grand Rapids, MI: Fleming H. Revell, 1993.

Crow, Gillian. *Orthodoxy for Today*. London: SPCK, 2008.

Davis, Charles A. *Making Disciples across Cultures: Missionary Principles for a Diverse World*. Downers Grove, IL: IVP, 2015.

Ellingsen, Mark. *African Christian Mothers and Fathers: Why they Matter for the Church Today*. Eugene, OR: Cascade Books, 2015.

Elowsky, Joel C. 'Early Alexandrian Theology as a Way of Life'. In *A New History of African Christian Thought: From Cape to Cairo*. David Tonghou Ngong, ed. Abingdon: Routledge, 2017, 39-53.

Ewell, Samuel E., III. *Faith seeking Conviviality: Reflections on Ivan Illich, Mission, and the Promise of Life Together.* Eugene, OR: Cascade Books, 2019.

Fitch, David. *Faithful Presence: Seven Disciplines that Shape the Church for Mission.* Downers Grove, IL: IVP, 2016.

Flett, John G. *The Witness of God: The Trinity,* Missio Dei, *Karl Barth and the Nature of Christian Community.* Grand Rapids, MI: Eerdmans, 2010.

Florovsky, Georges. *Bible. Church, Tradition: An Eastern Orthodox View.* Collected Works 1. Belmont, MA: Nordland, 1972.

Foster, Richard. *Celebration of Discipline: The Path to Spiritual Growth.* London: Hodder & Stoughton, 2008.

Garrett, Paul. *Saint Innocent: Apostle to America.* Yonkers, NY: St Vladimir's Seminary Press, 1979.

Ghosn, Margaret. *Samaritan Journey: Compassion, Subversion and Discipleship,* Coventry: Coventry Press, 2020.

Grass, Tim, Jenny and Paul Rolph, and Ioan Sauca, eds. *Building Bridges between the Orthodox and Evangelical Traditions.* Geneva: WCC Publications, 2012.

Griffith, Sidney H. *The Church in the Shadow of the Mosque.* Princeton, NJ: Princeton University Press, 2008.

Goheen, Michael W. *A Light to the Nations: The Missional Church and the Biblical Story.* Grand Rapids, MI: Baker, 2011.

Hagley, Scott. *Eat what is set before you: A Missiology of the Congregation in Context.* Skyforest, CA: Urban Loft, 2019.

Hardy, Andrew, and Dan Yarnell. *Missional Discipleship after Christendom.* Eugene, OR: Cascade Books, 2018.

Hauerwas, Stanley. *A Community of Character: Toward a Constructive Christian Social Ethic.* Notre Dame, IN: University of Notre Dame Press, 1991.

Heisey, Nancy R. *Origen the Egyptian: A Literary and Historical Consideration of the Egyptian Background in Origen's Writings on Martyrdom.* Nairobi: Pauline Publications Africa, 2000.

Holt, Simon Carey. *God Next Door: Spirituality and Mission in the Neighbourhood.* Brunswick East, Vic.: Acorn Press, 2010.

Hopko, Thomas. *All the Fulness of God.* Crestwood, NY: St Vladimir's Seminary Press, 1982.

Hopko, Thomas. *Speaking the Truth in Love: Education, Mission and Witness in Contemporary Orthodoxy.* Crestwood, NY: St Vladimir's Seminary Press, 2004.

Hull, Bill. *The Complete Book of Discipleship: On Being and Making Followers of Christ.* Colorado Springs, CO: NavPress, 2006.

Jennings, Willie James. *Acts: A Theological Commentary on the Bible.* Belief Series. Louisville, KY: Westminster John Knox Press, 2017.

Jillions, John A. 'Spiritual Guidance in Eastern Orthodox Christianity'. In *Spiritual Guidance Across Religions.* John R. Mabry, ed. Woodstock, VT: SkyLight Paths, 2014, 247-261.

Kadloubovsky, E., and G. E. H. Palmer, trans. *Writings from the Philokalia on the Prayer of the Heart.* London: Faber & Faber, 1979.

Kalu, Ogbu U., ed. *African Christianity: An African Story.* Africa World Press, 2005.

Kashouh, Hikmat. *Following Jesus in Turbulent Times: Disciple-making in the Arab World.* Carlisle: Langham Global Library, 2018.

Karekin II, Catholicos of Cilicia. *In Search of Spiritual Life: An Armenian Christian Miscellany.* Antelias, Lebanon: Armenian Catholicosate of Cilicia, 1991.

Kinlaw, Dennis F. *The Mind of Christ.* Nairobi: Evangel Publishing House, 1998.

Kinlaw, Dennis F. *Let's Start with Jesus: A New Way of doing Theology.* Grand Rapids, MI: Zondervan, 2005.

Krabill, James R., and Stuart Murray, eds. *Forming Christian Habits in Post-Christendom: The Legacy of Alan and Eleanor Kreider.* Harrisonburg, VA: Herald Press, 2011.

Kreider, Alan. *The Patient Ferment of the Early Church.* Grand Rapids, MI: Baker, 2016.

Leiva-Merikakis, Erasmo. *The Way of the Disciple.* San Francisco, CA: Ignatius Press, 2003.

Lewis, C. S. *The Screwtape Letters.* London: Century Press, 1942.

Louth, Andrew. *Modern Orthodox Thinkers: From the Philokalia to the Present.* London: SPCK, 2015.

Louth, Andrew. *The Wilderness of God.* London: Darton, Longman and Todd, 1991.

Matthew the Poor. *Orthodox Prayer Life: The Interior Way by Matthew the Poor.* Crestwood, NY: St Vladimir's Seminary Press, 2003.

Matthew the Poor. *If You Love Me: Serving Christ and the Church in Spirit and Truth.* Chesterton, IN: Ancient Faith Publishing, 2018.

Mbiti, John. 'African Concept of Human Relations'. *Ministry* 9 (1969).

McVey, K. E. *Ephrem the Syrian: Hymns.* New York: Paulist Press, 1989.

Meyendorff, John. *Living Tradition: Orthodox Witness in the Contemporary World.* Crestwood, NY: St Vladimir's Seminary Press, 1978.

Meyendorff, John. *Witness to the World.* Crestwood, NY: St Vladimir's Seminary Press, 1987.

Miller, Darrow L. *Discipling Nations: The Power of Truth to Transform Cultures.* Seattle, WA: YWAM Publishing, 1998.

Millward, C. *Disciplemaker.* Greenville, SC: 3DM Publishing, 2015.

Myers, Ched. *Binding the Strong Man: A Political Reading of Mark's Story of Jesus.* Maryknoll, NY: Orbis, 1988.

Nassif, Bradley. 'Orthodox Spirituality: A Quest for Transfigured Humanity'. In *Four Views on Christian Spirituality.* Bruce Demarest, ed. Grand Rapids, MI: Zondervan, 2012, 27-55.

Nassif, Bradley. 'Living the Gospel According to the Orthodox Tradition'. In *Living the King Jesus Gospel.* Nijay Gupta, Drew Strait and Tara Beth Leach, eds. Eugene, OR: Cascade Books, forthcoming.

Nassif, Bradley. *The Gospel in Eastern Orthodox Theology.* Crestwood, NY: St Vladimir's Seminary Press, forthcoming.

Nyman, James. *Stubborn Perseverance: How to launch Multiplying Movements of Disciples and Churches among Muslims and others.* Mount Vernon, WA: Mission Network, 2017.

Oden, Thomas C. *How Africa shaped the Christian Mind: Recovering the African Seedbed of Western Christianity.* Downers Grove, IL: IVP, 2007.

Oden, Thomas C. *The African Memory of Mark: Reassessing Early Church Tradition.* Downers Grove, IL: IVP, 2011.

Oden, Thomas C. *The Rebirth of African Orthodoxy: Return to Foundations.* Nashville, TN: Abingdon, 2016.

Orobator, Agbonkhianmeghe E. *Theology Brewed in an African Pot.* Maryknoll, NY: Orbis, 2008.

Oxbrow, Mark, and Tim Grass, eds. *The Mission of God: Studies in Orthodox and Evangelical Mission.* Oxford: Regnum, 2015.

Paavali, Archbishop. *The Faith We Hold.* Yonkers, NY: St Vladimir's Seminary Press, 1980.

Peppiatt, Lucy. *The Disciple: On Becoming Truly Human.* Eugene, OR: Cascade Books, 2012.

Peterson, Eugene. *A Long Obedience in the Same Direction: Discipleship in an Instant Society.* Downers Grove, IL: IVP, 2019.

Rogers, Cris. *Making Disciples: Elevating the Conversation around Discipleship and Spiritual Formation.* Uckfield: Essential Christian, 2018.

Rognlien, Bob. *A Jesus-Shaped Life.* Greenville, SC: 3DM International Publishing, 2016.

Rommen, Edward. *Get Real: On Evangelism in the Late Modern World.* Pasadena, CA: William Carey Library, 2019.

Rommen, Edward. *Into all the World: An Orthodox Theology of Mission.* Yonkers, NY: St Vladimir's Seminary Press, 2017.

Ross, Cathy, and Humphrey Southern. *Bearing Witness in Hope: Christian Engagement in Challenging Times.* London: SCM Press, 2020.

Roxburgh, Alan J. *Joining God, Remaking Church, Changing the World: The New Shape of the Church in Our Time.* New York: Morehouse, 2015.

Sanneh, Lamin O. *Disciples of All Nations: Pillars of World Christianity.* Oxford: Oxford University Press, 2008.

Schmemann, Alexander. *For the Life of the World.* Crestwood, NY: St Vladimir's Seminary Press, 1973.

Seamands, Stephen. *Ministry in the Image of God: The Trinitarian Shape of Christian Service.* Downers Grove, IL: IVP, 2006.

Shaw, Perry. *Transforming Theological Education: A Practical Handbook for Integrative Learning.* Carlisle: Langham Global Library, 2014.

Sheldon, Charles. *In His Steps: What Would Jesus Do? Illustrated Edition.* Kirkland, WA: Chump Change, 2020.

Shenk, David W. and Linford Stutzman, eds. *Practicing Truth: Confident Witness in our Pluralistic World.* Scottdale, PA: Herald Press, 1999.

Sine, Tom. *The New Conspirators: Creating the Future One Mustard Seed at a Time.* Downers Grove, IL: IVP, 2008.

Smith, Gordon T. *Called to be Saints: An Invitation to Christian Maturity.* Downers Grove, IL: IVP, 2014.

Smith, Luther E. *Intimacy and Mission: Intentional Community as Crucible for Radical Discipleship.* Scottdale, PA: Herald Press, 1994.

Soerens, Tim. *Everywhere You Look: Discovering the Church right where you are.* Downers Grove, IL: IVP, 2020.

Spidlik, Tomaš. *The Spirituality of the Christian East: A Systematic Handbook.* Trans. Anthony P. Gythiel. Cistercian Studies 79. Kalamazoo, MI: Cistercian Publications, 1986.

Stamoolis, James J. *Eastern Orthodox Mission Theology Today.* Eugene, OR: Wipf and Stock, 2001.

Stamoolis, James, ed. *Three Views on Eastern Orthodoxy and Evangelicalism.* Grand Rapids, MI: Zondervan, 2004.

Stott, John. *The Contemporary Christian.* Leicester: IVP, 1992.

Stott, John. *The Disciple: A Calling to be Christlike.* Downers Grove, IL: IVP, 2019.

Stott, John. *The Radical Disciple: Some Neglected Aspects of our Calling.* Downers Grove, IL: IVP, 2014.

Tiénou, Tite. 'Lessons from the Prayer Habits of the Church in Africa'. In *Teach us to Pray*. D. A. Carson, ed. Grand Rapids, MI: Baker / Exeter: Paternoster, 1990, 268-271.

Torrance, T. F. *Divine Meaning: Studies in Patristic Hermeneutics*. Edinburgh, T. & T. Clark, 1995.

Vasileios, Archimandrite. *Hymn of Entry: Liturgy and Life in the Orthodox Church*. Crestwood, NY: St Vladimir's Seminary Press, 1984.

Vassiliadis, Petros. *Eucharist and Witness: Orthodox Perspectives on the Unity and Mission of the Church*. Geneva, WCC Publications, 1998.

Vassiliadis, Petros, ed. *Orthodox Perspectives on Mission*. Oxford: Regnum, 2013.

Veronis, Luke A. *Go Forth: Stories of Mission and Resurrection in Albania*. Chesterton, IN: Conciliar Press, 2010.

Veronis, Luke A. *Lynette's Hope: The Witness of Lynette Katherine Hoppe's Life and Death*. Chesterton, IN: Conciliar Press, 2008.

Volf, Miroslav, and Matthew Croasmun. *For the Life of the World: Theology that makes a Difference*. Grand Rapids, MI: Brazos Press, 2019.

Walls, Andrew F. 'The Cost of Discipleship: The Witness of the African Church'. *Word and World* 25.4 (Fall 2005), 433-443.

Walton, Roger. *The Reflective Disciple: Learning to Live as Faithful Followers of Jesus in the Twenty-First Century*. London: SCM Press, 2009.

Ward, Benedicta, trans. *The Lives of the Desert Fathers*. London: Mowbray, 1981.

Ward, Benedicta, trans. *The Sayings of the Desert Fathers*. London: Mowbray, 1975.

Ward, Benedicta, trans. *The Desert Fathers: Sayings of the Early Christian Monks*. London: Penguin, 2003.

Ware, Kallistos. *The Inner Kingdom*. Collected Works 1. Crestwood, NY: St Vladimir's Seminary Press, 2000.

Ware, Kallistos. *The Orthodox Way*. Yonkers, NY: St Vladimir's Seminary Press, 1979.

Ware, Kallistos, G. E. H. Palmer, and Philip Sherrard, eds. *The Philokalia, Vols 1-4*. London: Faber & Faber, 1983.

Warren, Tish Harrison. *Liturgy of the Ordinary: Sacred Practices in Everyday Life*. Downers Grove, IL: IVP, 2016.

Watson, David. *Discipleship*. London: Hodder & Stoughton, 1983.

Watson, David L. and Paul D. Watson. *Contagious Disciple Making*. Nashville, TN: Thomas Nelson, 2014.

Wilhite, David E. *Tertullian the African: An Anthropological Reading of Tertullian's Context and Identities*. Berlin: Walter de Gruyter, 2007.

Wilk, Karen. *Don't Invite Them to Church: Moving from a Come and See to a Go and Be Church*. Grand Rapids, MI: Faith Alive Christian Resources, 2010.

Wilkins, Michael. *Following the Master*. Grand Rapids, MI: Zondervan, 1992.

Wilson, Tom. *Hospitality, Service, Proclamation: Interfaith Engagement as Christian Discipleship*. London: SCM Press, 2019.

Wright, Christopher J. H. *Cultivating the Fruit of the Spirit: Growing in Christlikeness*. Downers Grove, IL: IVP, 2017.

Wright, Christopher J. H. *'Here are your gods!': Faithful discipleship in Idolatrous Times*. London: Inter-Varsity Press, 2020

Wright, Christopher J. H. *The Mission of God's People: A Biblical Theology of the Church's Mission*. Grand Rapids, MI: Zondervan, 2010.

Wright, N. T. *God in Public*. London: SPCK, 2016.

Wright, N. T. *New Testament Prayers for Everyone*. London: SPCK, 2012.

Wright, N. T. *Simply Christian.* London: SPCK, 2006.
Wright, N. T. *Spiritual AND Religious.* London: SPCK, 2017.
Wright, N. T. *Virtue Reborn.* London: SPCK, 2010.
Zizioulas, John D. *Being as Communion: Studies in Personhood and the Church.* Crestwood, NY: St Vladimir's Seminary Press, 2002.

List of Contributors[*]

[*] The affiliations given were correct at 31 August 2020.

His Eminence Archbishop Angaelos is the Coptic Orthodox Archbishop of London and Papal Legate to the United Kingdom. He was conferred the honour of Officer of the Most Excellent Order of the British Empire by Her Majesty the Queen for Services to International Religious Freedom, the Lambeth Cross by the Archbishop of Canterbury for Ecumenism, and the Coventry Cross of Nails for Reconciliation.

Tekle Belachew is currently a PhD candidate in the history of exegesis, Concordia Seminary, St Louis, MO, researching the 6th-century Ethiopian poet-musician and hymnographer St Yared. He is also a researcher at Tibeb Research & Retreat Centre, Ethiopia. His research and teaching interests include patristics, African theology and Ethiopian Christianity.

Dr Joshua Bogunjoko has been the International Director of SIM since 2013. Since joining the mission in 1995, he has held several medical and leadership roles. Joshua is a family physician and holds a master's degree in Leadership and Management.

Leslie Doll was employed as an OTC Trader in New York City, and serves on the Board of Directors and Kingdom Investment Committee of Strategic Resource Group (SRG), a partnership of business people resourcing indigenous ministry in the Middle East. Leslie and her husband Bob are leaders in the New York Movement project convening Christians in cities around the world for gospel acceleration. She holds a BA from the University of Texas at Austin and an MBA from Southern Methodist University.

Dr C. Rosalee Velloso Ewell is a Brazilian theologian from the city of São Paulo. She has a PhD in biblical theology from Duke University, USA, and was the New Testament editor for the Comentário Bíblico Contemporáneo. Rosalee served as Principal of Redcliffe College and is the Director of Church Relations for the United Bible Societies.

Dr Tim Grass has been Facilitator of the Lausanne-Orthodox Initiative since 2016, and involved in Orthodox-Evangelical dialogue in Britain and internationally for over twenty years. A Fellow of the Royal Historical Society, he is a Senior Research Fellow at Spurgeon's College, London, and has published widely in the field of church history.

Prof. Nathan Hoppe was born and brought up in Colombia. After completing his education in the USA, he moved to Albania with his family, where he has served under Archbishop Anastasios since 1998. He has directed the Central Children's Office of the Orthodox Church of Albania since 2004, and has extensive ecumenical experience. Nathan teaches at Logos University in the Department of Theology and Culture.

Very Revd Dr John Jillions is past Chancellor of the Orthodox Church in America and the founding Principal of the Institute for Orthodox Christian Studies in Cambridge, UK. He is the author of *Divine Guidance: Lessons for Today from the World of Early Christianity* (Oxford University Press, 2020).

Dr Sergei Koryakin is a Protestant who joined the Orthodox Church in 2011. He teaches theology at Moscow Evangelical Christian Seminary. Teaching students of various Protestant denominations, he tries to combine the best of the two religious traditions, encouraging the learners to think ecumenically and seek paths to unity among Christians.

Dr Ralph Lee, a representative of The Navigators UK, started work as an engineer, moving to Ethiopia to lecture. Interest in Ethiopia's Christian tradition led to studies at the School of Oriental and African Studies in London, and PhD studies led to teaching at the Holy Trinity Theological College in Addis Ababa. Now settled in Cambridge, UK, he maintains broad interests in Christian discipleship and Orthodox Christianity.

Dr David Lyons serves as an International Vice President of The Navigators. He helped to create Orthonet, a network of Evangelicals and Orthodox faithful associated with The Navigators. His eldest daughter is Orthodox, and her husband graduated from St Vladimir's Orthodox Theological Seminary.

Dr Bradley Nassif is from the Antiochian Orthodox Church, and has taught at Holy Cross Greek Orthodox Seminary and the Patriarch Athenagoras Orthodox Institute. He is Professor of Biblical and Theological Studies at North Park University, and author of *The Evangelical Theology of the Eastern Orthodox Church* (forthcoming, St Vladimir's Seminary Press).

Deacon James R. Nicholas's personal experience includes service as a member, lay leader and clergyman in both the Anglican and Orthodox Christian faiths. More than forty years of work in developing and managing global church-planting and mission programmes in both traditions provides him with a unique perspective on mission and evangelism in various cultures.

Archpriest Michael Oleksa has served as a parish priest, seminary dean, and professor at the University of Alaska and Alaska Pacific University. He has written several books on Alaska Native history and culture, and presented a PBS television series, 'Communicating across Cultures'. Now he lives in Anchorage with his Yup'ik wife, Xenia.

Revd Canon Mark Oxbrow served in mission leadership for thirty years, as assistant general secretary of the Church Mission Society and international director of Faith2Share. He is currently the director of the Guided Study Programme at Oxford Centre for Mission Studies and serves as consultant to the Anglican Communion on discipleship issues.

Vladimir Strelov is rector of the Bible college 'Nasledie' (Heritage), and a member of the missionary-catechetical commission of the Moscow diocese of the Russian Orthodox Church. He has worked for the Department of Youth Affairs and the Missionary commission of the ROC, and aims to promote Bible study groups within the ROC.

Dr Irini Thabet is an assistant professor of English Literature and Western Culture at Ain Shams University, Egypt, and teaches biblical and liturgical English in the Coptic Orthodox Church Theological Seminary. She is also a press writer and in 2020 was elected to the Egyptian Senate.

Dr Myrto Theocharous was born in Cyprus and moved to Greece in 2001 for theological studies. A PhD graduate of the University of Cambridge, she writes on the Old Testament and teaches at the Greek Bible College in Athens. She is also the president of New Life Ministries against Trafficking and Prostitution in Athens, Greece.

Very Revd Dr Eric George Tosi is Rector of St Gregory's Orthodox Church and Chair of the Commission on Missions and Evangelism of the Orthodox Church in America; formerly he served the Church as its Secretary. He has a BA and MA from Fordham University, MDiv from St Vladimir's Seminary and a DMin from University of Toronto (Trinity). He is the Assistant Professor of Pastoral Theology at St Vladimir's Seminary.

Fr Luke A. Veronis serves as the Director for the Missions Institute of Orthodoxy Christianity at Holy Cross Greek Orthodox School of Theology, Brookline, MA, where he teaches as an adjunct instructor; he also pastors Saints Constantine and Helen Church in Webster, MA. He has been involved in the Orthodox Church's missionary movement since 1987.

Revd Dr Karen Wilk works with Resonate Global Mission and Forge Canada, teaching, coaching and practising what it means to discover and join the Spirit on God's mission in our neighbourhoods. She has a doctorate in Missional Leadership and has been a pastor for over thirty years in Edmonton, Alberta, where she also enjoys being a wife, mother and neighbour.

Revd Dr Christopher J. H. Wright is International Ministries Director of Langham Partnership, founded by John Stott. After ordained Anglican ministry in Tonbridge, England, he taught Old Testament in India and at All Nations Christian College, England. He now lives in London as an honorary curate at All Souls Church, Langham Place.

Rt Revd Prof N. T. Wright is Emeritus Professor of New Testament at St Andrews, and Senior Research Fellow at Wycliffe Hall, Oxford. He was formerly Bishop of Durham. He has published around ninety books and hundreds of articles, and has broadcast frequently on radio and TV.